Governors State University
Library Hours:
Monday thru Thursday 8:00 to 10:30
Friday 8:00 to 5:00
Saturday 8:30 to 5:00
Sunday 1:00 to 5:00 (Fall
and Winter Trimester Only)

On Our Own, Together

On Our Own, Together

Peer Programs for People with Mental Illness

Edited by Sally Clay

With Bonnie Schell, Patrick W. Corrigan, and Ruth O. Ralph

Vanderbilt University Press

NASHVILLE

This publication was made possible by the Consumer-Operated Services Program
(COSP), a multi-site collaboration funded by the U.S. Department of Health
and Human Services (DHHS), Substance Abuse and Mental Health Services
Administration (SAMHSA), Center for Mental Health Services (CMHS), grant
numbers: Coordinating Center Missouri SM52328; Penn SM52355; Florida (&
California) SM52332; Maine SM52362; Boston SM52352; Michigan/Tennessee
SM52367; Mt. Sinai SM52372; Chicago SM52363

The publication contents are solely the responsibility of the authors and do not
necessarily represent the official views of the DHHS, SAMHSA, CMHS, or the COSP
collaborating partners.

Library of Congress Cataloging-in-Publication Data

On our own, together : peer programs for people with mental illness / edited by
Sally Clay, with Bonnie Schell, Patrick W. Corrigan, and Ruth O. Ralph.—1st ed.
    p. cm.
    Includes bibliographical references and index.
ISBN 0-8265-1465-0 (cloth : alk. paper)
ISBN 0-8265-1466-9 (pbk. : alk. paper)
    1. Mentally ill—Rehabilitation. 2. Mentally ill—Services for. 3. Peer
counseling in rehabilitation. 4. Self-help groups.
RC480.5.O495 2005
362.2'04256—dc22

                                                          2004017371

Contents

Tables and Figures   vii

Acknowledgments   ix

Preface: Nothing About Us Without Us   xi

I. Introduction and Background

1   About Us: What We Have in Common   3
     Sally Clay

2   The Historical and Philosophical Development
     of Peer-Run Support Programs   17
     Jean Campbell

II. Drop-In Centers

3   Mental Health Client Action Network (MHCAN),
     Santa Cruz, California   67
     Bonnie Schell

4   Portland Coalition for the Psychiatrically Labeled,
     Portland, Maine   92
     Janine M. Elkanich

5   The St. Louis Empowerment Center, St. Louis, Missouri   108
     Helen Minth

6   PEER Center, Inc., Oakland Park, Florida   123
     Compiled by Bonnie Schell and Nancy Erwin
     from material supplied by PEER Center directors and staff

III. Peer Support and Mentoring Services

7   GROW In Illinois   141
     Lorraine Keck and Carol Mussey

8   The Friends Connection, Philadelphia, Pennsylvania   159
     Jeanie Whitecraft, James Scott, Joseph Rogers, Bill Burns-Lynch,
     Terrance Means, and Mark S. Salzer

IV. Educational Programs

9   Advocacy Unlimited, Inc., Connecticut   179
     Yvette Sangster

10   BRIDGES in Tennessee: Building Recovery of Individual
     Dreams and Goals through Education and Support   197
     Louetta Hix

V. Conclusion

11   Common Ingredients as a Fidelity Measure
     for Peer-Run Programs   213
     Matthew Johnsen, Gregory Teague, and Elizabeth McDonel Herr

12   With Us: Where Are We Going?   239
     Sally Clay, with contributions from Bonnie Schell,
     Patrick Corrigan, and Jean Campbell

     Epilogue: Ourselves and Others   259

Appendixes

A.   Guides to the Text   261
B.   Common Ingredients of COSPs, CAP Definitions   273
C.   National Directories   282

     Contributors   285
     Index   289

Tables and Figures

Tables

1.1. The Sites: Eight programs and three clusters   5

1.2. COSP Common Ingredients by Category   7

2.1. Reasons for Using Peer-Run Drop-In Centers   32

2.2. Operating Principles of Peer-Run Support Programs   35

2.3. Peer-support Competencies   42

2.4. Highest-ranked Individual Statements   43

2.5. Peer-run Programs Evidence Base   46

8.1. Skills Targeted by the Friends Connection   162

11.1. Organization of the COSP FACIT   226

11.2. Interrater Reliability and Item Means for COSP FACIT   228

11.3. Performance of COSPs and TMHS Programs
on FACIT (by Domain)   230

11.4. Performance of COSP Clusters on FACIT (Wave II)   234

A.1. Glossary   261

A.2. Peer-run Programs Contact List   268

A.3. Researchers in the COSP Study   273

B.1. Common Ingredients of COSPs, CAP Definitions

C.1. National Peer Organizations   282

C.2. Web Links for Peer Programs   283

Figures

A.1	Disability Rights Poster	x
1.1.	Common Ingredients Organized by Section, Category, and Core Ingredient	8
2.1.	Peer-Support Competencies Cluster Rating Map	43
3.1.	What Can a Typical Client Expect at MHCAN?	69
3.2.	"God Save the Mentally Ill," a painting by Sam Oastler	81
3.3.	Drop-in Center Rules	86
4.1.	An Untitled Painting by David Towne	96
4.2.	Rules for Behavior: Purpose and Philosophy of the Portland Coalition Code of Conduct	99
5.1.	Goals of the Empowerment Drop-in Center	112
6.1.	The First PEER Center	125
6.2.	The PEER Center in 2002	126
6.3.	Layout of the PEER Center	130
7.1.	The Twelve Steps of Recovery and Personal Growth	146
9.1.	AU Logo	180
9.2.	Advocacy Education Program	186
9.3.	Samples from Individual Advocacy Reports	191
9.4.	Samples from Individual Advocacy Reports of Legislative Advocacy	193
9.5.	Testimonials from AU Graduates	196
10.1.	The BRIDGES Course	205
10.2.	"A Voice from the Region," by Sam Viar	206
11.1.	Performance on FACIT by COSPs and TMHSs	231
11.2.	Performance on FACIT by COSP models and TMHSs	235

Acknowledgments

First, thanks go to Maine researcher Ruth Ralph, who made my work on this book possible. When I lost my affiliation with the PEER Center and thus with the Consumer Operated Services Program study (the COSP study), she organized the book project so that I could continue as editor. Many of the other principal investigators—including Susan Essock, Tom Summerfelt, Mark Salzer, Patrick Corrigan, and Sally Rogers—pitched in to support us.

Bonnie Schell and Patrick Corrigan, the other editors of this book, gave me prompt and thoughtful reviews of the chapters submitted, while Ruth helped in assembling and submitting the final manuscript. In addition, Bonnie wrote the chapter about her drop-in center, and she contributed her writing to two other chapters. Pat supplied much personal support, along with valuable guidance from his experience as publisher of another small press. Without these three editors—Ruth, Bonnie, and Pat—this book would not have come to be.

I am grateful to all of my peers who were members of the COSP Consumer Advisory Panel (CAP) and, as such, deeply involved in developing the list of common ingredients and often writing the individual chapters about their programs. Dianne Côté was a valued consultant every step of the way. The color scheme and type design on the book jacket are based on a graphic design by Kevin C. Murphy, an artist affiliated with MHCAN in California. Other consumer/survivors worked professionally as members of their site's research team, and at least three of the principal investigators for these teams were consumer/survivors, including Jean Campbell of the Coordinating Center.

I personally would like to express my appreciation to the people at the Center for Mental Health Services (CMHS), starting with Jackie Parrish and Neal Brown in the 1980s, for their support of consumer-operated projects.

The positive interplay between consumers and researchers on the multisite research project was, for me, inspiring to behold. I thank Rise Goldstein for her instructive presentations of research issues at CAP meetings; and Matt Johnsen and other members of the Common Ingredients Subcommittee for their support in developing the common ingredients and conducting the fidelity study described in Chapter 11.

I enjoyed working with the staff at the coordinating center, particularly Rita Atkins, who was always behind the scenes helping to plan and organize. More intangibly, I will always remember the informal peer support and friendship shared among all of us who contributed to this book—together.

Sally Clay
Lake Placid, Florida
September 13, 2004

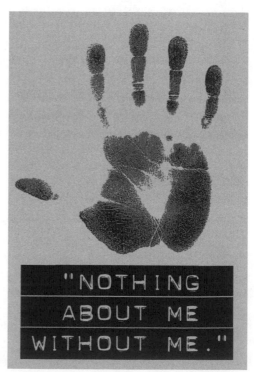

Figure A.1 Disability Rights Poster © *Mouth Magazine*

Preface:
Nothing About Us Without Us

This book is written by and for persons who have experienced what is generally known as "mental illness." We write in the tradition of *On Our Own*, a groundbreaking book by Judi Chamberlin (1978) that gave expression in the 1970s to a movement of people—sometimes called "consumers," "survivors," or "ex-patients"—who sought compassionate alternatives to the mental health system through peer-run programs.

As mental health clients, we are part of a larger disability movement that in the 1980s was part of the liberation struggle in South Africa, where the slogan "Nothing About Us Without Us!" became a rallying cry for persons with mental illness, as well as those with physical disabilities. William Rowland (2001), the first chairperson of Disabled People South Africa, refers to the slogan in a brief history of the disability rights movement in his country.

> Two initiatives took shape, a political one, to mobilize disabled people to claim their rights, and a developmental one, taking the form of income generation through self-help. We also articulated a new philosophy: that disability was not a health and welfare issue, but a human rights and development issue; that the medical model of disability was inappropriate and that doctors and social workers should not run our lives; that the pacifist methods of struggle would best serve our cause; and that we should align ourselves with the liberation movement. We became "conscientised" and adopted our now famous slogan: "Nothing About Us Without Us!"

The slogan soon crossed the ocean and was adopted by advocates for the disabled in the United States, who sometimes rephrased it as "Nothing About Me Without Me." The handprint on the cover of this book is taken from a poster created by Lucy Gwin, editor of *Mouth Magazine* (see Figure A.1).

It is a powerful reminder, even today, that we, as persons recovering from mental illness, are survivors of a mental health system that tends to objectify and coerce us. We have alternately been demonized and treated as wayward children, and until very recently had no say in the treatment formed "about us" but chosen "without us." We have thus been obliged to question the treatments that failed to heal us, and to seek and create methods and programs "on our own." This we have done for over twenty years, building peer-run services with little recognition and even less funding.

Sally Clay
Lake Placid Florida
September 13, 2004

References

Chamberlin, J. 1978. On our own: Patient-controlled alternatives to the mental health system. New York: Hawthorn Books. The book has been reprinted and continues to be available from the National Empowerment Center, 599 Canal St., Lawrence, MA 01840; *www.power2u.org*

Mouth Magazine, P.O. Box 558, Topeka, KS 66601 *www.mouthmag.com* Contact Lucy Gwin, Editor, Free Hand Press, fax 785-272-7348.

Rowland, W. 2001. "Nothing about us without us: Some historical reflections on the Disability Movement in South Africa," *Disability World, A Bimonthly Web-Zine of International Disability News and Views*, November–December 2001. *www.disabilityworld.org/11–12_01/il/southafrica.shtml*

PART I

Introduction and Background

1
About Us:
What We Have in Common

Sally Clay

In the winter of 1998, mental health consumers from eight different states met in Washington, DC, to join researchers and government representatives to begin a four-year federal study of the workings of peer-run programs. The Consumer Operated Services Program, known as the COSP study, was a large, multi-site project to examine successful programs run entirely by mental health consumers for their peers—adults with schizophrenia, bipolar disorder, major depression, and other serious mental illnesses.

We consumer/survivors who represented these programs joined with other consumers on research teams to form a Consumer Advisory Panel as part of our participation in the federal study. Our programs had been chosen because consumer/survivors controlled all of their operations and expenditures. Thus, the fundamental definition of a peer-run program is that it is operated by us and for us.

In the first ever major quantitative study of self-help mental health programs, peer-run programs were examined alongside traditional mental health programs to determine whether they contribute to the effectiveness of mental health services in the community and whether they are cost effective. The study was funded by the U.S. Substance Abuse and Mental Health Services Administration (SAMHSA) from 1998 to 2002, at a cost of over $20 million.

The purpose of this book is to describe the inner workings of consumer-operated services. At its heart are eight chapters about the programs in the federal COSP study, written by the people who developed them and who live them every day. Chapters 3–10 describe eight programs in detail and from personal experience, bringing to life what has previously been presented usually from a clinical perspective and by researchers not personally involved in the self-help programs. The authors of these chapters, all members of the Consumer Advisory Panel (CAP) of the COSP study, write about their own programs. They are the recipients and the providers of the mental health services researched in the study.

Jean Campbell, author of Chapter 2, on the history of consumerrun programs, was head of the coordinating center for the study. She is a consumer/survivor herself, as well as a recognized researcher in the field.

Chapter 11 is the only chapter written by nonconsumers. The three authors, Matthew Johnsen, Gregory Teague, and Elizabeth McDonel Herr, are all researchers who report the results of a fidelity measure designed to find out whether the programs "do what they say they do." Chapter 12 includes updates on how the eight programs have fared since the end of the COSP study.

Organizing the Programs into Clusters

At first, we consumers regarded each other with some misgivings. For one thing, our programs and our perspectives were different in many ways. Some of us were active members of the mental health consumer/survivor movement that had struggled since the 1970s to reform—some might say transform—the mental health system. Other peer leaders had established their programs independent of civil rights ideology and more in partnership with existing mental health services. Despite their superficial differences, however, each of the peer programs in the COSP study fell into one of the three clusters—drop-in, peer support, and education/advocacy (see Table 1.1). Later we would examine the different catagories of common ingredients that applied to all of these clusters.

The first cluster consists of drop-in centers that provide varied services, such as meals and housing assistance for members, as well as a place to meet friends and relax in a stigma-free environment. One can expect that a drop-in center will include a permanent environment, with norms and structures, but flexible choices in activities and a relaxed time frame for participation. For example, the St. Louis Empowerment Center is in the basement of a large building in downtown St. Louis. Although the center maintains rules of behavior, all rules and standards are "self-imposed and self-enforced." Likewise, a center member is free to come at any time during its hours of operation; he or she may participate in any activity or may choose simply to chat with other members and have a cup of coffee.

The second cluster includes two programs based on peer support and

Table 1.1. The Sites: Eight Programs and Three Clusters

Drop-in Centers

California   Mental Health Client Action Network (MHCAN) (1992)
             PEER Center/Louis de la Parte Florida Mental Health Institute

Maine   Portland Coalition for the Psychiatrically Labeled (1981)
             Edmund S. Muskie School of Public Service

Missouri   St. Louis Empowerment Center (1996)
             Boston University

Florida   PEER Center, Inc. (1992)
             PEER Center/Louis de la Parte Florida Mental Health Institute

Peer Support and Mentoring

Illinois   GROW in Illinois (1978)
             University of Chicago

Pennsylvania The Friends Connection in Pennsylvania (1989)
             Mental Health Association of Southern Pennsylvania/University
             of Pennsylvania Center for Mental Health

Education and Advocacy

Connecticut Advocacy Unlimited, Inc. (1994)
             Mount Sinai School of Medicine

Tennessee   BRIDGES in Tennessee (1995)
             Michigan State University

Note: Dates indicate the year the program was founded; the institutions conducting the evaluation in each state are paired with each consumer-operated program. PEER = personal empowerment, education, and recreation; GROW = goals, reframe, options, and wellness; BRIDGES = building recovery of individual dreams and goals through education and support.

mentoring. The Friends Connection in Pennsylvania provides mentoring services to persons with dual diagnoses who are living in private houses or apartments. GROW in Illinois is part of an international program of recovery with residential services, peer support, and recreational activities based on peer support within the larger community. Programs in the peer support cluster are frequently conducted in discrete locations, such as individual homes, and these programs generally emphasize one-on-one relationships. For example, the Friends Connection links someone seeking recovery from mental illness and substance abuse with a peer support staff person who is already in recovery.

The third cluster consists of two training programs in which mental health consumers attend time-limited classes to learn recovery skills for themselves or advocacy for themselves and other consumers. BRIDGES in Tennessee conducts a ten-week course on mental health treatment and recovery, as well as ongoing support groups. Advocacy Unlimited, in Connecticut, conducts training in individual and systems advocacy and supports continuing advocacy by its graduates. Both projects are facilitated and attended by consumers, and both are statewide programs. In these, as in other education-based programs, one can expect to find a process that emphasizes a fixed timeline and a specialized location, such as a classroom for the conduct of groups or classes.

The two longest running of our programs are GROW in Illinois and the Portland Coalition for the Psychiatrically Labeled in Maine. Both of these have been in operation for more than twenty years, and the Portland Coalition was one of the first consumer-run drop-in centers in the country.

In describing these three clusters of peer-run services—drop-in centers, peer support programs, and education programs for life skills or advocacy—our intention is not to include every possible kind of program that mental health consumers might create. We omit, for example, consumer-run businesses and art projects. Our goal is simply to present the successful consumer-run programs involved in the COSP study and to examine the conceptual underpinnings and operational policies that make them work. We look for the common ingredients in these particular programs that distinguish them from professional mental health programs. In doing this, we hope that we have found qualities that apply to other consumer endeavors, while at the same time we agree that it is the prerogative of any peer-run program to define itself without having to rely on "politically correct" rules and credentials.

Listing the Common Ingredients

Despite our initial differences, the consumer/survivors in the COSP study enthusiastically worked with each other as well as with the researchers, and together we found that underlying the different programs and separate strategies are common characteristics that describe a consumer/survivor's way of working to help himself or herself and others. In the end, we arrived at twenty-six common ingredients, which we refined into a table with comprehensive definitions of the ingredients. This document, entitled "Common Ingredients of COSPs (CAP Definitions)," is reproduced in Appendix B. The table shown below (Table 1.2) is a more compact list of the twenty-six ingredients in the CAP document, organized into five categories.

Although the CAP members agreed that each common ingredient is important, we labeled some as "core ingredients" because they are fundamental to all peer-run programs and essential to the peer-run concept (these are marked with an asterisk in Table 1.2). Noncore ingredients, in contrast, are those that might have greater or lesser emphasis among programs, depending on the cluster, or type of program, involved. For example, a program cannot be designated peer-run unless it is governed and administered by consumers—thus, "consumer operated" is a core ingredient. Some so-called consumer programs cannot be referred to as consumer operated because they are controlled or staffed by mental health

Table 1.2. COSP Common Ingredients by Category

Program Structure	Peer Support
*Consumer-operated Participant responsive Linkage to other supports	*Peer support Telling our stories Consciousness raising Crisis prevention Peer mentoring and teaching
Environment	**Education/Advocacy**
Accessibility *Safety Informal setting Reasonable accommodation	*Self-management and problem- solving strategies Education
Belief Systems	
*Peer principle *Helper's principle *Empowerment Creativity and humor Choice Recovery Acceptance and respect for diversity Spiritual growth	*Self-advocacy Peer advocacy Systems advocacy Community education

*Core ingredients.

professionals. This use of professionals is one of the ways the clubhouse model differs from the peer-run model; a clubhouse is similar to a drop-in center but it is not governed by its consumer members, and consumers do not manage its budget.

An educational program may offer classes in peer counseling, and an advocacy program may teach its members to do systems advocacy, but such trainings are not always available in a drop-in or mentoring program and so are not core ingredients.

The five categories of common ingredients emerge naturally from three different sections:

1. *Structure:* how peer programs are organized. This section includes the categories of Program Structure and Environment.
2. *Values:* how the programs reflect a uniquely consumer philosophy. This section includes the single category of Belief Systems.
3. *Process:* what programs or activities they offer. This section includes the categories of Peer Support and Education/advocacy.

This scheme for organizing the CAP common ingredients is shown in Figure 1.1 (below). Common ingredients are subdivided by section and then by catagory. For example, "Consumer Operated" is listed under Program Structure, "Safety" is under Environment, and both of these catagories are under the Strucure section. Researchers used this setup to create the Fidelity Assessment Common Ingredients Tool (FACIT) for their fidelity study. The FACIT allowed them to assign measurable units to all of

Figure 1.1. Common Ingredients: Section/Category/Core Ingredient

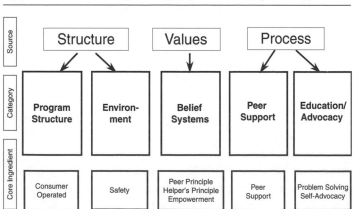

the common ingredients and thus to analyze them when the researchers made site visits at each COSP location. The entire FACIT document is not reproduced in this book because of its length, but its use is described in detail in Chapter 11.

The list of common ingredients in the FACIT is somewhat different from the CAP definitions in Table 1.2 and in Appendix Table B.2. The FACIT lists education and advocacy as separate categories, and it describes two "overarching domains" (structure and process) rather than three sections (structure, values, and process). It omits three ingredients: "creativity and humor," "systems advocacy," and "community education." Nevertheless, the FACIT scheme is essentially the same as the CAP lists, and it follows the same configuration in Figure 1.1. The minor differences between the lists do not present a problem to CAP members, since we agreed from the beginning that none of our definitions should be "set in stone," and all such lists should include flexibility in their definitions and in describing the ways that our programs operate.

Defining the Common Ingredients

Program Structure

Tables and figures used to describe the various common ingredients apply to all of the clusters in the COSP study. The most important ingredient of any consumer-run program is that its administration and primary activities are independent of provider organizations and that consumers control its board of directors, its staff, and its budget. This is the definition of *consumer operated* that SAMHSA used to determine whether a program qualified to participate in its 1998–2002 COSP study. Consumer operated is also the first common ingredient, labeled as core, in the CAP list (Table 1.2), and it follows one of the most honored principles of the disability rights movement: "Nothing About Us without Us."

Most of the programs in the study have achieved not-for-profit status, and most manage their own budget. Two who do not manage their own budget—the St. Louis Empowerment Center and Friends Connection—each operate under the aegis of a larger consumer-run program, which in turn fulfills the definition of consumer operated. The St. Louis program is administered by the Depressive and Bipolar Support Alliance, and the Friends Connection by the Mental Health Association of Southeastern Pennsylvania.

All of the programs in the COSP study included the other ingredients in the category of Program Structure—they are *participant* (or member) *responsive,* and they include *linkage to other supports.*

Environment

The core ingredient in the Environment category is *safety,* which for mental health consumers means a noncoercive milieu that soothes fears resulting from past trauma, including trauma induced by the mental health system. There is no threat of commitment, clinical diagnosis, or unwanted treatment except in cases of suicide attempt or physical danger to other participants. Participants draw up their own rules and norms of behavior in order to protect the well-being of themselves and others.

Even peer programs such as educational trainings that meet in classrooms endeavor to provide an *informal setting.* According to this characteristic, a peer-run program should provide an environment that is people-friendly and comfortable. Rigid distinctions between staff and client do not exist, and there is a sense of freedom, fellowship, and belonging. Participants feel supported and free to express themselves. They care about each other and create community together. Most participants readily identify their sense of belonging as the first and perhaps most important benefit of joining a peer-run program.

Other elements of a peer environment borrow terms from the disability movement, such as accessibility and reasonable accommodation. For mental health consumers, *accessibility* refers to transportation and meeting times, which should be convenient to consumers, as well as wheelchair accommodation. *Reasonable accommodation* applies to mental as well as to physical disabilities.

Belief Systems

The largest number of common ingredients falls under the section Values, which heads the single category of Belief Systems. This is not surprising, for consumers are an idealistic lot—we have experienced disruptions in our lives that put our identities and all of our relationships in question. Most of us, after going through such experiences, come out philosophizing. The core ingredients under "Belief Systems" are the peer principle, the helper's principle, and empowerment, concepts that emphasize the equality and mutuality of relationships among all consumers in a program, and the strength derived from these values.

According to the *peer principle,* relationships are based on shared experiences and values and are characterized by reciprocity and mutuality. *Peer* is defined in the dictionary as "a person who has equal standing with another in rank or class." Within the consumer/survivor movement, a peer is not just someone with equal standing but also someone who has shared similar experiences and challenges. A peer relationship implies equality, along with mutual acceptance and unconditional respect. Any group of self-identified peers, whether it is within a twelve-step meeting, cancer support group, or a mental health group, creates a palpable feeling of hope and belonging.

The *helper's principle* is a corollary of the peer principle. It means acting for the benefit of both oneself and others. Consumer/survivors believe that working for the recovery of others, especially one's peers, facilitates personal recovery for both. Help or advice is friendly rather than professional and does not demand compliance the way that much formal treatment does. All peer-run services are based on peer-to-peer relationships, as part of the peer principle and the helper's principle. Most successful peer-run programs in mental health have been started by persons who were themselves still on the road to recovery. In the process of creating a program to help others, they find that that they themselves achieve wisdom and satisfaction in their lives.

Empowerment is honored as an important basis of recovery. Personal empowerment is defined as a sense of personal strength and efficacy, with self-direction and control over one's life. It produces hope, an element indispensable to independent living and recovery. Consumers believe that recovery and well-being are not possible unless we begin with a strong sense of hope. The sense of ownership felt by participants in a peer-run program is an important source of empowerment as well.

Empowerment is a two-way street—participants in a peer-run program are expected, but not forced, to be accountable for their actions and to act responsibly. Self-reliance is encouraged. Group empowerment comes from belonging to an organized group that is recognized by the larger community. The legitimacy of any group contributes both to the personal empowerment of the individuals within it and to improvements in social systems. Consumers participate in systems-level activities at their own pace.

All of our belief systems operate from a strong sense of personal ethics and an unconditional respect for each person as an individual with the right to make decisions for himself or herself. Thus, our values include not just the philosophies of peer principle, helper's principle, and empowerment but also creativity and humor, choice, recovery, acceptance and respect for diversity, and spiritual growth. Many of us have found that *creativity* comes naturally to those who experience madness, and pursuing artistic endeavors such as writing and painting can be healing. Likewise, *humor* is healing. Joking with our peers deepens friendships, and barriers of stigma dissolve when we can laugh together with so-called normal persons.

Mental health clients believe in the element of *choice* largely because we know from experience that involuntary treatment has failed to heal and may even damage us. Thus, participation in a peer-run program is completely voluntary, and all activities are elective and noncoercive. Choice of services includes the right to choose none. Consumers are regarded as experts in defining their own experiences and choosing the peer-run or professional services that best suit them. Problems to be addressed are those identified by the consumer, not by professionals or other external persons. For example, a client in a community mental health clinic may be required to participate in assigned appointments and activities and to reach certain goals and self-improvement within a set period of time. In contrast, in a consumer-run drop-in center, a member can follow his or her own schedule and goals. If she is not yet ready to move forward, for example, she can just sit and drink coffee until she is ready to go on to something else. Often drop-in centers are criticized for the number of people who seem to just sit around and do nothing. But often it is precisely because we are allowed to "take our time" that we can find the feeling of safety and freedom necessary to pursue true healing.

Often members of our Consumer Advisory Panel expressed the belief that *acceptance* and *respect for diversity* were essential components of peer support. As peers, we are able to tolerate people whose actions and beliefs in a professional setting might be labeled "symptomatic" or considered "inappropriate." Since we have been crazy ourselves, we feel compassion for the confusion of others rather than fear of their madness, and we strive to offer unconditional respect to those who are "in the same boat" as we are.

It was surprising to some of us that we could not come up with satisfactory definitions for recovery and spirituality. We all agreed that *recovery* is an important component of peer-run programs, but we could not pin down exactly what it is. In the end, we agreed that recovery is a process, not an outcome, and that each individual defines recovery in his or her own terms. There was similar uncertainty over the role of *spiritual growth* in peer-run programs. Although we could not arrive at a way to identify true spirituality, we did agree that the subjective beliefs and experiences of each person should be respected, and not labeled as symptoms of illness.

Peer Support

The idea of peer-facilitated recovery really began with Alcoholics Anonymous and has been adopted by other peer groups of every kind. In mental health, *peer support* is the core and the mainstay of any consumer-run program. Individual participants are available to each other to listen with empathy and compassion based on common experience. Similar support may be provided in formal support groups, such as those that meet at scheduled times or are conducted with a peer facilitator.

Small support or conversation groups allow participants to share common experiences. These groups may be formal peer support groups or casual, ad hoc conversations. *Telling our stories* is a common way for mental health consumers to share personal feelings and information with each other. We also use the technique of telling our stories to take our message to the larger community and to raise the consciousness of other people and agencies, as well as ourselves. Personal accounts of life experiences are embedded in all forms of peer support and education. Sharing life experiences is a powerful tool for public education and an effective means of eliminating stigma. An excellent example of personal story-telling may be found in Chapter 10, in a story entitled "A Voice from the Region" by Sam Viar.

The same skills used in peer support allow peer-run programs to provide formal or informal *crisis prevention* and inspire persons in recovery to act as role models for their peers, and even mentors or teachers. Through *peer mentoring and teaching* participants receive information about the consumer movement, and new participants discover commonality with others. This peer support often produces the first dramatic change in a consumer's perspective, helping him or her move from despair to hope and empowerment. Consumers often report that joining a peer-run program gave them a sense of belonging that replaced their previous loneliness and isolation.

Education and Advocacy

The core ingredients in this category are *self-management and problem-solving strategies* as well as *self-advocacy,* and these ingredients apply, for the most part, to all of the programs in our study. Most peer-run programs provide some way of learning self-management skills, and most encourage participants to identify their own needs and to advocate for themselves when there are gaps in services. In one way or another, all peer-run programs allow participants to develop and improve social skills in a natural environment in which they feel comfortable. This is often a first step toward creating or re-establishing valued roles in the community and reintegrating into community life. The focus is on practical solutions to human concerns.

The cluster of programs under Education/advocacy also contains elements that are sometimes particular to education classes or advocacy training and not as prominent in drop-in centers and peer support programs. Educational programs, various kinds of advocacy, and community education are projects that may or may not be present in a drop-in center or a mentoring program. For example, training models of peer-run programs such as BRIDGES in Tennessee are more likely to offer formal instruction in daily living skills, such as job readiness, communication skills, and assertiveness skills.

Most programs encourage consumers to practice self-advocacy by becoming active partners in developing their service plans with traditional agencies or mental health professionals. However, some peer-run agencies also feature well-defined programs in which individual advocates work on behalf of their peers to assist them in resolving problems encountered with entitlement programs, medical institutions, community agencies, residences, and even their own families. In our study, for example, educational programs such as Advocacy Unlimited and drop-ins such as MHCAN both teach and practice self-advocacy and individual peer advocacy. These peer-run advocacy programs also use a number of tools to carry out *systems advocacy,* to bring changes at the societal and legislative levels. Such tools may include testifying before the legislature; participating on boards, committees, and task forces; and communicating directly with policy and lawmakers.

Finally, *community education* is practiced by all programs to some degree through newsletters and other methods of outreach to the public. Some programs, however, such as the four drop-in centers in our group, go a step further by creating a bureau that provides speakers to make formal presentations before local community groups or nationally held conferences for consumers, families, and mental health professionals. Speakers such as these, or such as individual consumers who tell their stories, are probably the single best stigma-destroying tool available to us. Remarkable changes can occur when we just make the point that we are human beings with the same needs and aspirations as everyone else.

In the end, we discovered that most of the eight consumer-operated services programs observe most of the processes of Peer Support and Advocacy/Education. And the reason for this consistency, we found, was recognition of the value of the peer principle—identifying oneself with others—which leads a consumer to seek support from likeminded persons and to offer peer support in return. Likewise, peer-run programs observe the processes of advocacy and education because they recognize the value of the helper's principle—benefiting oneself by helping others—which leads consumers to both teach and learn from peers and to advocate for the benefit of themselves and others.

Assessing the Eight Peer-Run Programs

As mentioned earlier, one result of the dialogue between CAP members and researchers about common ingredients was the FACIT document that was adopted by the COSP Multi-Site Research Initiative as the basis for its fidelity measure. The FACIT measured the presence of the Common Ingredients in all of the peer-run programs. Researchers from the Coordinating Center visited all of the sites and examined the degree to which they followed the Common Ingredients that they themselves had identified.

A less tangible result of our CAP dialogues was that consumers from the different clusters of programs and different areas of the country found that not only could we work successfully together but that we could reach consensus on the definitions of core principles and structures that applied to all of us.

In our updates on how the eight programs have fared since the end of the COSP study in Chapter 12, we identify obstacles and setbacks that appeared during the course of this study and that are common to peer-run programs in general. It is our hope that by assembling and naming the common structures, principles, and foibles that make up peer-run endeavors, we will encourage other consumers who endeavor to start new peer-run programs of their own. We urge our consumer readers to network with the programs in this book and with other programs around the country and in other parts of the world. As consumers who have experienced empowerment and recovery, we now seek to impart our acquired knowledge and courage to others who may continue this pioneering journey. We hope that you, too, will learn the ropes about peer support and leadership, and that this knowledge will lead to the funding and establishment of many more peer-run programs.

We live in an era in which peer-run self-help and recovery programs are under attack by those who believe that mental health consumers should be treated only by professionals, only in formal systems, and sometimes against their will. Peer-run programs are always in danger of losing their funding; they are often the last to be funded and the first to be cut when budgets are tight. Perhaps this will always be true where the stakes are so high, and because the stakeholders in mental health services cover such a broad spectrum, from families to law enforcement to government to mental health professionals, and all the way down to ordinary citizens in individual households. Let us never forget, however, that mental health consumers are the primary stakeholders. We are the ones who have experienced mental illness, and we are the ones who are most qualified to evaluate what has helped us and what does not help. We present the common ingredients through the CAP definitions in Appendix B as an informal guideline to what has led us to well-being and recovery. A glossary of terms used in this book and among consumers may be found in Appendix Table A.1.

Before we look at the eight consumer-operated services programs and how they operate, however, we review in Chapter 2 the history of the consumer/survivor movement and the principles that have guided and informed us in creating programs that not only supplement the work of conventional services but add an indispensable element of our own.

2
The Historical and Philosophical Development of Peer-Run Support Programs

Jean Campbell

The general public thinks of people with mental illness as the quintessential "Other"—persons who represent the subterranean depths of humanity and whose differentness makes us not really human at all. It is common practice to call us by our diagnoses rather than our names. Usually we are simply referred to as "the mentally ill."

Mental health professionals subsume our identity with a global sentence of illness and disability. It is often presumed that we do not know what is in our own best interests. Our feelings of anger and joy are scrutinized for signs of pathology and violence. Our needs and desires are imputed for us, as if we were mute. We are routinely consigned to everyday lives emptied of quality, vitality, and dignity.

When you look closer, however, to the margins of society, you find us speaking for ourselves. By forming peer relationships, we have created a dynamic way of life that embraces cooperation, connection, and community. Our social relations are complex. We build networks of support and service, produce culture and research, and dream of a liberated future. Collectively we choose to call ourselves *persons* diagnosed with a mental illness, *people* with psychiatric disabilities, *persons* who have experienced madness, mental health consumers, psychiatric survivors, or mental health clients. But most important, each person has a name; each person has a story.

As mental health systems have matured, professionals have begun to change their views about the abilities of people with mental illness. They have started to include consumer/survivors as partners in the design, delivery, and evaluation of services (Campbell 1996, 1997). Progressive forces in the mental health community recognize that differences in perspective between mental health professionals and persons who have been institutionalized are "valuable, worthwhile, and important" (McCade and Unzicker 1995, 61). In describing a framework for the role of consumers as providers of psychiatric rehabilitation, Mowbray and Moxley (1997, 39) suggest that one rationale for peer-run support programs is that "consumers have the ability to form creative, nontraditional, and more beneficial alternatives or adjuncts to formal mental health services. . . . Since the consumer-controlled program is developed and delivered by consumers, it has the potential of contributing something that is very different in rehabilitation and community support than what individuals with professional training can do within existing structures."

The delivery of mental health care in the United States today is being challenged. On one hand, professionals and policymakers acknowledge that mental health services have failed to help people get the level of care that research has shown to be effective. Financial resources are limited and traditional mental health programs are both fragmented and strained by growing demands for services. On the other hand, the recovery model of service delivery suggests that "adjuncts and alternatives to formal treatment, involvement in self-help groups, and social opportunities at local drop-in centers foster empowerment and provide opportunities for a more meaningful life" (Forquer and Knight 2001, 25). Further, many peer-run programs serve persons who will not accept, or who do not choose to participate in, traditional services (Segal, Silverman, and Temkin 1995). Therefore, when peer support services are included within the continuum of community care, the mental health system expands quantitatively, by reaching more people, and qualitatively, by helping people become more independent and interdependent (Gartner and Reissman 1982).

As a result, mental health administrators are increasingly open to shifting resources to a recovery-based model of community services (President's New Freedom Commission for Mental Health 2002). Such a shift presents a compelling case for dialogue between traditional mental health providers and mental health consumer/survivors about what promotes and deters recovery, and the inclusion of persons with mental illness as partners in collaborative systems of service and support.

By responding to the experiences of people with mental illness, peer-run programs provide the needed support for people in their struggles to live with dignity and hope. Consumer/survivors have discovered that recovery is not a state that impinges on everyday life from the outside. Rather, the inherent dynamics of recovery are grounded in a person's mind and body—in his or her hopes, needs, preferences, and choices. Most important, peer support service providers treat consumer/survivors as full human beings rather than disease entities. They believe that each person is capable of entering communities of his or her choice (Ahern and Fisher 2001) and are promoting recovery from mental illness through voluntary forms of assistance directed by individuals who have had similar experiences. According to Ahern and Fisher (1999, 4), "The cornerstone of this assistance is the development of trusting relationships, which in turn allows people to (re)capture their dreams and enables them to (re)gain a valued social role."

This chapter traces the remarkable development of peer-run support programs as they emerged from a legacy of abuse, dehumanization, and coercion that was found in traditional mental health service systems. It illuminates the beliefs, values, and customs that bind consumers in an evolving "empowerment culture of recovery" (Ahern and Fisher 2001) by examining the operating principles of peer-run support services and the unique forms of mutual support that have arisen as alternatives to professional mental health programs. It shows how the early alternative programs are linked to contemporary peer support program goals of empowerment, personhood, and recovery and provides studies of the effectiveness of peer support approaches. Looking to the future, the chapter concludes with a discussion of the tensions embedded in the movement of the peer-run support programs toward partnership with traditional mental health service systems, and the benefits and dangers of professionalization of peer-run services as they become integrated within the continuum of community care.

Rehabilitation Is Not Enough

Several forces converged over the past century to foster peer-run support programs as they exist today for people with psychiatric problems:

- the growth of self-help groups that address a broad range of life crises, medical conditions, and disabilities;
- the struggle of persons with mental illness to re-enter community life following deinstitutionalization and the development of psychosocial rehabilitation programs to address the need for life-skill training and socialization; and
- the rise of the mental patients' rights movement, anti-psychiatry, an consumer/survivor alternatives to traditional mental health treatments.

In some ways, all of these forces reflect the natural human tendency to seek others with problems and concerns similar to one's own in order to make sense of one's experiences and to be empowered by that knowledge. Although seeking the company of others was once considered a social trait of the species and of less importance than the basic human need for food and shelter, we now know that being with another person or group of people is of primary importance to people confronted with life-challenging events. Clinicians and researchers have found ample evidence that people confide in relatives and friends as a way of coping with emotionally stressful events and that those who are isolated suffer greater stress and are at higher risk for a variety of physical and emotional problems than those who have a social network. Thus, the company of others has a functional value, and those elements that sustain social connections to everyday life are necessary for one's physical and emotional health. Within the context of social relationships—parenthood and friendships, civic memberships, and even chance meetings on a neighborhood stroll or casual words around the coffee machine at work—people are nourished as human beings.

Americans Discover the Power of Self-Help

Over the past thirty years, participation in self-help groups has become an increasingly important way for people to help each other cope with various problems and life crises. Approximately 7.5 million Americans belong to as many as one-half million self-help groups, addressing a range of illnesses, addictions, disabilities, and conditions (Lieberman and Snowden 1994). Members of such groups come together to share experiences, feelings, and practical ways of handling problems, and the two-way interaction of giving and receiving help is therapeutic in itself (Mental Health Policy Resource Center 1991). Durman (1976) found that most self-help groups developed in response to the need for human interaction, for the quick availability of others in a crisis, and for a place where the focus is not on making basic changes in outlook or personality but in sustaining the ability of members to cope with difficult situations.

With the proliferation of these groups, researchers and policymakers began to recognize the therapeutic value of being with others through various life crises (Gartner and Riessman 1982). According to Medvene's (1986) review of the literature on the effectiveness of self-help groups, "numerous research studies show that participation in self-help groups can help people improve the quality of their lives significantly" and that "support groups reduce the need for medical care and hospitalization." Cobb (1976, 300) reported that "social support can protect people in crisis from a variety of pathological states: from low birth weight to death, from arthritis through tuberculosis to depression, alcoholism, and the social breakdown syndrome. Furthermore, social support may reduce the amount of medication required, accelerate recovery, and facilitate compliance with prescribed medical regimens."

Ample evidence has established that personal networks and social activities are important for the well-being of people with mental illness. Family and friends are characterized as "good medicine" in a publication of the California Department of Mental Health (1981, 17): "The good news is that friends, family, and other support groups help protect us from the harmful effects of stress. In fact, their presence even helps reduce stress in our lives by helping us care about ourselves, anticipate change, and cope with our crisis and transitions."

Grusky et al. (1985, 49) observed that "social ties provide mentally ill individuals with opportunities for appropriate behavior, nondependent relationships, and reciprocal social exchange—all of which are essential for normal functioning." In addition, studies of decision-making in psychiatric emergency rooms indicated that "hospitalization could have been avoided if there had been a more supportive and protective milieu" (Marson, McGovern, and Pomp 1988, 921).

Some people are reluctant to join a self-help group because membership could confer identification with a stigmatized group. Still, the emotional support between people who have gone through similar experiences is very powerful. One mental health consumer/survivor remarked, "I feel good with the people there, I like them and I feel they like me. I feel like we respect each other and that we have the same things in common, that there is more sameness about us than there are differences, and that's a good feeling to me" (quoted in Campbell and Schraiber 1989, 51).

A Loneliness That Humbled the Spirit

Paralleling the rise of self-help groups, in the 1970s large numbers of psychiatric patients were discharged from psychiatric hospitals only to find themselves adrift in uncaring communities: isolated, lonely, and lacking meaningful relationships (Campbell and Schraiber 1989; Baker and Intagliata 1984). Limited financial resources restricted their social activity. The media's frequent portrayals of persons with mental illness as dangerous validated community rejection, and prejudice and discrimination polluted public and private spaces. Community and mental health professional stereotyping altered the quality and spontaneity of interpersonal relationships as negative attitudes were internalized (Reidy 1994; Campbell and Schraiber 1989). Zinman (1987, 8) wrote, "For us as people, we have internalized the dehumanizing stereotypical images propagated by our families, the mental health system, and society at large."

Bernikow (1987, 222) reported that mental health clients at a Settlement House lived together in a community made up of "individual little lonelinesses." One resident said, "I keep thinking if I can make it past breakfast without lying down and crying because I feel so lonely ... if I can make it past lunch ... if I can make it past coffee break."

The Well-Being Project survey of attitudes of mental health consumer/survivors in California (Campbell and Schraiber 1989) found that respondents were primarily searching for community and mutual support in a hostile world. One person remarked, "We have this thing in our society that you have to be with somebody all the time, but I think that there's a real lack of intimacy. I felt alone, lonely in the crowd. We live among missions of strangers, and where people are very uptight" (47).

Organized Socialization

Early professional psychiatric rehabilitative programs recognized the need for autonomy and free association among individuals who had been socially disabled by institutionalization. Socialization was taught, promoted, and evaluated as part of rehabilitation initiatives. In the 1950s a group of consumers calling themselves We Are Not Alone developed a clubhouse approach to provide mutual support after they left a state hospital. This program was adapted by professionals to build an intentional therapeutic community comprising both people who had a serious mental illness and general staff who worked within the clubhouse (Beard, Propst, and Malamud 1982; Beard 1976).

Participation in activities that provide social support is sometimes prescribed as part of an individual treatment plan. For example, rehabilitation programs provide training in common living skills, such as riding the bus, paying bills, and grocery shopping. Thus, professionally constructed social relationships become opportunities for both the delivery of mental health rehabilitative services and various types of human interaction. The value of socialization services is revealed in the comment by one consumer/survivor, "When my friend calls me, it's as though he accepts me in spite of my craziness and I, therefore, can feel better about myself" (quoted in Breirer and Strauss 1984, 950).

The process of formalizing social support through professional mental health programs, however, strips relationships of intimacy, closeness, affection, and sexual contact. Often when mental health consumer/survivors identify social relationships as important to improving their lives, they mean that they want to get married or be part of a loving family. Yet, rehabilitative programs that offer social interactions on one hand are often fraught with denial on the other because they exclude the possibility of intimacy by maintaining boundaries between people. Reflecting the pervasive clinical beliefs of the 1970s and 1980s that people cannot manage their psychiatric problems and will remain chronically mentally ill, professional rehabilitation programs often sustain low expectations for members to recover and occupy meaningful roles within society, including as partners within the mental health system itself.

Reaching Across

As some consumer/survivors reacted with dissatisfaction to professional mental health treatments and services, they autonomously began to seek the company of their peers for validation and support. Lack of understanding, respect, and trust between mental health clients and professionals prompted clients to reject both clinical and rehabilitation programs and to develop peer-run alternatives. One person interviewed by the Well-Being Project (Campbell and Schraiber 1989, 60) explained:

> As clients we contend that treatment should not be forced upon us, especially treatment that we do not want. We believe in the freedom to be able to choose the kind of services that are going to make us feel like worthwhile adults in the community, and feel like we're contributing members to society. We feel the best way to do that is to allow us to make our own choices. Our lives have more meaning than a diagnosis. We need to be treated as whole people, to be included in that treatment, and to be able to make the decisions. Clients have real needs. The reason why we clients have sort of taken it upon ourselves to start organizations is because our needs aren't being met by the professionals in mental health.

Early attempts at peer support led to the organization of patients' rights groups, such as the Insane Liberation Front in Portland, Oregon, and the Mental Patient's Liberation Project in New York City. These were civil rights activist groups (Van Tosh, Ralph, and Campbell 2000; Chamberlin 1988, 1997) in the tradition of the liberation movements of blacks, women, and gays in the sixties and the seventies. "We are like colonized people," Zinman (1987, 7) explained, "struggling to be free, to reclaim from psychiatry ownership of our lives. We are fighting for autonomy."

Local groups were the heart of the patients' rights movement. They were started by small numbers of people who would come together through a common sense of injustice and the belief that through organization they could bring about change in the mental health system. Known by a variety of names (Mental Patients' Alliance; Network Against Psychiatric Assault Independent; Project Acceptance; Reclamation, Inc.; Take A Loving Look At Yourself) these loosely linked associations developed different ideologies, styles, and goals. Some operated within traditional hierarchies, selecting officers and holding formal meetings. Others had more egalitarian structures with shared decision-making and no formal leadership. The groups communicated through *Madness Network News,* a newspaper nationally distributed by and for people with mental illness, and they met at conferences. Activities included "organizing support groups, advocating for hospitalized patients, lobbying for changes in laws, public speaking, publishing newsletters, developing creative and artistic ways of dealing with the mental patient experience" (Chamberlin 1997).

In 1977, the Community Support Program (CSP), now located within the U. S. Substance Abuse and Mental Health Services Administration's Center for Mental Health Services, provided further impetus to the growing movement through a variety of initiatives. CSP funded the first annual National Consumer Alternatives Conference in 1985, and from 1988 to 1991 it supported fourteen service demonstration projects designed to implement and evaluate consumer-operated peer support services, including drop-in centers, outreach programs, businesses, employment and housing programs, and crisis services (Van Tosh and del Vecchio 2000; Kaufmann, Ward-Colasante, and Farmer 1993; Mowbray and Tan 1992; Lieberman, Gowdy, and Knutson 1991). Centers for self-help research and self-help technical assistance centers run by mental health consumer/ survivors, such as the National Empowerment Center in Lawrence, Massachusetts, and the National Mental Health Consumers' Self-Help Clearing House in Philadelphia, Pennsylvania, were also federally funded.

In a study of 104 self-help groups, Emerick (1990) classified groups according to structure, affiliation, and service model along an ideological continuum from radical, separatist groups, such as the National Alliance of Psychiatric Survivors, to conservative groups that allow professionals to act as leaders in partnership with consumer/survivors, such as Recovery, Inc. and Emotions Anonymous. Social movement and individual therapy were found to be the two major service models. The social movement groups offer legal advocacy, public education, technical assistance, and information-referral networking. The individual therapy groups offer more "inner-focused" individual change through group support meetings. Two-thirds of the groups were identified as social movement groups and of these more than 70 percent were found to have little to no interaction with mental health professionals. In fact, 43 percent held antiprofessional attitudes.

From Separatism to Inclusion

Throughout the 1990s, people with mental illness began to organize on a national level around the issues of empowerment and strengthening the consumer voice (Chamberlin 1997), championing the South African disability motto, "Nothing About Us, Without Us." Groups opposed traditional mental health system treatments, such as day treatment, involuntary commitment, forced drugging, and the use of seclusion and restraints, but they also began to emphasize concepts such as "service recipient," choice, and treatment "partnerships" of clinicians and clients within the mental health system. Some consumer/survivor leaders started to advocate for consumer inclusion in the administration, provision, and evaluation of mental health services as a tool of system reform (Campbell 1996, 1997; Campbell and Johnson 1995; Campbell, Ralph, and Glover 1993; Scott 1993).

The transformation of the healthcare delivery system to a managed care environment during this period also produced an unintended opportunity for mental health consumer/survivors to demand responsibility for making decisions in the medical marketplace as customers. The argument that persons who seek mental health services are just like persons who seek other types of services was strengthened by the call of consumer/survivors for inclusion in research and policy decisions that affect their treatment options. Consumerism implies that the "values derived from principles of good medical care must be interpreted and operationalized through reference to the patient's personal health care values and desires" (Beisecker and Beisecker 1993, 53). This view overturned the "expert knows best" rationale for paternalistic models of service delivery that excluded shared decision-making.

In 1989, the National Association of State Mental Health Program Directors (NASMHPD) approved a position paper that "recognizes that former mental patients/mental health consumers have a unique contribution to make to the improvement of the quality of mental health services in many areas of the service delivery system." The paper recommends that consumer contributions be valued and sought in areas of program development, policy formation, program evaluation, quality assurance, systems designs, education of mental health service providers, and provision of direct services.

With the support of the Mental Health Statistics Improvement Program at the Center for Mental Health Services, the Consumer/Survivor Mental Health Research and Policy Work Group was organized in 1992 to promote the inclusion of mental health consumers in policy and research. One of the projects of the group was to define desired outcomes of state mental health service from the perspective of consumers. Another effort was to initiate a series of "Pioneer Dialogue" meetings between members of the consumer work group and state mental health commissioners. The response from the commissioners, according to Bevilaqua (1993, 2) was "excellent" and included "a willingness to engage openly consumer/survivor representation in the various activities of NASMHPD with a shared concern for governance, policy, and research."

Over the past two decades, mental health consumer/survivors have built a national presence within the public mental health sector, with growing numbers now participating in research and evaluation (Van Tosh, Ralph, and Campbell 2000) and taking leadership roles in policy and administration of public mental health services (McCabe and Unzicker 1995). They have led efforts to determine housing preferences (Tanzman 1993), to define outcome measures (Campbell 1997; Trochim, Dumont, and Campbell 1993), and to develop partnership models with public mental health professionals (Campbell 1996). Some professionals and policymakers responded to consumer inclusion by redesigning professional roles and creating opportunities for people who receive services to provide input and perspective. Consumer/survivors carved out an expanding role in lecturing, conducting grand rounds, teaching continuing education classes, and offering workshops at national professional conferences. In 1993 consumer-practitioners and psychiatrists engaged in a dialogue in New York regarding coping strategies and recovery from mental illness (Blanch et al. 1993). The proliferation of offices of consumer affairs in state mental health agencies, statewide consumer conferences, consumer-directed technical assistance centers, and peer-run support services, and the growing respect for consumer/survivor research and policy professionals are indicators of a vibrant culture of collaboration today among consumer/survivors and professionals.

Peer support services, once separate from mainstream mental health services, began to develop partnerships with traditional mental health providers. Some professional mental health agencies employ consumers in designated positions to provide peer services, such as case management or crisis intervention (Arntsen et al. 1995). Peer support services are also offered as part of an array of services designed and delivered through a traditional mental health agency, and staffed with mental health consumer/survivors who share administrative and fiscal authority with nonconsumers (Solomon and Draine 2001).

Some types of peer support programs remain autonomous and are staffed solely by mental health recipients, with decision making and service delivery responsibility shared among the members. But most of these peer-run support programs no longer consider themselves alternatives to traditional treatment, since their membership appears to make notable use of the mental health system. Chamberlin, Rogers, and Ellison (1996) found that members in the peer-run groups they studied used about seven mental health services in one year, and about half were currently taking psychiatric medications. In most instances, the relationship of peer-run support programs and professional services have not been formalized within an integrated system of care but maintain ad hoc or informal relationships.

The Vision of Recovery

Rehabilitation literature began to define a new vision of recovery from mental illness that was shaped more and more by the ideas and needs of mental health consumer/survivors who in the 1990s were participating in mental health systems in a variety of leadership roles (Anthony 1993). Epidemiological studies of long-term recovery (DeSisto et al. 1995; Harding et al. 1987) found evidence that people could recover fully from the most severe forms of mental illness. Yet, most providers still limited the concept of recovery to functioning while remaining mentally ill. Some rehabilitation approaches also began to recognize the value of building on the strengths of persons (Rapp 1998), while others remained focused on the remediation of deficits (Cook, Jonikas, and Solomon 1991).

The ambivalence within professional services meant that the cutting edge of recovery was not situated in the engineered interventions offered by mental health rehabilitation programs. For those labeled with psychiatric disorders, learning to live with a mental disease still meant remaining an outcast from society—subjected to intense prejudice and discrimination and denied meaningful work and decent housing. To consumer/survivors, recovery implies having hope for the future, living a self-determined life, maintaining self-esteem, and achieving a meaningful role in society. Rather than a model of rehabilitation, the process is deeply personal and different for everyone. Based on choice, acceptance, and healing, it is "facilitated or impeded through the dynamic interplay of many forces that are complex, synergistic, and linked" (Onken et al. 2002). A combination of recovery-based beliefs, relationships, skills, and community were to be found in the humanized environments of modern peer-run support programs.

Description of Peer Support Services

Tan, Mowbray, and Foster (1990) describe the goals of peer-run programs as providing a safe, supportive, and normalizing community environment; providing an atmosphere of acceptance; helping consumers feel needed and helping to promote their self-worth, dignity, and respect; and increasing knowledge about the community by learning from one another. A self-help group, according to Zinman (1987, 13), "can take many different forms; its parameters are limited only by the desires, energy, and possibilities of its members."

Peer support involves a wide range of services. Almost all provide members with opportunities to tell their stories to other members and to wider audiences. Through personal narrative, consumer/survivors combat societal stereotypes and begin to rebuild a sense of self within a consumer/survivor community (Mead, Hilton, and Curtis 2001; Skillman-Campbell 1991). Since societal problems and injustices are commonly viewed as major contributors to members' individual problems (Zinman 1986, 1987; Chamberlin 1988), learning to speak for themselves encourages members to act on their own behalf and to begin to advocate for the rights of others (McLean 1995). Some programs also formalize the role-modeling function of consumer/survivor staff and assign peer mentors to individual participants. Peer mentors speak openly about their personal struggles and use their own experience to provide encouragement and technical assistance to participants (Salzer and Liptzin-Shear 2002).

Mutual support groups, such as GROW in America, and *mentoring services,* such as Friends Connection in Philadelphia (see Chapters 7 and 8), typically consist of individual or group-based assistance and encouragement organized around empowerment and recovery (Rappaport, Reischl, and Zimmerman 1992). Following a small group dynamic, members help each other manage a range of personal concerns, including those associated with their psychiatric symptoms, prejudice and discrimination, work, housing, health, and personal relationships. Such groups differ from naturally occurring social support since the process is intentional and includes "standard procedures, routines, and prescriptions for addressing problems and issues of everyday life" (Davidson et al. 1999, 168). Mutual support groups expose members to successful role models and offer information on coping strategies and survival skills (Kaufmann, Freund, and Wilson 1989; Keogh 1975; Rootes and Aanes 1992; Stewart 1990) and present an alternative worldview to assist persons in making sense of their experiences (Chamberlin 1988; Kennedy and Humphreys 1994).

Peer-run multi-service agencies encourage and support persons with mental illness who have been underserved and require assistance to obtain vital services through peer advocacy (Trainor et al. 1997; Chamberlin, Rogers, and Ellison 1996), outreach (Lieberman, Gowdy, and Knutson 1991), case management (Nikkel, Smith, and Edwards 1992) and related services. Such agencies function as an open door to the mental health system—they require few pre-requisites for service and usually charge no fees for services. Each service has a different focus, but they complement each other by having the same basic goal: teaching people how to find and use community resources.

Peer-run drop-in programs (LeDoux 1997; Silverman 1997; Meek 1994; Mowbray, Wellwood, and Chamberlain 1988), such as the Mental Health Client Action Network in Santa Cruz, California, the Portland Coalition for the Psychiatrically Labeled in Portland, Maine, the St. Louis Empowerment Center in Missouri, and the PEER Center, Inc., in Oakland Park, Florida (see Chapters 3–6) are also multi-service agencies that provide an open venue for consumers to receive a variety of services as needed within a centralized location. Individuals participate in drop-in activities on a voluntary, at-will, and noncoercive basis. Service components may include support and activity groups, access to telephones, laundry facilities, and computers, and assistance with moving and with entitlements, medication education, clothing, and bus or transportation passes. Many have an educational component, since their members frequently request assistance in developing problem-solving skills (Silverman 1997). Some programs provide their membership with instruction in coping skills, wellness, available services, their rights and other advocacy issues, leadership skills, and the nature of the illness itself (Copeland 1997; Diehl and Baxter 1999).

Specialized supportive services tend to focus on developing supports to address a single problem, such as an emotional crisis (Dumont and Jones 2002; Prout 1997), unemployment (Kaufmann 1995), or inadequate housing and homelessness (Silverman 1997; Besio and Mahler 1993; Long and Van Tosh 1988). These peer-run programs generally offer services and training to assist persons in attaining employment, housing, or education. Supportive housing programs link affordable housing with supportive services, helping people to live stable and independent lives in community settings. Consumer/survivors may form an organization to purchase and maintain safe, affordable housing. Others may help individual recipients of mental health services choose, obtain, and keep regular integrated independent housing by working with the recipient and his or her traditional service provider to offer flexible personalized assistance. Supportive employment programs emphasize competitive employment and provide a place for consumers to gain skill and confidence, educate themselves about work and disability, and get help over the course of a career. Supportive education encourages people with psychiatric problems to enter or re-enter college or technical school programs. Services include academic and career counseling, assistance with obtaining financial aid, study skills, stress control, and tutoring and coaching. Crisis intervention is provided in an informal, nonclinical environment, where people can stabilize with the help of peer counselors (Dumont and Jones 2002; Burns-Lynch and Salzer 2001).

Peer-run education/advocacy programs, such as Advocacy Unlimited, Inc., in Wethersfield, Connecticut, and BRIDGES in Nashville, Tennessee (see Chapters 9 and 10), are based on the belief that consumers are best able to address their own recovery needs and to advocate for change within the mental health system when they have accurate and comprehensive knowledge about mental illness and psychiatric services, and strategies to support wellness. Education/advocacy programs use well-defined curricula to teach consumers this kind of information, sometimes in short-term classroom settings. Participants have commented that this knowledge enables them to make choices and begin to regain control over their lives (Trainor et al., 1997).

Research on Peer-Run Support Services

The emerging Peer-run Programs Evidence Base (see Table 2.5 at the end of this chapter) shows that the current state of research on thee programs is expanding and indicates positive outcomes in current studies of peer support services. Two recent reviews of the literature (Davidson et al. 1999; Solomon and Draine 2001) have established that there is preliminary evidence to support the effectiveness of peer-run support services to help people with mental illness. However, most studies have been descriptive or qualitative, seeking to identify the characteristics of people who choose to participate in these programs, the processes that lead to change, and the service recipient's perspective on benefits of program participation (Chamberlin, Rogers, and Ellison 1996; Segal, Silverman, and Temkin 1995; Kaufmann, Schulberg, and Schooler 1994; Mowbray and Tan 1993).

There are many reasons people with mental illness seek out peer-run support services. Campbell and Schraiber (1989) found that 38 percent of mental health recipients surveyed in California ($N = 331$) felt safe talking about personal matters or their innermost feelings to peer counselors and people in self-help groups. Thirty-two percent reported that they call or see a self-help group if they are having emotional or psychological problems. In research on six peer-run drop-in centers in Michigan, Mowbray and Tan (1992) identified social support as the dominant reason consumer/survivors attended (see Table 2.1).

Although there is little empirical data describing the basic characteristics of people who use peer-run support groups, two studies provide some information. Segal, Silverman, and Temkin (1995) surveyed 310 long-term members of four peer-run support programs in the San Francisco Bay area on their characteristics and service use. These programs were found to serve a primarily African American population (64 percent), many who were homeless (46 percent). A high portion of the persons served (50 percent) had a dual diagnosis with moderate to severe substance or alcohol abuse. This group indicated that they sought help for resources such as food and clothing and "a place to be."

Chamberlin, Rogers, and Ellison (1996) found that the six peer-run support programs they surveyed served a largely middle-aged, single or divorced, white male population, although over a third of the membership was African American. Most members had a high school diploma, were unemployed, received a monthly income of less than six hundred dollars, and lived in a private home or apartment. They participated in

Table 2.1. Reasons for Using Peer-Run Drop-In Centers $N = 120$

For social support, such as seeing friends, feeling a sense of family, or having the chance to socialize, converse, and exchange ideas	53.3%
For something to do	25.0%
For a place to go (e.g., away from the streets)	23.3%
To fulfill responsibility as a volunteer or worker at the center	19.1%
To relax	14.2%
For coffee and doughnuts	13.3%
To get help and encouragement	6.7%
Other reasons	4.2%

Source: Mowbray and Tan 1992.

self-help an average of over fifteen hours a week and had been involved in self-help almost five years. In terms of outcomes, most appeared satisfied with their housing, social situation, and physical well-being but were dissatisfied with their work and finances. Over 90 percent reported that they felt more positive about themselves as a result of participation.

Research using nonrandomized control groups or pretest scores for comparisons has shown that participation in these services yields improvement in psychiatric symptoms and decreased hospitalization (Galanter 1988), larger social support networks (Carpinello, Knight, and Janis 1992; Rappaport et al. 1985), and enhanced self-esteem and social functioning (DeMasi et al. 1997; Kaufmann, Schulberg, and Schooler 1994).

Recognizing the need to expand the evidence base for peer-run programs by researching outcomes and service costs, researchers have begun to conduct randomized, controlled studies. One research demonstration project developed a five-bed residence operated as an alternative to psychiatric hospitalization and evaluated the outcomes (Dumont and Jones 2002). Those with access had better healing outcomes and greater levels of empowerment than the comparison group. Length of hospital stays were also shorter and resulted in lower service costs overall. In 1998 the Center for Mental Health Services funded the Consumer-Operated Services Program (COSP) Multi-Site Research Initiative to study the cost effectiveness of existing consumer-operated service programs for adults with serious and persistent mental illness when offered as an adjunct to traditional mental health services. Another goal of the multisite study was to create strong, productive partnerships among consumers, service providers, and researchers (Campbell 2000). Enrolling 1,827 participants, the four-year randomized controlled trial is currently analyzing baseline characteristics of participants and longitudinal change in well-being, recovery, empowerment, housing, employment, social inclusion, and satisfaction with services, as well as costs and cost off-sets at four drop-in centers, two educational programs, and two peer support programs, in addition to the traditional mental health service partners. This book is a description of the participating peer-run programs in the multisite study and details the development and analysis of the common ingredients of these peer-run program study sites (see Chapter 11).

In the past decade, the study of peer support has enabled the mental health community to ask new questions and to come to new conclusions. That is how the hope of recovery for people with mental illness found its way into collective discourse. When deciding what programs should be studied, what outcomes should be included in the research, and what practices should be funded, policymakers have looked for evidence of high quality in study design and methods, and positive results in outcomes. However, the focus on evidence-based practices has neglected to consider important service elements valued by consumers in selecting treatments and services—whether, for example, the program's goals are consistent with the consumer's goals; whether kindness, respect, and cooperation are expressed by program staff; and whether the consumer feels a level of comfort with the program. The emerging evidence of positive outcomes from recent studies of peer support services has enabled consumer providers to claim a voice in determining how research will shape the content and character of community mental health services.

The Philosophy of Peer Support Programs

The philosophy of modern peer-run support programs is grounded in the earliest writings of mental health consumer/survivors. A review of the consumer/survivor literature shows that no matter how diverse these programs are today, they share common emancipatory and caring functions that define their operating principles. Emancipatory functions evolved from the struggle for rights and equality evident in the patients' liberation movement, an advocacy approach to peer support with theory and practice rooted in the civil rights movement. Caring functions are the foundation of individual mutual support and reflect the need for empathetic services and supports in response to social isolation and the failures of the community mental health system to provide services responsive to consumer needs and preferences (see Table 2.2).

Emancipatory Functions

Now called empowerment, the struggle for rights and advocacy services at the individual, interpersonal, organizational, and societal levels of society is often a stated goal of peer support services. It is incorporated in program mission statements (Chamberlin, Rogers, and Ellison 1996) that support asserting one's rights and obtaining needed information and resources (Rappaport 1987). In defining mutual support groups, Budd (1987, 43) writes, "A mutual support group can provide you with a place to give as well as to receive, a place to feel useful and to affirm your self-respect. A mutual support group can, thus, help you explore your self-identification and to be a role model for your peers. This can be very empowering." Riessman (1965, 1990) identifies this shift in roles as the "helper therapy principle," and the consumer/survivors who drew up the Common Ingredients used in the COSP study called it simply the "helper principle" (see Chapter 11). Through a structured social interaction people provide feedback and assistance to others and receive support for their own efforts to address their problems. By assuming socially valued identities, they are no longer restricted to passive patient roles relying solely on mental health professionals for direction and advice (Roberts et al. 1991).

The organized struggle for the civil rights of people with mental illness developed in the early 1970s, influenced by the black, women's, and gay liberation movements and the concept of self-determination. Organizing required consciousness-raising, a process borrowed from the women's movement, to enable people with psychiatric problems to understand their lived experiences within an ideological framework of oppression called mentalism. Mentalism reinforced the idea that mental patients are unequal. As consumers shared their life stories, they realized that their psychiatric problems were not a result of personal deficits but were instead indicators of society's systematic oppression supported by the prac-

Table 2.2. Operating Principles of Peer-Run Support Programs

Emancipatory Functions	Caring Functions
Offering autonomy, voluntariness, choice, personal control, noncoercive practices	Offering empathic social support, availability as a caring friend, listening
Offering equal power of members, horizontal decision-making, democratic structure, reaching across person-to-person, back and forth	Insuring that there is no pressure to take advice, non-judgmental; encouraging experimentation with what works and what does not
Organizing against forced treatments, stigma, discrimination, and mentalism; anti-psychiatry; advocating for social justice and system change	Encouraging movement from patienthood to personhood; taking a wholistic approach; demystifying emotional life
Restoring collective and individual power (empowerment)	Being responsive to "special populations" (e.g., bilingual, disadvantaged, physically disabled, black, gay)
Encouraging self-definition of needs	Being part of a supportive larger group
Role modeling	Insuring mutual respect to people as people—not as clinical diagnoses; proving validation to people as human beings; nurturing positive self-images
Providing information, transportation, housing, employment, education, benefit supports	Promoting the belief that those who have had a mental illness are in a better position to know the needs and desires of people with similar experience (peer principle)
Promoting inclusion in research and policymaking in the mental health system	Promoting a recovery orientation; providing hope
Consciousness-raising; sharing knowledge of common experiences; providing opportunities to tell one's story, give testimony	Encouraging personal growth by providing help to others (helper principle)
Defining consequences of actions; learning to take responsibility	Creating a safe place to be when in crisis

tices of the mental health system. Consciousness raising demystified experiences in the mental hospital and enabled consumers to decide what treatments and procedures were harmful or helpful. Chamberlin (1988, 189) believes that "an ongoing consciousness-raising process is essential for building self-confidence and counteracting the effects of mentalism. Like racism and sexism, mentalism infects its victims with the belief in their own inferiority, which must be consciously rooted out. By working together in self-help organizations, ex-patients can gain experience in helping themselves and one another. But the belief in one's own inferiority can continue unless active efforts are made to combat it."

Ending involuntary treatment became the long-term goal of the mental patients' liberation movement, and many peer support groups today continue to focus on advocacy to oppose all laws and practices that promote discrimination and coercion. Advocacy within *peer groups emphasizes freedom of choice for people wanting to receive psychiatric services through true informed consent to treatment and includes the right to refuse any unwanted treatments in the hospital and community.* The goal of these advocacy efforts is to create a society where a psychiatric diagnosis has no impact on a person's citizenship rights and responsibilities.

Allowing consumer/survivors to make their own choices in peer support programs has become a fundamental value. "The consumer-run alternative model," according to Stroul (1986, 50), "is based on a set of basic values. First and foremost is freedom of choice. Participation is completely voluntary, and only the consumer decides whether to participate, which aspects of the program to take advantage of, and what other types of services to participate in."

Zinman (1987) organized brainstorming sessions with consumers attending the Alameda County Consumer Speaks Conferences in California in 1984 in an effort to identify the characteristics self-help groups share. She identified equality, volunteerism, choice, and the personhood of each member as essential beliefs. The consumer-run groups represented by those she polled were controlled by members, based on the self-determination of the group and the individual, and opposed to all forms of coercion to get people into treatment situations. Attendance was voluntary and consumers chose to participate in only the parts of the services or programs they desired. "Supporting individuals where they are ... and in the choices they make is essential to self-help groups," Zinman (1987, 9) concludes. The groups also shared power, responsibility, and skill. Relationships were horizontal; no person could make decisions for another because "no person has the power over another person to write records about, diagnose, or commit her/him." Most important, throughout the years consumer/survivors have maintained that peer support groups treat people as human beings with real life needs. The shift away from focusing on patienthood to promoting personhood was a significant conceptual development that was not to be found within the traditional mental health system. Consumer/survivors have consistently reported that their need for respect, dignity, and choice is more significant than the treatment needs that mental health professionals identify as primary. They have a global view of mental health that encompasses the needs to recognize and nourish personal strengths and personhood, and support a high quality of life (Campbell and Schraiber 1989).

Caring Functions

It is not surprising that mental health consumers, as an act of empowerment, turned away from the psychiatric system and established mutual support groups as alternatives to traditional treatments and services. However, without an understanding of the importance of the need for affiliative relationships in providing help and care, the rise of peer-run programs and their unique qualities could only partially be explained. Research on patient-provider communications indicated that the manifestation of power, authority, professional detachment, and status in medical interactions was widespread (Street and Wiemann 1987; Lane 1983; Hall, Roter, and Rand 1981; Korsch and Negrete 1972). Studies of patient satisfaction with health services found that most persons put an intense emphasis on a provider's personality or caring functions. Among the caring functions recipients identified as the most important were personal contact, communication, and concern (Lewison 1975; Cartwright 1964; Skipper, Taglacozzo, and Mauksch 1964). Ben-Sira (1980, 173) stresses the importance of "behavior directed by the physician toward the patient as a person rather than as a case."

In three decades of research, the quality of the therapeutic relationship was acknowledged as an essential component in mental health treatment (Gelso and Carter 1985; Greenberg and Pinsof 1986; Gurman 1977; Rogers 1957). The psychodynamic concept of the therapeutic alliance was used in studying the quality of client-provider relationships (Greenberg and Pinsof 1986; Marziali 1984; Bordin 1979) and was found to be the common factor that accounted for therapy outcomes regardless of treatment approach (Horvath and Luborsky 1993; Styles, Shapiro, and Elliot 1986; Hartly and Strupp 1983).

Chamberlin (1988, 163) points out that in the mental health system "detachment and impartiality, which mental health professionals believe are the proper therapeutic attitudes, become, in practice, either cold formality or the shallow pretense of friendliness. Alternative services replace medical and bureaucratic distance with real friendliness—not the bland, impartial 'friendliness' of a person behind a desk but the open give-and-take of a relationship between equals. Having problems is seen as a normal component of living in a sometimes difficult and threatening world and not as part of an illness existing only in some unfortunate people."

Peer support programs cultivate an atmosphere that is entirely different from that of professionally provided services. The traditional mental health system considers every difficulty people with psychiatric problems experience as an indication of mental illness requiring professional expertise. Even practical problems, such as finding a job or a place to live, are handled within the context of disability. People come out of hospitals with little faith in their own ability to deal with life. When they turn to the traditional mental health system for assistance, this perception of themselves as hopeless, helpless individuals is further reinforced. In psychiatric encounters, biomedical statements direct the responses of consumer/survivors to objectified symptoms, signs, and treatments and shift attention away from the totality of social relations and the social issues that are often root causes of psychiatric problems. Instead, attention is focused on individual pathology and personality. Symptoms, signs, and treatment take on an aura of scientific fact, rather than being treated as manifestations of a troubled social reality, and traditional mental health treatments reduce the potential for positive client-provider relationships.

Most of the problems facing mental health consumer/survivors are purely practical ones–where to live, how to get a job, or how to obtain welfare. Thus, when people go to peer support programs they find new ways to deal with problems as they watch people like themselves helping one another to find solutions. They learn that they too have the capacity to help others that goes beyond the biomedical "illness model" of mental disease.

A diagnosis of mental illness permeates all aspects of a mental health consumer's life, constricting the ideological, material, and emotional resources that give people meaning in everyday life and allow them to act as the historical subject of their own lives. A psychiatric diagnosis strips away a person's objective power and will to power as he or she encounters the social world and participates in the reproduction of daily life. Kate Millet recounts from her experience in the mental health system, "We are taught to distrust our mind, our intellect" (quoted in Bielski and Fraser 1990, 18).

The mental health system manages the interior life of the mental health consumer through careful monitoring of feelings and thoughts, and through the use of psychiatric medications, hospitalization, and other treatment modalities. Consumers report that once their psychiatric diagnosis is known, other people do not accept the range of their emotions as legitimate feelings. In a survey of consumers by Campbell and Schraiber (1989) 70 percent said that people "never," or "seldom" accept their feelings of sorrow, despair, anger, or frustration. Mary Lee Stocks, a mental health consumer who works as a licensed social worker, relates that in order to be looked on as normal or functioning by her colleagues in the mental health system, she had to maintain a level of "evenness" of mood (quoted in Ninde 1990). By controlling interior life, the mental health system subverts a person's relationship to the public and private spheres of experience.

Once the mental health system situates itself between the subjective experience of living and what that experience means, it supplants the power of persons with mental illness to define themselves. No longer are persons primarily concerned with how bills are paid or how one maintains a job, gets married, buys a car, raises children, or plans for the future. Existence is organized around therapeutic values rather than human values and citizenship. The mediation of the mental health system separates the consumer from both public and private life, muting their connection to experiences of poverty, loss, pain, hope, and possibility. This separation is much more profound than a physical separation from everyday experiences (as when one is in a psychiatric hospital).

Peer support allows autonomous moments for people to control their lives with acts of affirmation and resistance and to find legitimacy and hope in their own ways of experiencing and understanding. The interaction between peers provides a way for consumers to reclaim mental subjectivity by producing native wisdom. Such wisdom is not developed for the sake of abstract knowledge but to transcend one's condition. In sharing experiences, consumers revise the image of their past, and meaningfulness surfaces to bind past and present together. By telling their stories, consumers also can make order and get on top of things. When order is organized from without, as in a clinical relationship, one's experiences become a tool of control; in contrast, within a peer support group, collective points of references are a means of liberation. The consumer culture constitutes itself within the consciousness of each member of the group. "Self-help groups," Zinman (1987, 11) writes, "demystify our emotional life, giving back to us the knowledge and tools to help ourselves. Our emotional life is no longer somebody else's, the medical profession's specialty. We are the experts."

The free-flowing give and take between people gives peer support some of its unique characteristics. Support, however, is not therapy. As Budd (1987, 43) observed, "in support, the goal is to comfort, to be available as a caring friend, to listen, and to share the knowledge of common experiences. In any natural relationship, it is common for friends to make suggestions of multiple options, to listen to another's troubles, to offer encouragement, to comfort by expressing empathy and sympathy, and to have common experiences and knowledge about available resources."

Peer support programs have developed a recovery orientation and are helping members gain hope, a sense of personhood and meaning in life outside identification with mental illness (Mead, Hilton, and Curtis 2001; Ralph 2000; Baxter and Diehl 1998). The experience of recovery is deeply personal, different for everyone; thus, a range of service models can support recovery. As a paradigm for achieving emotional, financial, and social empowerment, recovery is not necessarily contingent on scientific breakthroughs or the discovery of new therapies. Rather, it is an organizing principle for peer support that is based on the values of choice and self-determination, acceptance and healing. Recovery requires being part of active, interdependent social relationships at the workplace, school, and neighborhood, and within psychiatric services.

Through peer support, people with mental illness have learned that recovery does not come only from without but taps into an inner life force. They have discovered that giving feels good because it nurtures a sense of self-worth. Self-worth is also developed in peer support by learning about one's strengths and weaknesses within a supportive environment. This process gives one power to change and to manage the challenges of everyday life. The mental health system tends to define caring as protecting rather than supporting people's efforts when they take chances, even if they may fail. In peer support, failure is seen as a natural learning process in gaining power over one's life, rather than diminishing one's life.

Defining Peer Support Competencies

As peer-run support programs developed, there occurred a natural evolution of consumer/survivors in peer support roles. Campbell, Dumont, and Einspahr (1999) conducted a comprehensive review of both published and unpublished literature on peer support services and identified seventy-three statements of peer competencies emerging in peer support service provision. Nineteen peer providers were recruited from throughout the United States to rank the importance of these statements and to sort them into clustered statements or domains (see Tables 2.3 and 2.4). Using a computerized software program called concept-mapping (Trochim and Linton 1986), Campbell and colleagues combined this structured group process with several multivariate statistical analyses in the mapping program to yield a variety of maps that graphically show how the group of peer providers perceived the ranked statements to be interrelated within domains and between domains. This ground-breaking research to define peer support competencies was a key starting point for the COSP Multisite Research Initiative to identify the common ingredients of consumer-operated service programs and evaluate program fidelity (see Chapter 11).

The highest ranked domains of peer support competencies were "Encouraging independence," "Beliefs supporting recovery," and "Interpersonal skills" (Table 2.3), and the highest ranked individual statements were "Support for choice-making and risk-taking as leading to growth" and "Foster a sense of hope" (Table 2.4).

Numbered statements are distributed across a map (Figure 2.1). Some statements appear in close proximity to one another, indicating they are considered by the peer providers to be more conceptually similar than statements that are on the opposite side of the map from one another. The concept-mapping software program also organizes the clustered statements into conceptual domains that are titled through a group consensus process assisted by the mapping program.

In the eastern area of the map, statement #19, "Know recovery triggers and structure settings so recovery triggers are present" is in close proximity to statement #13, "Know how peers live with and manage their disorders" and statement #16, "Know and support the coping strategies of peers." This grouping suggests that there are recovery triggers that are shared by many persons who have had the mental illness experience, and that a helper supports the coping strategies of peers by drawing on these shared learnings. While statements in the eastern area appear to have more to do with understanding a person's own management or coping strategies, statements in the southern area concern the attitudes and beliefs peer providers have that make recovery possible. In the southern area one finds statement #6, "Provide choice by avoiding controlling behaviors" near statement #17, "Accept a peer's feelings (sorrow, despair, anger, joy)

Table 2.3. Peer-Support Competencies

Domain	Statements
Encouraging independence	"Support choice-making and risk-taking as leading to growth"; "Encourage independent thinking of peers"; "Give peers freedom to make their own mistakes."
Beliefs supporting recovery	Foster a sense of hope"; "Behave in ways that indicate that peers can share their own future"; "Believe in the peer's ability to recover."
Interpersonal skills	"Avoid treating peers as children"; "Accept a peer's feelings of sorrow, despair, anger, joy without pathologizing"; "Provide choice by avoiding controlling behaviors."
Peer-based program support	"Understand that the episodic nature of mental illness does not prevent recovery"; "Know the signs and impact of sexual and physical trauma"; "Learn how recovery changes the frequency and duration of symptoms."
Understanding how peers cope	"Know and behave in ways that help the recovery process of peers"; "Know non-threatening crisis response techniques"; "Know recovery triggers, and structure settings so recovery triggers are present."
Advocacy	"Recognize the effects of trauma and re-traumatization induced by seclusion and restraints"; "Be both informed and able to educate peers about their rights"; "Know about nontraditional alternatives to mental health services."
Legal rights and antidiscrimination	"Learn and follow rules regarding the privacy and confidentiality of peer records and data"; "Be able to identify sexual harassment and know how to initiate the appropriate policies and procedures"; "Be able to identify racial discrimination and know how to initiate the appropriate policies and procedures."
Training for work and family life	"Know how to work with peers so they can find the resources they need"; "Base job development and placement on the expressed need and demonstrated interest of peers"; "Know and be able to educate peers on the history and organization of the consumer/survivor/ex-patient movement."

Source: Campbell, Dumont, and Einspahr 1999.

Table 2.4. Highest-ranked individual statements $N = 19$

Support for choice-making and risk-taking as leading to growth	4.92
Foster a sense of hope	4.92
Encourage independent thinking of peers	4.85
Give peers freedom to make their own mistakes	4.85
Use people-first language	4.85
Behave in ways that indicate that peers can shape their own future	4.77
Believe in the peer's ability to recover	4.77
Listen to peers and consider what they say to be valid and important	4.69
Avoid treating peers as children	4.69
Understand and support the peers' need to regain "critical consciousness" or self-awareness	4.62
Look at and recognize a peer's abilities	4.62
Understand how recovery from the consequences of treatment are often more difficult than recovery from the illness itself	4.62
Understand the feelings, thoughts, values, goals, and roles that enhance recovery throughout peer support	4.62
Build choice into program planning	4.62
Know ways to support rather than punish peers who relapse	4.62

Source: Campbell, Dumont, and Einspahr 1999.

Figure 2.1. Peer-support Competencies Cluster Rating Map

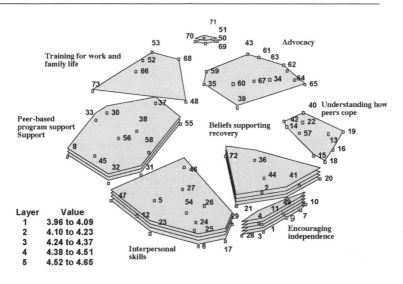

without pathologizing." On one hand, this relationship implies that when a person experiences feelings that are part of the human condition, even extreme feelings, he or she does not necessarily view them through the lens of illness. On the other hand, because people are subject to the views of others, a person may be led to consider his or her feelings an expression of a psychiatric diagnosis. A psychiatric diagnosis may contribute to a greater amount of pathologizing feelings and treatments that can have a serious controlling function. Therefore, part of providing choice would be for peer providers to avoid this practice. The western area of the map has more to do with programmatic issues than person-centered competencies, as illustrated in statement #8, "Practice the 'strength model' of rehabilitation" and #45, "Build choice into program planning." The northern area includes a group of nearly overlapping statements that involve policy or legally related competencies: #71, "Learn about informed consent protocols and how to provide informed consent to peers for data collection activities," #70, "Learn the provisions of the Americans with Disabilities Act (ADA)," and #69 "Learn and follow rules regarding the privacy and confidentiality of peer records and data."

Using this map, Campbell, Dumont, and Einspahr (1999) concluded that peer providers know intuitively about recovery triggers that are shared by many persons who have had mental illness, and that peer providers support the coping strategies of others by drawing on these shared understandings. In programs and trainings, however, they need to explicate these processes, bringing them to the surface so they can be shared one-to-one and through training and evaluation. Similarly, advocacy efforts involve formal competencies to assist persons in actualizing their rights—specialized knowledge in legal rights and antidiscrimination policies—as well as the informal skill of understanding the needs of persons as they express themselves.

Conclusion

Today people with mental illness are looking for greater ownership and control over their lives, individually and collectively through the enactment of public mental health policy. An essential component of empowerment is the opportunity to speak for ourselves about those issues that directly affect our daily lives and well-being. Many mental health consumer/survivors feel satisfaction in their success and believe, with consumers interviewed by Campbell and Schraiber (1989, 58) that peer support is moving in the right direction. "It's going to take years for people to respond to what we're trying to do. People don't believe us, that we're capable of doing anything. They consider us irresponsible, incompetent, crazy, insane. But the trouble is, self-help works."

In the past thirty years, peer-run programs have matured, diversified, and increased their numbers across the United States. Some have developed management information systems to track utilization, performance and membership characteristics, and service outcomes. Others have certified staff, created peer specialist positions, written program manuals, and achieved accreditation.

Programs developed and administered by mental health consumers/survivors have built a self-help service infrastructure that helps people recover from psychiatric problems, in addition to providing supports for housing, employment, and education. Peer providers have created community links with traditional mental health providers through service referrals. They have also educated mental health professionals about the experience of living with a psychiatric diagnosis and about the struggle to live a good quality life in the face of prejudice, discrimination, isolation, and poverty. By providing opportunities for consumer/survivors to interact with their peers, peer-run support services have been shown to have a positive impact on recovery, including increasing empowerment, hopefulness, and informal learning of adaptive coping strategies for people diagnosed with serious mental illness.

Still, there are barriers to establishing a strong network of peer support services and including them in the continuum of community services. In addition to continued skepticism about the effectiveness of peer support programs by some mental health professionals, lack of solid, ongoing funding for such programs, which are often supported through time-limited special project grants, threatens to cripple their future. States are beginning to fund peer support services with federal dollars available through the Medicaid rehabilitation option (Koyanagi and Semansky 2001), though this option is limited. Peer-run support programs can offer Medicaid-covered rehabilitation services only if they meet certain federal program requirements, peer providers receive standardized skill-building, and programs bill only for services that assist with problems or provide other services that are not purely social events.

Can and should peer-run support programs be classified, evaluated, and understood by the same measures that govern the kind of services provided in the traditional mental health system? Are the important aspects of peer support programs related more to how something is done and by whom, than to what services are offered? Would standardization of services supplant the healing bond of peer-to-peer relationships as units of time become billable hours and empathy is certified through training and testing? Like gardening, peer support works best by establishing favorable conditions, planting more seeds than one expects to sprout, and nurturing the ones that do. There is a danger that the professionalization of services and the establishment of partnerships with traditional mental health systems would undermine the emancipatory and caring functions of peer support programs that have inspired consumer/survivors to ask, "Who can I become, and why should I say yes to life?" On one hand, if peer-run programs become part of a continuum of mental health services, consumer leaders caution that peer support would be linked to involuntary hospitalization and treatments and, therefore, no longer totally voluntary. Also, consumer leaders worry that partnerships with traditional providers would be inherently unequal, with peer providers having little real power and responsibility. Although most mental health systems

Appendix 2.5. Peer-Run Programs Evidence Base

Study	Sample	Program Description
Corring 2002	18 people with mental illness and 21 family members	Chatham/Kent Consumer/Survivor Network, Inc., and Chatham/Kent Family Network commissioned the study of quality-of-life issues and formed the participant group
Dumont and Jones 2002	265 participants with a *DSM* diagnosis	Research demonstration project to determine whether people with access to a crisis hostel would experience greater recovery and increased empowerment, lower use of crisis services, and reduced total mental health treatment costs when compared with persons without access
Forquer and Knight 2001		Equal partnership between ValueOptions, a national behavioral managed-care company, and 8 community mental health centers that integrated recovery and self-help into the routine care delivery

boast that they are consumer-directed, real progress toward collaboration is uneven, and partnerships are difficult, as many service providers continue to perpetuate mentalism. On the other hand, it is doubtful that peer programs can continue to grow beyond current operations if they lack valid, reliable skill assessment tools and training protocols to help them improve the quality of their work forces, and if they lack management information systems to measure program outcomes and thus to evaluate program effectiveness.

As a consumer/survivor community, we must thoughtfully consider what partnerships between peer-run support programs and the mental health system have to offer in the way of a recovery-based future for people with mental illness. But we must also consider the hazards of such a partnership. Staying the course will certainly take creativity, courage, and leadership.

Method	Conclusions
Qualitative methods using 3 focus groups that were audiotaped, transcribed, and coded; member checks conducted	Results supported the need for continued peer support and advocacy services along with a continued focus on promoting and supporting recovery
Randomized, experimental design with assessment at baseline, 6 months and 12 months	Experimental group had better healing outcomes, greater levels of empowerment, shorter hospital stays, and fewer hospital admissions than control group, which resulted in lower costs
Evaluation of the impact of Colorado's Mental Health Assessment Agencies Under Capitation Financing (FY97–98 to FY 98–99), which included the creation of more than 70 self-help groups and 4 consumer-operated drop-in centers	Number of persons with severe mental illness served by the Colorado managed-care capitation project increased significantly; suicide rate and substance abuse decreased significantly, as did hospitalization; social contacts increased significantly, as did participants' ability to carry out activities of daily living

Study	Sample	Program Description
Yanos, Primavera, and Knight 2001	60 participants with past or present psychiatric diagnosis	Recruitment from a mental health center and 2 consumer-run programs to determine whether involvement in consumer-run services is positively associated with recovery
Campbell 2000; Consumer-Operated Service Programs Multi-Site Research Initiative	1,827 participants with serious mental illness receiving mental health services within the year previous to enrollment; funded by SAMHSA	7 study sites and a coordinating center funded to study cost-effectiveness of 8 consumer-operated programs when offered as an adjunct to traditional mental health services; models of consumer-operated service programs included drop-in centers (4), mutual support groups (2), and educational/advocacy programs (2)
Van Tosh and del Vecchio 2000	Descriptions of 13 demonstration projects from the Community Support Program Initiative	Project materials from the projects were examined to provide in-depth, cross-program evaluation of each individual initiative; documents reviewed were original applications, annual continuation applications, NIMH correspondence, final project reports, and evaluation findings
Klein, Cnaan, and Whitecraft 1998	10 dually diagnosed clients from a peer social support program and 51 who had been in community care one year prior to the investigation	Friends Connection is a consumer-operated program that provides mutual support for persons with mental illness and a substance use problem
DeMasi et al. 1997	Statewide sample of New York public mental health service recipients	New York Office of Mental Health service recipients

Method	Conclusions
Random selection from CMHC and screening of self-selected participants from consumer-run programs; selected scales administered face-to-face at one time	Participants in consumer-run programs had better social functioning than those in CMHC; psychological variables associated with social functioning and mediated by problem-centered coping strategies
Randomized, controlled trial with common assessment protocol administered face-to-face at baseline, 4 months, 8 months, and 12 months, along with a fidelity assessment of intervention; outcomes included empowerment, social inclusion, well-being, housing, employment, recovery, program satisfaction	Baseline, outcome, cost, and fidelity analyses currently under way
Program elements were explored: project goals and objectives, program description, implementation issues and problems, and evaluation findings	75% of the programs provided mutual support, 85% provided direct services, 50% indicated that empowerment was a major focus, 90% cited public education as a goal, 75% also indicated rights protection was a project goal; programs served people who were in poverty (30%), as well as veterans (30%); all projects reported their participants showed greater levels of independence, empowerment, and self-esteem; over 60% indicated increased development of social supports
61 dually diagnosed clients who had been receiving ICM services were randomly selected and 10 participants were assigned to Friends Connection for 6 months; data from pre- and post-client interviews and case records were compared	Findings suggest that coupling peer support with ICM is associated with positive system outcomes: number of crisis events and hospitalizations of the comparison group was higher; those in the peer program showed improved quality of life and perceived physical and emotional well-being
Data from a statewide, two-wave mail survey were analyzed to develop a conceptual model of the recovery process; study examined how participation in self-help and traditional services contributes to recovery, investigated ways individuals are referred to self-help groups, and identified most persuasive referral sources	Findings on the role of self-help in the recovery process indicated that traditional services have a slight negative impact on self-concept and social outcomes; the relationships among symptoms, self-evaluation, and quality of life proved significant; the effects of one's beliefs about stigma on self-concepts varied according to individual symptoms; there are significant differences between members and nonmembers of self-help groups in the ways referral sources are used; the most persuasive methods that influenced individuals to join self-help groups came from recommendations made by peers through distribution of printed materials describing self-help groups

Study	Sample	Program Description
Kessler and Mickelson 1997	3,032 respondents recruited from a random digit dial sampling frame from the United States; ages ranged from 25 to 74; men and older respondents were over-sampled	Data reported came from the Midlife Development in the U.S. survey, a nationally representative telephone-mail survey carried out in 1995–96 under the auspices of McArthur Foundation Network on Successful Midlife Development
Trainor et al. 1997	Over 600 consumers from CSDI of Ontario, Canada	CSDI directly funded 36 organizations at the time of the study, including cooperative businesses (6), generic consumer/survivor organizations (28), a provincial business council (1), and a diagnostically focused organization (1)
Carpinello et al. 1996	554 persons from mental health service sites (33%) and self-help groups (67%)	Mental health service sites and self-help groups in western region of New York State
Chamberlain, Rogers, and Ellison 1996	271 members of self-help programs were sampled; funded by a grant from the National Institute for Disability Rehabilitation Research	A survey of 6 self-help programs in the United States was conducted to collect information about users of such programs, their demographics, quality of life, and program satisfaction
Kaufmann 1995	146 clients with serious mental illness	Self-Help Employment Center in Pennsylvania provided vocational services based on self-help principles

Method	Conclusions
Survey in two phases: telephone interview and self-administered mail questionnaire	18.1% of sample participated in a self-help group at some time in their life and 6.9% did so in the past year; large proportions of people who use self-help groups for substance (50%) and emotional (76%) problems also see a professional for these problems; those reporting less support and more conflict in their social networks are more likely to participate than those with more supportive networks; those with a lower sense of personal control are more likely to participate
The impact of CSDI membership on the use of Mental Health Services was examined; also looked at the importance attached to various components of the mental health system	CSDI members used fewer mental health services, noted an increase in community involvement and contacts, found consumer/survivor organizations to be more helpful than traditional mental health services, and found other consumer/survivors as individuals to be more helpful than professionals with mental health issues
Two substudies investigated the decision-making process that leads to the use of self-help strategies: a cross-sectional survey and a cohort study	Findings from cross-sectional study indicated that self-help participants tend to be older, white, and married and to have a higher level of education; diagnosis and symptoms were not related to participation; participants were less likely than nonparticipants to have been hospitalized in the past 5 years; these findings suggest that self-help programs aid in the recovery process and reduce overall use of mental health services
Survey data and descriptive data from each of the programs were collected and descriptive results calculated	This sample averaged 4.8 lifetime hospitalization; 34.5% were unemployed at the time of the survey; 48.1% lived in private homes or apartments; used programs 15.3 hours/week; used both self-help and traditional services; 46% indicated that self-help involvement had changed the amount of contact with family in a way they liked; and that it had a salutary effect on quality of life
Outcome assessment sought to determine % working, % in new jobs, hours worked, time to present job, and time in present job; participants were randomly assigned to experimental and control groups and were assessed at baseline, 6 months, and 12 months	Not many significant differences on employment variables; center members were significantly more improved at 12 months on a vocational status scale

Study	Sample	Program Description
Segal, Silverman, and Temkin 1995	310 clients participated for at least 3 months in selected self-help agencies in the San Francisco Bay area	4 consumer-run self-help agencies
Luke, Roberts, and Rappaport 1994	861 people attending at least one GROW, Inc., meeting	15 self-help groups from GROW, Inc., an organization for people with serious mental illness or psychiatric hospitalizations located in southern Illinois
Kaufmann, Ward-Colasante, and Farmer 1993	478 consumers (psychiatric patients, excluding substance abusers, homeless) across 9 centers during a 6-month period	Centers provided social support and employment services
Mowbray and Tan 1993	120 consumers attending self-help centers in the Justice in Mental Health Organization	Six self-help centers in Justice in Mental Health Organization
Carpinello, Knight, and Janis 1992	25 adults sampled from self-help groups (10 group leaders, 11 group members, 4 parents)	48 self-help groups representing 7 classes of self-help: advocacy/legal, educational/technical, information/referral, drop-in centers, group support, alternative therapy, and service provider

Method	Conclusions
Survey of members of self-help agencies randomly selected from the total population was conducted to characterize service utilization, psychiatric history, functional status, symptoms, diagnosis, and health issues	Typical center members were found to be poor, African American, and homeless and to have a serious mental illness
This study was part of an assessment of GROW, Inc. conducted during a 27-month period by trained observers/ participants who collected data as members attended 527 meetings	Participants ranged in age from 15 to 85 and tended to be single, Caucasian, and female and to have some education beyond high school; participation of the member can be influenced by the "fit" between the member and the particular self-help group (e.g., self-help group/specific person, characteristics of the first meeting attended by the individual, and individual/other group members); participants most likely to drop out were (1) younger, less educated, currently or previously married, and high functioning; (2) members who attend meetings that are more than 2:1 female; (3) members who attended group with persons who had different hospitalization history, different marital status
Conducted interviews and focus groups with members and tracked attendance to evaluate centers	Members liked the "relaxed atmosphere," being with similar people, having a place to go; clients wanted more equitable enforcement of rules, support, and expanded hours of activities; components of a successful center were identified as participatory management, strong volunteers, relationships with other provider systems, resources, social activities, special events, and ongoing recruitment
Study conducted structured interviews using the Group Environment scale, Community Oriented Program Environment scale, and the Client Satisfaction Questionnaire	Most consumers believed they had input into center operations, felt supported, learned from one another, were encouraged to be independent, and participated more in positive activities and less in negative activities; 80% reported being more confident in several life domains; 75% perceived the centers more positively than other mental health services in the area
Qualitative research methods including focus group and key informant interviews, member checking, and negotiation discussions	Participants reported positive outcomes related to self-help membership, such as empowerment, and felt that self-help worked; self-help success related to formation of a social network, change in role from person helped to helper, sharing of coping behaviors, presence of role model, and existence of a meaningful group structure

Study	Sample	Program Description
Emerick 1990	104 self-help groups	The social movement groups offered legal advocacy, public education, technical assistance, and information-referral networking; the individual therapy groups offered more "inner-focused" individual change through group support meetings
Campbell and Schraiber 1989	331 past and present mental health consumers who had been labeled chronically mentally ill; 53 family members of mental health clients; 150 mental health professionals and caregivers; funded by the California Department of Mental Health	Qualitative and quantitative consumer-directed survey research on what factors promote or deter well-being of people in California with severe mental illness
Galanter 1988	201 recovery group leaders and 155 recent recovery members (joined 6–12 months previously)	Study designed to ascertain whether mental health self-help groups can serve as an adjunct or alternative to professional care; group leaders selected at random in each of the 211 Recovery Inc. administrative areas in North America; member participants selected by group leaders
Kurtz 1988	188 participants in the founding chapter of DMDA, including people with mental illness and family members	Survey of mutual-aid group for mental disorders to describe membership, examine member satisfaction with the association, and to elicit members' perceptions of benefits to them as a result of participation

Method	Conclusions
By conducting key informant interviews, classified groups based on structure, affiliation, and service model along an ideological continuum from radical, separatist to conservative groups that allowed professionals to act as leaders in partnership with consumer/survivors	Social movement and individual therapy were found to be the two major service models; two-thirds of the groups were identified as social movement groups and of these more than 70% were found to have little to no interaction with mental health professionals; 43% held antiprofessional attitudes
Consumer-developed client questionnaire (151 items); family-member questionnaire (76 items); mental health professional questionnaire (77 items)	Descriptive self-reported statistics found significant correlation between poor well-being of clients and stigmatizing professional attitudes and behaviors; fear of involuntary treatment reported as deterring clients from seeking professional mental health; peer support identified as promoting well-being
211-item multiple choice questionnaire completed anonymously included demographics, general well-being schedule, neurotic distress scale, social cohesiveness scale, ideological commitment to recovery, and psychiatric treatment	Decline in both symptoms and concomitant psychiatric treatment after participants joined Recovery Inc.; responses to items reflecting affiliative ties toward Recovery predicted an appreciable portion of the variance in respondents' well-being and reported improvement after joining
Anonymous 36-item questionnaire included demographic data, history of illness, rating of satisfaction with the association and perceptions of outcome (CSQ-8) mailed to 578 individuals on the DMDA mailing list; 41% response rate	Length of membership and intensity of involvement was related to global satisfaction and information/support provided; 81.5% of consumer respondents coped better with the illness after participation and 83% better accepted their illness; weak positive indication of medication compliance and participation

Study	Sample	Program Description
Mowbray, Wellwood, and Chamberlain 1988	Over 1,800 consumers, most with previous mental health experience, desiring mutual support; funded by the Michigan Department of Mental Health	Daybreak Drop-In Centers offered an unstructured setting that included recreational, cooking, housing assistance, and employment activities
Rappaport et. al 1985	Over 100 meetings representing 12 different GROW groups in Illinois; Funded by NIMH	GROW group meetings follow the method suggested by the founder, including personal testimonials, mutual support, education, presenting coping strategies, and personal development

CMHC	Community Mental Health Center
CSDI	Consumer/Survivor Development Initiative
DMDA	Depressive and Manic Depressive Association
DSM	American Psychiatric Association, Diagnostic and Statistical Manual (1994)

References

Ahern, L., and D. Fisher. 1999. *Recovery at your own PACE.* Lawrence, MA: National Empowerment Center.

———. 2001. Recovery at your own PACE. *Journal of Psychological Nursing and Mental Health Services* 39(4):22–31.

American Psychiatric Association Diagnostic and Statistical Manual for Mental Disorder. 1994. 4th ed. Washington, DC: American Psychiatric Press.

Anthony, W. 1993. Recovery from mental illness: The guiding vision of the mental health service system in the 1990s. *Psychosocial Rehabilitation Journal* 16:11–23.

Arntsen, B., T. Greenfield, A. Harris, and E. Sundby. 1995. CRF: Early experiences at Sacramento's consumer run crisis residential program. *CAMI Journal* 6(3):35.

Baker, F., and J. Intagliata. 1984. A comparative analysis of the young adult chronic patient in New York State's community support system. *Hospital and Community Psychiatry* 35:45–50.

Method	Conclusions
Surveyed program members, tracked attendance, and calculated costs per month	Averaged over 150 persons a month for 12 months; high member satisfaction; cost was $470/month
Trained observers completed the Observer Rating Form, an observational coding system designed to record verbal interactions of group members during meetings; a coding strategy was developed to allow analysis of the observed group interactions	Mutual self-help organizations such as GROW are a viable alternative to fill the gap created by funding cuts and policy changes in professional Mental Health Services provisions

ICM   Intensive Care Management
NIMH   National Institute for Mental Health
SAMHSA   U.S. Substance Abuse and Mental Health
            Services Administration

Baxter, E., and S. Diehl. 1998. Emotional stages: Consumers and family members recovering from the trauma of mental illness. *Psychiatric Rehabilitation Journal* 21:349–55.

Beard, J. 1976. Psychiatric rehabilitation at Fountain House. In *Rehabilitation medicine and psychiatry,* ed. J. Meislin, 393–413. Springfield, IL: Charles C. Thomas.

Beard, J., R. Propst, and T. Malamud. 1982. Fountain House model of psychiatric rehabilitation. *Psychosocial Rehabilitation Journal* 5:47–53.

Beisecker, A., and T. Beisecker. 1993. Using metaphors to characterize doctor patient relationships: Paternalism versus consumerism. *Health Communication* 5(1):41–58.

Ben-Sira, Z. 1980. Affective and instrumental components in the physician-patient relationship: An additional dimension of interaction theory. *Journal of Health and Social Behavior* 21:170.

Bernikow, L. 1987. *Alone in America: The search for companionship.* Boston: Faber and Faber.

Besio, S., and J. Mahler. 1993. Benefits and challenges of using consumer staff in supported housing services. *Hospital and Community Psychiatry* 44:490–91.

Bevilaqua, J. 1993. Consumerism is not a fad. *Resources* 5:1–2.

Bielski, V., and L. Fraser. 1990. Beyond the looney bin. *San Francisco Guardian,* June 6.

Blanch, A., D. Fisher, W. Tucker, D. Walsh, and J. Chassman. 1993. Consumer-practitioners and psychiatrists share insights about recovery and coping. *Disability Studies Quarterly* 13(2):17–20.

Bordin, E. 1979. The generalizability of the psychoanalytic concept of the working alliance. *Psychotherapy: Theory, research, and practice* 16(3):252–60.

Breier, A., and J. S. Strauss. 1984. The role of social relationships in the recovery from psychotic disorders. *American Journal of Psychiatry* 141:949–55.

Budd, S. 1987. Support groups. In *Reaching across: Mental health clients helping each other,* ed. S. Zinman, H. Harp, and S. Budd, 41–55. Riverside: California Network of Mental Health Clients.

Burns-Lynch, B., and M. Salzer. 2001. Adopting innovations: Lessons learned from a peer-based hospital diversion program. *Community Mental Health Journal* 37(6):511–21.

California Department of Mental Health. 1981. *Friends can be good medicine.* San Francisco: Pacificon Productions.

Campbell, J. 1996. Towards collaborative mental health outcomes systems. *New Directions for Mental Health Services* 71:69–68.

————. 1997. How consumers/survivors are evaluating the quality of psychiatric care. *Evaluation Review* 21(3):357–63.

————.. 2000. MIMH coordinates multi-site consumer studies research initiative. *Mental Health American,* 11.

Campbell, J., J. Dumont, and K. Einspahr. 1999. *Peer core competencies project.* Philadelphia: Center for Mental Health Policy and Services Research, University of Pennsylvania.

Campbell, J., and J. R. Johnson. 1995. Struggling to reach common ground. *Behavioral Healthcare Tomorrow* 4(3):40, 45–46.

Campbell, J., R. Ralph, and R. Glover. 1993. From lab rat to researcher: The history, models, and policy implications of consumer/survivor involvement in research. In *Proceedings: Fourth Annual National Conference on State Mental Health Agency Services Research and Program Evaluation,* 138–57. Alexandria, VA: National Association of State Mental Health Program Directors.

Campbell, J., and R. Schraiber. 1989. *In pursuit of wellness: The Well-Being Project.* Sacramento: California Department of Mental Health.

Carpinello, S. E., E. L. Knight, and L. Janis. 1992. A study of the meaning of self-help, self-help processes, and outcomes. In *Proceedings: Third Annual Conference on State Mental Health Agency Services Research,* 37–44. Arlington, VA: National Association of State Mental Health Program Directors Research Institute, Inc.

Carpinello, S., E. Knight, L. Videka-Sherman, C. Sofka, and F. Markowitz. 1996. Self-selection distinguishing factors: Participants and non participants of mental health self-help groups. Report prepared for the Center for the Study of Issues in Public Mental Health.

Cartwright, A. 1964. *Human relations and hospital care.* London: Routledge and Keegan.

Chamberlin, J. 1988 *On our own: Patient-controlled alternatives to the mental health system.* Manchester, Eng.: Mind Publications.

———. 1997. *The ex-patient movement: Where we've been going and where we're going.* Lawrence, MA: National Empowerment Center.

Chamberlin, J., E. S. Rogers, and M. Ellison. 1996. Self-help programs: A description of their characteristics and their members. *Psychiatric Rehabilitation Journal* 19:33–42.

Cobb, S. 1976. Social support as a moderator of life stress. *Psychosomatic Medicine* 38(5):300–314.

Cook, J., J. Jonikas, and M. Solomon, M. 1991. Models of vocational rehabilitation for youth and adults with severe mental illness. *American Rehabilitation* 17(1).

Copeland, M. E. 1997. *Wellness Recovery Action Plan.* W. Dummerston, VT: Peach Press.

Corring, D. 2002. Quality of life: Perspectives of people with mental illnesses and family members. *Psychiatric Rehabilitation Journal* 25.

Davidson, L., M. Chinman, B. Kloos, R. Weingarten, D. Stayner, D. and J. Tebes. 1999. Peer support among individuals with severe mental illness: A review of the evidence. *Clinical Psychology: Science and Practice* 9(2):165–87.

DeMasi, M., S. Carpinello, E. Knight, L. Videka-Sherman, C. Sofka, and F. Markowitz. 1997. The role of self-help in the recovery process. Report prepared for the Center for the Study of Issues in Public Mental Health.

DeSisto, M., C. Harding, R. McCormick, T. Ashikaga, J. Strauss, and G. Brooks. 1995. The Maine and Vermont three-decade studies of serious mental illness. *British Journal of Psychiatry* 167:331–41.

Diehl, S., and E. Baxter. 1999. *BRIDGES: A Journey of Hope, a peer-taught curriculum on mental illness, mental health treatment, and self-help skills.* Knoxville: Tennessee Alliance for the Mentally Ill.

Dumont, J., and K. Jones. 2002. Findings from a consumer/survivor defined alternative to psychiatric hospitalization. *Outlook,* Spring, 4–6.

Durman, E. 1976. The role of self-help in service provision. *Journal of Applied Behavioral Science* 12:433–43.

Emerick, R. 1990. Self-help groups for former patients: Relations with mental health professionals. *Hospital and Community Psychiatry* 41:401–7.

Forquer, S., and E. Knight. 2001. Managed care: Recovery enhancer or inhibitor? *Psychiatric Services* 52:25–26.

Galanter, M. 1988. Research on social supports and mental illness. *American Journal of Psychiatry* 145:1270–72.

Gartner, A., and F. Riessman. 1982. Self-help and mental health. *Hospital and Community Psychiatry* 33:631–35.

Gelso, C., and J. Carter. 1985. The relationship in counseling and psychotherapy: Components, consequence, and theoretical antecedents. *Counseling Psychologist* 2:155–243.

Greenberg, L., and W. Pinsof. 1986. Process research: Current trends and perspectives. In *The psychotherapeutic process: A research handbook*, ed. L. Greenberg and W. Pinsof, 3–20. New York: Guilford.

Grusky, O., K. Tierney, R. Manderscheid, and D. Grusky. 1985. Social bonding and community adjustment of chronically mentally ill adults. *Journal of Health and Social Behavior* 26:49–63.

Gurman, A. 1977. The patient's perception of the therapeutic relationship. In *Effective psychotherapy: A handbook of research*, ed. A. Gurman and A. Razin, 503–43. New York: Pergamon Press.

Hall, J., D. Roter, and C. Rand. 1981. Communication of affect between patient and physician. *Journal of Health and Social Behavior* 22:18–30.

Harding, C., G. Brooks, T. Ashikaga, J. Strauss, and A. Breier. 1987. The Vermont longitudinal study of persons with severe mental illness. *American Journal of Psychiatry* 144:718–26.

Hartley, D., and H. Strupp. 1983. The therapeutic alliance: Its relationship to outcome in brief psychotherapy. In *Empirical studies in analytic theories*, ed. J. Masling, 1–37. Hillsdale, NJ: Erlbaum.

Horvath, A., and L. Luborsky. 1993. The role of the therapeutic alliance in psychotherapy. *Journal of Consulting and Clinical Psychology* 61:561–573.

Kaufmann, C. 1995. The self-help employment center: Some outcomes from the first year. *Psychosocial Rehabilitation Journal* 18:145–62.

Kaufmann, C., P. Freund, and J. Wilson. 1989. Self-help in the mental health system: A model for consumer-provider collaboration. *Psychiatric Rehabilitation Journal* 13:520.

Kaufmann, C., H. Schulberg, and N. Schooler. 1994. Self-help group participation among people with severe mental illness. *Prevention in Human Services* 11:315–31.

Kaufmann, C., M. Ward-Colasante, and M. Farmer. 1993. Development and evaluation of drop-in centers operated by mental health consumers. *Hospital and Community Psychiatry* 44:675–78.

Kennedy, M., and K. Humphreys. 1994. Understanding worldview transformation in mutual help groups. *Prevention in Human Services* 11:181–89.

Keogh, C. 1975. *Readings for mental health*. Sydney: GROW.

Kessler, R., and K. Mickelson. 1997. Patterns and correlates of self-help group membership in the United States. *Social Policy* 27:27–47.

Klein, R., R. Cnaan, and J. Whitecraft. 1998. Significance of peer support with dually diagnosed clients: Findings from a pilot study. *Research in Social Work Practice* 8:529–51.

Korsch, B., and V. Negrete. 1972. Doctor-patient communication. *Science American* 227:66.

Koyanagi, C., and S. Semansky. 2001. Recovery in the community: Funding mental health rehabilitative approaches under Medicaid. Washington, DC: Bazelon Center for Mental Health Law.

Kurtz, L. 1988. Mutual aid for affective disorders: The Manic Depressive and Depressive Association. *American Journal of Orthopsychiatry* 58:152–55.

Lane, S. 1983. Compliance, satisfaction, and physician-patient communication. In *Communication yearbook,* ed. R. Bostrom, 7:772–99. Beverly Hills, CA: Sage.

LeDoux, E. 1997. Revitalizing a consumer-controlled alternative. In *Consumers as providers in psychiatric rehabilitation,* ed. C. Mowbray, D. Moxley, C. Jasper, and L. Howel, 142–47. Columbia, MD: International Association of Psychosocial Rehabilitation Services.

Lewison, D. 1975. An analysis of the components of inpatient satisfaction. Master's thesis, Johns Hopkins University School of Hygiene and Public Health.

Lieberman, A., E. Gowdy, and L. Knutson. 1991. The mental health outreach project: A case study in self-help. *Psychosocial Rehabilitation Journal* 14:100–105.

Lieberman, M., and L. Snowden. 1994. Problems in assessing prevalence and membership characteristics of self-help group participants. In *Understanding the self-help organization: Frameworks and findings,* ed. T. Powel, 32–49. Thousand Oaks, CA: Sage.

Long, L., and L. Van Tosh. 1988. *Program descriptions of consumer-run programs for homeless people.* Vol. 2 of 3 pts. Contract no. 304666. Rockville, MD: Division of Education and Service Systems Liaison, National Institute of Mental Health, June.

Luke, D. A., L. Roberts, and J. Rappaport. 1994. Individual, group context, and individual-group fit predictors of self-help group attendance. In *Understanding the self-help organization: Frameworks and findings,* ed. T. J. Powell, 88–114. Thousand Oaks, CA: Sage.

Lyons, J., J. Cook, A. Ruth, and M. Karver. 1996. Service delivery using consumer staff in a mobile crisis assessment program. *Community Mental Health Journal* 32:33–40.

Marson, D., M. McGovern, and H. Pomp. 1988. Psychiatric decision-making in the emergency room: A research overview. *American Journal of Psychiatry* 145:918–25.

Marziali, E. 1984. Predication of outcome of brief psychotherapy from therapist interpretive interviews. *Archives of General Psychiatry* 41:301–5.

McCabe, S., and R. Unzicker. 1995. Changing roles of consumer/survivors in mature mental health systems. *New Directions for Mental Health Services* 66:61–73.

McLean, A. 1995 Empowerment and the psychiatric consumer/ex-patient movement in the United States: Contradictions, crisis, and change. *Social Science Medicine* 40:1053–71.

Mead, S., D. Hilton, and L. Curtis. 2001. Peer support: A theoretical perspective. *Psychiatric Rehabilitation Journal* 25:136.

Medvene, L. 1986. Research studies examine the effectiveness of self-help groups. *Self-Helper* 1(4):6.

Meek, C. 1994. Consumer-run drop-in centers as alternatives to mental health system services. *PRO/CON* 3(1):49–51.

Mental Health Policy Resource Center. 1991. The growing mental health self-help movement. Policy in Perspective. Washington, DC: Author, May.

Mowbray, C., and D. Moxley. 1997. A framework for organizing consumer roles as providers of psychiatric rehabilitation. In *Consumers as providers in psychiatric rehabilitation,* ed. C. Mowbray, D. Moxley, C. Jasper, and L. Howel, 35–44. Columbia, MD: International Association of Psychosocial Rehabilitation Services.

Mowbray, C., and C. Tan. 1992. Evaluation of an innovative consumer-run service model: The drop-in center. *Innovations and Research* 1(2):19–23.

———. 1993. Consumer-operated drop-in centers: evaluation of operations and impact. *Journal of Mental Health Administration* 20(1):8–19.

Mowbray, C., R. Wellwood, and P. Chamberlain. 1988. Project Stay: A consumer-run support service. *Psychosocial Rehabilitation Journal* 12:33–42.

National Association of State Mental Health Program Directors (NASMHPD). 1989. *NASMHPD Position Paper on Consumer Contributions to Mental Health Delivery Systems.* Arlington, VA: NASMHPD.

Nikkel, R., G. Smith, and D. Edwards. 1992. A consumer-operated case management project. *Hospital and Community Psychiatry* 43:577–79.

Ninde, N. 1990. *Yes I can! Seven true stories of persons coping with mental and emotional illness.* Franklin County, OH: Alliance for the Mentally Ill.

Onken, S., J. Dumont, P. Ridgway, D. Dornan, and R. Ralph. 2002. *Mental health recovery: What helps and what hinders?* Alexandria, VA: National Technical Assistance Center for State Mental Health Planning.

President's New Freedom Commission for Mental Health. 2002. *Interim report.* Washington, DC: Office of the President, October 29.

Prout, N. 1997. Offering sanctuary and safety: Rainbow House, a peer support facility. In *Consumers as providers in psychiatric rehabilitation,* ed. C. Mowbray, D. Moxley, C. Jasper, and L. Howel, 148–54. Columbia, MD: International Association of Psychosocial Rehabilitation Services.

Ralph, R. 2000. Recovery. *Psychiatric Rehabilitation Skills* 4:480–517.

Rapp, C. 1998. *The strengths model: Case management with people suffering from severe and persistent mental illness.* New York: Oxford University Press.

Rappaport, J. 1987. Terms of empowerment/exemplars of prevention: Toward a theory of community psychology. *American Journal of Community Psychology* 15:121–44.

Rappaport, J., T. Reischl, and M. Zimmerman. 1992. Mutual help mechanisms in the empowerment of former mental patients. In *The strengths perspective in social work practice,* ed. D. Saleebey, 84–97. White Plains, NY: Longman.

Rappaport, J., E. Seidman, T. A. Paul, L. McFadden, T. Reischl, L. J. Roberts, D. Salem, C. Stein, and M. Zimmerman. 1985. Collaborative research with a self-help organization. *Social Policy* 15:12–24.

Reidy, D. 1994. Recovering from treatment: The mental health system as an agent of stigma. *Resources* 6:3–10.

Riessman, F. 1965. The helper-therapy principle. *Social Work* 10:27–32.

———. 1990. Restructuring help: A human services paradigm for the 1990s. *American Journal of Community Psychology* 18:221–30.

Roberts, L., D. Luke, J. Rappaport, E. Seidman, P. Toro, and T. Reischl. 1991. Charting unchartered terrain: A behavioral observation system for mutual help groups. *American Journal of Community Psychology* 19:715–37.

Rogers, C. 1957. The necessary and sufficient condition of therapeutic personality change. *Journal of Consulting and Clinical Psychology* 22:95–103.

Rootes, L., and D. Aanes. 1992. A conceptual framework for understanding self-help groups. *Hospital and Community Psychiatry* 43:379–81.

Saltzer, M. and S. Liptzin-Shear. 2002. Identifying consumer-provider benefits in evaluation of consumer-delivered services. *Psychiatric Rehabilitation Journal* 25:281.

Scott, A. 1993. Consumers/survivors reform the system, bringing a "human face" to research. *Resources* 5:3–6.

Segal, S., C. Silverman, and T. Temkin. 1995. Characteristics and service use of long-term members of self-help agencies for mental health clients. *Psychiatric Services* 46:269–74.

Silverman, S. 1997. Recovery through partnership: "On Our Own, Charlottesville, Virginia." In *Consumers as providers in psychiatric rehabilitation,* ed. C. Mowbray, D. Moxley, C. Jasper, and L. Howel, 126–41. Columbia, MD: International Association of Psychosocial Rehabilitation Services.

Skillman-Campbell, J. 1991. *Towards undiscovered country: Mental health clients speak for themselves.* Ann Arbor: UMI.

Skipper, J., D. Taglacozzo, and H. Mauksch. 1964. Some possible consequences of limited communication between patients and hospital functionaries. *Journal of Health and Human Behavior* 6(10):34.

Solomon P., and J. Draine. 2001. The state of knowledge of the effectiveness of consumer provided services. *Psychiatric Rehabilitation Journal* 25:20–27.

Stewart, M. 1990. Expanding theoretical conceptualizations of self-help groups. *Social Science and Medicine* 31:1057–66.

Street, R. L. Jr., and J. Wiemann. 1987. Patients' satisfaction with physician interpersonal involvement, expressiveness, and dominance. In *Communication yearbook,* ed. M. McLaughlin, 10:591–612. Beverly Hills, CA: Sage.

Stroul, B. 1986. *Models of community support services approaches to helping persons with long-term mental illness.* Boston: Boston University.

Styles, W., D. Shapiro, and R. Elliott. 1986. Are all psychotherapies equivalent? *American Psychologist* 41:165–80.

Tan, C., C. Mowbray, and J. Foster. 1990. *Consumer-run drop-in center study: Technical report, executive summary.* Detroit: Michigan State University.

Tanzman, B. 1993. An overview of mental health consumers' preferences for housing and support services. *Hospital and Community Psychiatry* 44:450–55.

Trainor, J., M. Shepherd, K. Boydell, A. Leff, and E. Crawford. 1997. Beyond the services paradigm: The impact of consumer/survivor initiatives. *Psychiatric Rehabilitation Journal* 21:132–40.

Trochim, W., J. Dumont, and J. Campbell. 1993. A report for the state mental health agency profiling system: Mapping mental health outcomes from the perspective of consumers/survivors. Technical report series. Alexandria, VA: National Association of State Mental Health Program Directors Research Institute.

Trochim, W., and R. Linton. 1986. Conceptualization for planning and evaluation. *Evaluation and Program Planning* 9(4):289–308.

Van Tosh, L., and P. del Vecchio. 2000. *Consumer-operated self-help programs: A technical report.* Rockville, MD: Center for Mental Health Services.

Van Tosh, L., R. Ralph, and J. Campbell. 2000. The rise of consumerism. *Psychiatric Rehabilitation Skills* 4:383–409.

Yanos, P., L. Primavera, and E. Knight. 2001. Consumer-run service participation, recovery of social functioning, and the mediating role of psychological factors. *Psychiatric Services* 52:493–500.

Zinman, S. 1986. Taking issue: Self-help; The wave of the future. *Hospital and Community Psychiatry* 37:213.

———.. 1987. Definition of self-help groups. In *Reaching across: Mental health clients helping each other,* ed. S. Zinman, H. Harp, and S. Budd, 7–15. Riverside: California Network of Mental Health Clients.

PART II
Drop-In Centers

3
Mental Health Client Action Network (MHCAN), Santa Cruz, California

Bonnie Schell

The Mental Health Client Action Network (MHCAN) is a drop-in center in Santa Cruz, California, run by adults diagnosed with major mental disorders who want to create a healing place for themselves and their peers. Our program began in the 1970s as part of an anti-psychiatry political group and evolved through four historical phases to become a contractor providing consumer-operated services for North County Mental Health in Santa Cruz, California.

In the first phase of consumer organizing, adults who had been diagnosed with major mental disorders met together informally in the community as members of the Psychiatric Inmates Rights Collective (PIRC). Their energy stemmed primarily from anger at the formal mental health system, with the certainty that consumers could treat patients in a more sensitive, respectful manner. I was angry because when medication mistakes were made or when my friends were physically and emotionally abused in the hospital, providers never apologized. I also took exception to the practice of routinely handcuffing persons in front of their neighbors when police took them to the hospital for observation.

PIRC's focus changed significantly in 1991, beginning MHCAN's second phase of development, when the group decided to attend a national consumer conference, Alternatives, in Berkeley. Raising funds to attend the conference required collaboration with non-PIRC members and the mental health system in Santa Cruz. A third phase began after the conference, when MHCAN split from PIRC and cooperated with county mental health services to start a consumer-operated drop-in on site at the county clinic. Consumer leaders approached and retreated and bargained for their own drop-in center with their own rules, with the result that MHCAN moved away from the clinic and achieved consistency in its program and staff. MHCAN, in its fourth phase, is now a nonprofit organization and operates a stand-alone community drop-in that provides mutual support to others, including those who are homeless and those not receiving services. Figure 3.1 lists what clients of mental health services find when they arrive at our community-centered drop-in.

The fourth and most recent phase of our development was initiated by MHCAN's selection to participate in the federal Consumer-Operated Services Programs (COSP) Multi-Site Research Initiative in 1998. As a half-time research staff person, I was put on a steep learning curve to make reports, hire non-consumers for research staff, look at factors which attracted consumers to the drop-in, record their participation, and evaluate our program. Participation in the research study equipped MHCAN as an organization to take charge of its own well-being and survival. The remainder of this chapter describes more fully these four phases of MHCAN's development.

Phase I: Anger and Certainty (1975–90)

The most vocal group of town radicals met monthly in John Stuart's rented front room in a big house in downtown Santa Cruz, a California beach town with a population of fifty-five thousand. Jane Kysor's blue VW station wagon, covered in anti-psychiatry stickers ("Housing, not Haldol!"), brought six people, all outpatients of the public mental health system. Other members came by bus, calling themselves "ex-patients." Both the ex-patients and the outpatients living in board and care homes called themselves "survivors," meaning that they had survived mental health treatments. At a typical meeting, the first item of business was for all to "check in," reporting on how their lives were going. Then Jane would list the needs in the survivor community—who needed clothes or shoes, who wanted to be visited in locked facilities, and when hearings about conservatorship of a person were scheduled in Superior Court.

This was the PIRC, formed in 1975 by former mental patients, aided by students in a community services class at the University of California at Santa Cruz. PIRC members were later to be present at the founding of MHCAN. PIRC took an anti-psychiatry position, contrary to the biological-medical model of mental illness, that left them unlikely to be funded by state and county traditional services. PIRC's specific purpose was to educate the public about abuses in the traditional mental health system, to promote the civil rights and liberties of those institutionalized,

FIGURE 3.1. What Can a Typical Client Expect at MHCAN?

Two staff members open up and make coffee by 9 a.m. A driver is available to bring clients to the center if they request a ride. The clients check in with the receptionist. Those who are new are asked whether they have Medicaid, whether they have had a physical examination in the past year, and whether they have housing. The receptionist points out that there is coffee and pastry in the kitchen and a free telephone for client use.

The client then has the following options:

- Read the newspaper or books and magazines or use the phone.
- Use the computer lab to play games, check e-mail, or receive instruction on one of the ten computers.
- Print out homework or employment applications or housing applications and make copies.
- Play chess or ping pong in the community room.
- Sleep on one of four couches.
- Play the piano or guitar or listen to tapes or radio.
- Watch cable television.
- Use art materials: pens, acrylic, charcoal.
- Talk to others; ask for advice about problems with Social Security or landlords or case managers.
- Get a ride to medical appointments or a payee's office.
- Attend any of two or three peer counseling groups scheduled each day and run by other clients.
- Walk to retail businesses within a few blocks: fast food restaurants, a grocery store, two pharmacies.
- Smoke outside at a picnic table and talk and listen to others.
- Get a ride home or to the homeless shelter in the late afternoon.

_____

Note: Clients may use MHCAN as a mailing address and those looking for housing may have messages left there.

and to create alternatives to the current system. David Williams, a member of the Boston Mental Patients Liberation Front, had brought some of these ideas to Santa Cruz.

PIRC was responsible for lobbying for a local patient advocate for inpatients, through a program of Protection & Advocacy, Inc., in Santa Cruz. Over the years, PIRC wrote various grant proposals for treatment and respite centers that were voluntary, free, and run by other mental patients. Their proposals were all turned down, primarily because they lacked a feasible budget. Living on Supplemental Security Income (SSI) or disability benefits, a group of ex-patients could not afford a house or liability insurance. Not being professionally licensed counselors, they could not bill any insurance for their peer counseling or for sitting and listening all day and night to a person who was suicidal or manic.

PIRC members all felt they had been traumatized by the public and private mental health system and had not received help for real problems they did acknowledge. The experience most shared was that of having a mental health diagnosis interrupt their lives. In one of their news sheets, *Where We Stand,* PIRC members wrote: "We are mental patients. . . . We know what it is like to be . . . treated as an object. . . . And we know what it's like to leave the hospital to find that we can't get a job, that the police are suspicious of us, and that we have lost old and valued friends." I have known this acquired stigma in my life. When I was first diagnosed with schizophrenia at age seventeen, the doctor told my parents never to turn in an insurance claim if I ever wanted to be a schoolteacher. Forty-five years later, when my neighbor and good friend heard me on a radio panel about mental health services, she told her children to stop coming to my house because they might bother me.

Every month PIRC received a packet from the National Teleconference, sponsored by the Psychosocial Rehabilitation Department at Boston University. It contained newspaper articles and essays on patient rights and legislation dealing with the public mental health system that the consumer leader Judi Chamberlin and her staff assembled. We decided which articles to copy and distribute around town. Three years' worth of teleconference packets, as well as issues of *Madness Network News* (first issue, 1972) and *Phoenix Rising,* our seminal movement newspapers, were stacked in John Stuart's back room. We always had chapter reprints from Judi Chamberlin, David Cohen, Leonard Frank, J. C. Mancuso and J. R. Adams-Webber, T. R. Sarbin, and Thomas Szasz (see Selected Readings at the end of this chapter), as well as Dr. Caligari's anonymous treatise on the side effects of psychotropic medications. We photocopied drawings by the local artist Ruth Saffen showing her electroshock treatments with family members and doctors standing around, as well as her poignant portraits of labeled people with split heads and missing fingers. We shared the poetry from little newsletters that arrived from survivor groups all over the country. In the 1980s we subscribed to and sold copies of David Oaks's *Dendron,* a quarterly published in Oregon.

PIRC's chief expense was thirty-six dollars to pay for our post office box. We paid printing and copying costs by charging a dime for the materials we distributed at local events and consumer conferences. John designed standing display boards out of cardboard on which he glued pivotal mental illness articles. An interested citizen simply requested an article by its number, and John pulled the text from his portable cardboard box filing system. PIRC also collected signatures on petitions against electroshock. Money for Jane Kysor's gas and for the small needs of individuals was all contributed by PIRC members from their Veteran's and SSI benefits and housecleaning jobs.

Because Jane had been a kindergarten teacher, she helped PIRC mix simple ways to have fun with politics, arranging horseback riding in the park and trips to the beach, making spoof videos of hospital experiences, designing message buttons, and holding dances that always included the homeless. The organization did not have liability insurance and did not have to worry about causing a public disturbance that would embarrass a funding agent.

Five or six PIRC members who were knowledgeable in the politics of mental-labeling theory frequently were called on as speakers for university classes that focused on the sociology of psychotherapy, women and seniors in the mental health system, the politics of homelessness, mind control, the marginalization of groups, power dynamics, and the treatment of spiritually sensitive people, as well as gays, lesbians, transgender, and bisexual people.

Over lots of coffee, PIRC members had disagreements over our confrontational political style. In ten years, where had it gotten us? If we picketed outside the office of a doctor who ordered electroshock for a senior patient, how could we expect him to listen when we begged him not to commit someone to a locked facility? Who would pay for what we said we wanted—safe places where people could get well, not a punitive system that strapped them with a stigmatizing diagnosis for life? We could not visit everyone in the hospital or find an apartment for everyone or give everyone transportation to get groceries. What about the thousands of mental health clients in Santa Cruz who were assisted by case managers and were dependent on the traditional system for their housing and entitlements, but who were subjected to mostly involuntary treatment? How could people with mental illnesses advocate within the formal system for more respectful treatment? I thought that we somehow needed to demonstrate respectful social interactions with our peers and professional providers, too. I believed we needed another type of organization that focused on meeting daily needs rather than rights advocacy that took the form of fist raising.

In April 1983 the California Network of Mental Health Clients was established as an independent organization, sharing some founders with the Network Against Psychiatric Assault, another anti-psychiatry organization in northern California. Most PIRC members joined and we began to participate in monthly self-help and public policy teleconferences. Self-help groups were springing up all over the state and getting assistance from one another without much leadership or assistance from the formal system. Most of these groups lasted three to five years until their leader burned out or until there was an incident, such as a suicide or arrest, that brought them bad publicity.

In August 1987, Sylvia Caras (a member of PIRC and the California Network of Mental Health Clients, and later founder of the "People Who" listserv), after being advised by a professional that people who had manic depression would never be able to meet together, formed Mood Matters Association, an evening support group in Santa Cruz. Mood Matters meetings encouraged attentive listening and examined new material on the latest medications. The group talked, not about no treatment, but about treatment choices. Under three changes of leadership, Mood Matters has continued to meet at MHCAN.

Mirroring the state network, the Santa Cruz Network of Mental Health Clients was formed in 1988 by Cindi Klein Peck and former PIRC members. The group entered into friendly conversation with the administration of North County Mental Health, but they did not hold regular meetings. Jane, John, and I, as well as others went every Saturday to socialize at a lunch and bingo event for all clients in board and care homes and supported housing run by Community Support Services, a branch of Santa Cruz Community Counseling Center, Inc. I applied for a job with the center as a community organizer (a nonconsumer position), but my application was never acknowledged.

Among all of the Santa Cruz mental health client activists, we had two computers (Sylvia's and mine), lots of yard-sale typewriters, one filing cabinet, and many marking pens. We had regular contacts with the community at large—with the city library for displays, with the university, with senior citizens, through groups such as the Seniors' Commission and the Gray Bears, with the Commission to Prevent Violence Against Women, with the Ombudsman Advocate, Inc., office, and with the courts. We also had anger that was focused on specific wrongs and injustices, legal knowledge of mental patients' rights, and the practice of listening to one another without voicing judgment. Meanwhile, it seemed to me that client groups, including PIRC, were wearing themselves out trying to support fellow members who were hospitalized annually or who were losing housing and all their worldly possessions and having to start over again and again. When an earthquake ruptured Santa Cruz in 1989, John lost his apartment and PIRC, its meeting space. Many mental health clients were displaced, although, strangely enough, the census on the Behavioral Health Unit at Dominican Hospital was the lowest it had been for some time. PIRC's phone tree was active day and night, checking on people.

Phase II: Collaboration and Compromise (1991–93)

In 1990, word had spread that Alternatives, the annual national conference for mental health clients, was going to be held at the University of California in Berkeley, home of the Free Speech Movement. In April 1991, members of Mood Matters, the Santa Cruz Network, and PIRC met with the executive director of Ombudsman Advocate, Inc., to discuss forming a coalition to seek funding for a client affairs coordinator and to ask for county funds to be used to send as many mental health clients as possible to the conference. The meeting bogged down over the meaning of self-help—how to separate our views from those of all the 12-step groups pledging to give up bad habits, make amends to those they had wronged, and give their problems over to a higher power. Were we to give up hearing voices and make amends to family members who had locked us out of their homes? The different consumer factions could only agree that listening to people and treating them with kindness was better than giving forced injections. Then accusations were made that not everyone in the room had had a true madness experience, that voyeurs were present. The coalition agenda was tabled.

A remnant task force of Jane, Sylvia, Cindi Peck, and I decided to seek funding for Alternatives '91. Sylvia drew up a budget. The county mental health director, Dr. Rama Khalsa, helped publicize the conference. However, when PIRC and the Santa Cruz Network members gathered before the County Board of Supervisors to request money for self-help programs, an argument over leadership and accepting government money erupted. Our division was obvious in public testimony. Nevertheless, Santa Cruz County budgeted $5,500 to send twenty-three people to Berkeley, to pay a client coordinator $500 to organize consumer meetings, and to supply an office for fiscal year 1991–92.

At Alternatives '91, Santa Cruz clients connected with two thousand clients from all over the United States who were running their own programs and workshops. I can still recall the tremendous sense of belonging and possibility we felt. PIRC women met Gayle Bluebird of Altered States of the Arts and, calling themselves the "Haldol Sisters," presented a song in the talent show. Attendees stayed in university dormitory rooms and cheaper student hostels.

After Alternatives '91, Cindi was elected coordinator of the Santa Cruz Network because of her experience on the local Mental Health Advisory Board. She was given a tiny office on the same hall as the psychiatrists in the county clinic. Our meetings, as well as those of Mood Matters, were held at London Nelson Community Center in downtown Santa Cruz in space arranged by Rama Khalsa. We again formed a liaison support group with university students called "Mad Womyn United." I started an eight-to-twelve-page newsletter called the *Alternative Report.* The county assumed all printing and mailing costs until, after two years, the newsletter printed a durable power of attorney packet for mental health care. Within a week, the county decided to withdraw funding.

The fledgling group continued PIRC's practice of hospital visiting. At Dominican Hospital and Harbor Hills, an Institute for Mental Disease, we tried to find out what patients thought would help them and to assist the patients in communicating their wishes to staff. If patients wanted to be released, we helped them file writs of habeas corpus. The hospital wanted outside visitors to come only at certain times on certain days. Then they wanted to interview and approve visitors. Cindi Peck set up a hospital visiting committee to work out an agreement with Dominican administration for visiting. After three years the rules were solidified to stipulate that visitors could not wear denim, had to wear a bra and close-toed shoes, could not visit patients in their rooms, and could not bring in coffee. We let Cindi agree to abide by these rules while Jane and I visited a patient in her room. We became attorneys in fact for this patient and eventually went to court with a plan of third party assistance for her. The Superior Court judge, observing that thirteen hospitalizations had not been helpful, released the patient to peer assistance. Twelve years later, this woman continues to live in her own apartment.

By the 1990s, inclusion of mental health patient input on state and community boards and councils had become a policy in California. Instead of organizing and doing more outreach in the community, we spent a lot of time commenting on the county's draft manuals for the Rehabilitation Option (which allowed counties to bill Medicaid for living skills and employment readiness training) and Coordinated Care Services (in which the psychiatrist, case managers, and other support persons delivered client-directed services as teams). While these efforts made us feel important, none of our comments were ever acknowledged or implemented. We did not have letterhead or a real place at the policy-making table. If we did a really competent job on a report, our work was seen as a symptom of mania and we were told to get more rest.

In April 1992, Sylvia and I invited Jay Mahler and Sally Zinman from the California Network of Mental Health Clients in Berkeley and Contra Costa to conduct an all-day workshop in Santa Cruz to help draft a mission statement for a new organization to be called Mental Health Client Action Network of Santa Cruz County. We paid them two hundred dollars, which seemed exorbitant. That meeting happened in the education building next to a United Methodist Church that MHCAN would move into eight years later. Ninety patients of the county system came and their wishes were subsequently honed into a mission statement:

> The Mental Health Client Action Network of Santa Cruz County is a client-run organization designed to empower with dignity through inter-dependence & in-dependence
>
> 1. By providing mutual support and networking,
> 2. By having a voice in all matters which affect us,
> 3. By creating programs controlled by clients,
> 4. By advocating for the right to choose and refuse care, the right to adequate housing, & the right to full and timely access to personal records & full and timely access to service options.
> 5. By educating the public from our perspective as well as providing information and sharing resources among ourselves.
> 6. By confronting discrimination against mental health clients.

For a year we debated whether to say we were "independent" or "interdependent." We liked to think of ourselves as independent agents, but those of us functioning well depended on the support of friends and family and a good psychiatrist or therapist. In 1992, being interdependent with the traditional provider service system was a process we could not picture.

Having seen so many of our brothers and sisters hospitalized by their families, we would not have gone to a meeting of the Alliance for the Mentally Ill. Later that year the alliance gave me an award for community service and outreach. I went to their meeting to accept my plaque and signed a sheet saying I was interested in membership. They never called. (By 2001 MHCAN and the Alliance for the Mentally Ill were jointly publishing an annual newsletter.)

At our first drop-in we simply made coffee and had two people there at all times to hear people's concerns or simply to be friendly. Cindi had a car and when other clients dropped by her office, they were soon off visiting someone on the locked unit or helping someone look for housing. The next year, the county moved us out of their building to a little house painted blue in the parking lot behind the mental health building. The Blue House was next to Community Connection, a socialization and mailroom employment program in the psychosocial rehabilitation model. We found their staff comfortable to be with, and they told us whom to contact in the medical-clinical system to obtain what we needed. The younger, friendly social workers from County Mental Health, as well as older staff who did outreach to the homeless, were soon hanging out on MHCAN's porch talking to consumers. MHCAN shared the four-room Blue House and one telephone with the Alliance for the Mentally Ill and a new group called the Mental Health Resource Center for families, all funded by the county. We had a kitchen counter for coffee and a little room for support groups and creative writing classes, but no office. We paid a few people a $65 monthly stipend to keep the drop-in open, we paid a coordinator, and we had a budget for coffee. We were not charged rent. Our budget was $19,000 in fiscal year 1992–93.

On a visit to my youngest daughter at Boston University in 1991, I sought out the Ruby Rogers Drop In Center, started by Judi Chamberlin. Knowing the address in a Cambridge residential neighborhood, I found the center by going to the back of the house, down some steps to the basement. The center was on a major bus line. I copied their rules off the wall and refrigerator, collected their schedule of events, and talked to consumers.

Meanwhile I used PIRC's nonprofit status to apply for a grant from the Cultural Council for a diary-writing class and later for an art show at the downtown County Government Building. In 1994 we sponsored art classes and held a month-long show on the theme Women and Psychiatry at the Women's Center at the University of California, Santa Cruz. Trying to break free of PIRC as a nonprofit sponsor, MHCAN attempted to get a local nonprofit agency for supported housing to back a grant application for a poetry teacher for consumers from the university and a public reading. The executive director would not accept the liability for a project without case management. On our own, we packed Bookshop Santa Cruz downtown for a reading and sold copies of our first chapbook of poetry. "Voices & Visions II" was printed in August 1994 and sold in local stores. Writing and publishing poems became a common activity among members at MHCAN. The following poem by Bonnie Schell is an example of our work.

Simple Event 2/02/02

He broke into my office
and I didn't press charges
against the thin man curled like a semicolon,
with a sack of clothes dotting his head.

He broke into my office
the night of blowing rain and thunder
opened the check book drawer
but touched nothing except
my illusion of locked separateness.

When discovered sleeping, Thomas ran
but followed the police car
back into the parking lot
and held out his wrists to be cuffed.

When the sun began to dry the puddles
Thomas returned, stayed outside
parceling crumbs to pigeons and gulls
throwing me a God Bless as I ignored him.

Today he asked how to make coffee
scrubbed the counters, poured
his brew for those with trembling hands.
He asked for duct tape
to mend a man's shoes.

Although PIRC leadership, now meeting at the library, refused to come onto county mental health property, where our little drop-in was located, their presence was still politically threatening to mental health administrators. Whenever the county discussed opening an adolescent wing at the hospital or administering electric shock treatment locally, I would spread the rumor that PIRC and all the radical groups in Berkeley and Oakland (now mostly defunct) were planning to march, picket, and call the newspaper. It always worked. To avoid public controversy, county administration seemed to table their action item.

In the mid 1990s the rhetoric from federal mental health agencies was way ahead of the local and state agendas. Jackie Parrish of the Center for Mental Health Services, for example, wrote in the first National Empowerment Center newsletter (April–May 1994), "Self-help is the basic value of the movement, but the major impact on people's lives is still from the formal system with all its resources, so without advocacy that's not going to change, and people will continue to get hurt."

Space for self-help was not in local planning. Santa Cruz County, in an effort to expand outpatient services, built a new mental health office facility. When grading began on the parking lot, the Blue House had to come down. MHCAN was urged to "look downtown" for space, such as a storefront, to rent. But finding a place was not that simple. We did not have nonprofit status, a car, a budget, or a checkbook, and we were mental health clients knocking on the doors of a downtown that served a tourist industry still rebuilding after the earthquake. As soon as we said, "drop-in center for mental health clients, you know, psychiatric outpatients," faces clouded over. We were fish out of water with no connections or mentoring about how to represent ourselves.

When we could not find a place to rent, we were invited back into the old mental health building to a room called the Solarium. But the invitation was only temporary and only for times when doctors and case managers were not using the room. When the county staff were there, we waited in the hall, pacing and noisy. The Solarium had been a sunroom for tuberculosis patients, and the county morgue was in the basement. We served popcorn and coffee but had no privacy for support groups or walls for artwork. Under the direction of co-coordinators, who changed three times in one year, MHCAN started a fund-raising project to sell one dollar tickets for homemade pies. This project was popular with the county staff but did not last long because it was construed to be taking advantage of client labor, as was selling our paintings to staff. Then the county hired a nonclient to monitor us. One morning a robust client hit the monitor over the head with a chair when the monitor would not let the client get a cup of coffee a little bit early, even though it was already made. Security was called. The county again seriously considered moving us out.

While we rarely looked at our mission statement, and seemed to be always reacting to someone's crisis, the two things we managed to do consistently were to welcome all people and to visit patients in the hospital every week. During drop-in hours on county property, it was hard to be relaxed and not to feel watched. Whether we were shouting in anger or gushing in excitement over an idea, staff would come running in, in reaction to our "symptoms."

Two of our coordinators and our bookkeeper became ill and had to be replaced. The next coordinator made an advisory committee of all her boyfriends. Once we spent our Client Advocacy budget on flip-flops and lipstick for people in the hospital and we bought cigarettes for patients, too, with county money. The first year our budget was managed by the Ombudsman Advocate office, and the next year by the William James Association, a nonprofit that sponsored art classes in prisons. Both agencies refused to continue. We were disorganized, very emotional when questioned about our decisions, and haphazard about keeping receipts for expenses. To some extent we were "playing store."

Administrators could see that outpatients who came to the drop-in hours were happier and took more active responsibility for their mental health. Our budget was increased to $39,000 and the Santa Cruz Community Counseling Center became our funding agent, assigning one of their program support staff to set up MHCAN time cards, personnel records, and petty cash forms and to sign off on all expenditures and cut our payroll checks. Our staff was inexperienced with office procedures, but we began to follow consistent policies, such as requiring two signatures on every check and coding all expenses according to our budget line items. At the end of fiscal year 1992–93 we had saved enough money to buy a used Plymouth van, bulletin boards, and two meeting tables. Again we went looking for a home with a 1993–94 budget of $56,000. I said to Dr. Rama Khalsa, "Don't give up on us, but let us take some risks," and she never interfered with our program.

Phase III: Stability and Consistency (1994–98)

In July 1993 MHCAN moved, with the county's blessing, into the basement of Grace United Methodist Church, of which I was a recent member. The space reminded me of the Ruby Rogers Center. The church was on the same corner as the Sunday school building where we had our Mission Statement Workshop. I had been teaching creative writing classes at MHCAN, and now I negotiated the lease and chaired the Advisory Council of clients. Staff interactions under co-coordinators were volatile, but MHCAN managed to be open consistently four days a week, to fix coffee, to give everyone a listening ear, and to continue the Hospital Visiting Committee, whose message had changed. Whereas PIRC focused on informing the inpatient of ways to be released, MHCAN's message was, "This is not the end of the world. It will take a while to find medications that work and a case manager who understands you, but you can still go to school and have a job because others with a serious diagnosis have done it. Have hope."

The Advisory Board met regularly, posted minutes, and contracted with an outside consultant, suggested by the mental health director, to help us apply for state and federal tax exemptions as a non-profit. Our bylaws specified that the board should consist of at least two-thirds primary consumers and stated that "consumer members are defined as those individuals who are identified by the majority of the Board as consumers." This stipulation was a carryover from both PIRC and the California Network of Mental Health Clients, who held that a consumer was anyone the community of consumers takes to be a consumer, whether or not he or she is receiving traditional services.

The first MHCAN Board meeting was June 19, 1995. I was offered the position of half-time executive director and accepted. The basement of the church, which developed soggy carpets every time it rained, was sixteen hundred square feet divided into five rooms: an office, a TV room, an art room, a kitchen, and a central meeting-reception room. For the next two years the budget remained stable at $84,823, and staff turnover was zero. Besides providing coffee, microwaves, a separate client telephone, the daily newspaper, and a library, MHCAN offered drawing, painting, folk guitar, knitting, and creative writing classes. Sam Oastler's painting "God Save the Mentally Ill" (Figure 3.2) was inspired by our art classes.

We hired a receptionist, a bookkeeper, a kitchen monitor, and a driver for the van. We were tolerant when consumers were upset, angry, or yelling, as long as they did not take their feelings out on anyone else. We posted no rules. We did not require that visitors sign in.

When we gave a reading from our new chapbook, "Voices & Visions III," offering a free salad lunch for county staff in their lunchroom, no one came except a few parents of readers. It felt as though, by funding us, the county had gotten rid of hearing our voices. We attended local Mental Health Board meetings and were invited to occasional county adult planning meetings. We did not know how to make our points without interrupting, raising our voices, sulking, or stalking out. We had a self-righteous tone or extreme timidity, but no moral agency.

Besides Mood Matters, we did not have any support groups. Women wanted a group that focused on abuse issues, but the county said, "Not a good idea" because abuse is not important in the biomedical model of mental illness. Our mental health director said she fully supported peer counseling and would put extra money in the budget for training. That happened for three years, and during that time I learned the value of writing a Memo of Understanding after important conversations, followed by a Proposal with a Budget. I also learned to document our suggestions to committees. We began to be people with skills and insights instead of people with bothersome (to others) symptoms.

We went to any mental health meeting the county invited us to. We provided speakers whenever asked. We distributed paperbacks on medi-

Figure 3.2. "God Save the Mentally Ill." Gouache on watercolor paper by Sam Oastler, 2002.

cation and symptom management that the county sent us. We tried to offer classes from these books, but clients were not interested. Always we were afraid of making a mistake, of not preparing a perfect flyer, of bouncing a check, or causing an incident. We were afraid to close the drop-in for a day to use our van to carry clients to a fair housing conference or patient rights workshop, events PIRC would have been able to attend without the responsibility of keeping a drop-in activities center open. We did not want to be criticized for not being at our jobs. We were trying to earn respect from our funder which, after all, had enormous power over us—the power to conserve the person and the power to withdraw services from individuals who were uncooperative.

We liked our little drop-in center. We could see that consumers appreciated its safety off the streets. Our county contract monitor, Karolin Schwartz, MSW, said it was a comfort to be in our accepting space. Once she had to step over a passed-out, inebriated client in the kitchen, but she never brought up the incident. While we counseled clients on how to tell their psychiatrists what they wanted and did not want, as an organization, our staff members had trouble telling peers that their behavior was sometimes not okay. In our new monthly newsletter, the *We Can Courier,* I used the term "ghettoes" to describe the housing for mental health clients clustered together in certain parts of town. Some of our funders said the word was unfortunately chosen and our attitude ungrateful. We countered by pointing out the parts of town where people with HUD (Housing and Urban Development) Section 8 vouchers or on SSI never lived. Once we were urged to go to the state's first Partnership Conference for providers and clients, particularly those working in the system, but none of us was offered a ride with county staff. We grumbled behind the scenes to one another and over the telephone about the lack of partnership but said nothing to those with the power to change our invisibility. I kept asking myself, Are we no more than a client daycare center-sitter to the county? I wondered whether we had become the good-hearted pet dog that could be let out once a year to be shown off—to do our pity stories for the County Board of Supervisors during budget hearings.

Through our hard-earned experiences from 1993 to 1997 we slowly earned the respect of some traditional service providers and came to understand some of their problems as well. Like county treatment staff, we came to prefer the easy, cooperative clients and to discourage the client who wanted to store seven bags of her worldly goods in our closet and use our address, then disappear for six months. We did not want to claim the client who cursed out his case manager, who had problems with alcohol and marijuana, who had no manners, who stank, who was grossly overweight with clothes that did not button, who took the hinges off our doors, who messed up our computers trying to check on whether the FBI was checking on him, who did not wear a watch, who never took his medications until the day before a blood lab, who played his boom box in front of the funeral parlor across the street. We starting using the descriptors "manipulative," "high functioning," "borderline," "sociopath." Some personalities made it hard for staff to concentrate on our real work. I sorely missed the PIRC discussions that could have examined what our real work was.

Sometimes the staff felt overwhelmed. We had to intensely raise our own self-esteem to believe that we were doing something important. Because the self-help consumer movement was traditionally against hierarchal structure, I had trouble being a boss or making someone supervisor over others. Employees could rewrite their job descriptions at any time. Yet every day a new client would volunteer to clean up or make coffee or help someone with a problem. Consumers began to thank us for creating a special safe place. We made the rule that staff would never be too busy to listen to another consumer who wanted to talk. At the same time, while we produced calendars, brochures, and newsletters, we kept asking ourselves, What is the special work that we alone can do best?

We had a librarian and a room of books. We had educational self-help videos, and clients who wanted instead to rent thriller videos. We proclaimed that we were a community, and yet some clients stole from other clients. We filled bulletin boards with legislative analyses and state program changes and updates to the Americans with Disabilities Act, but no one seemed interested. When we took people on overnight trips to state client forums, some spent all their time in the pool or sitting outside in the sun. So, what did clients really want? Ralph Hernandez one day told me. In the middle of a meeting, he shouted, "When are we going to do Life?" Life? I mulled over his question because to me it meant that we needed to move beyond talking about symptoms and pills all the time and talk instead about friends and family, recreation, education, valued jobs, and service to the community.

The organization had to divest itself of the romantic notion that all consumers, by virtue of being called seriously and persistently mentally ill, were wounded, misunderstood, innocent beings who would be valuable, cooperative employees or guests. We were not all persecuted geniuses, enemies of the status quo, or prophetic poet seers. To maintain a safe community, we developed rules of conduct (see Figure 3.3), which we try to enforce without favoritism.

The county wanted us to be the handmaiden of their case management in order to fulfill for them the state mandate to provide family and client self-help. They wanted us to check on people or to assign them a "buddy." I declined because I had observed that only if clients ask for help do they benefit from it. When it is forced on them, they resist. How degrading is it to be assigned a friend? Old PIRC members would drop in briefly to bring someone to use the telephone or get food or request transportation for someone. Setting up information tables that blocked tourists was now as illegal in Santa Cruz as sleeping in the park or in a car from 11:00 P.M. to 8:30 A.M. At the front and back door of the drop-in, and under the church eaves, the number of homeless clients increased. Vietnam veterans, usually drunk, came by for strong coffee and sugar and we made them stay outside but served them. In the rainy season we collected men's socks to give out as we took their wet ones to dry. While the county took eleven holidays, we observed only four so we could be open when clients had no other place to go and no case manager to reach. Only the mental health director and our contract monitor, of the county staff, had ever stopped in for a visit. We were good tenants but reluctant to put out a sign that said "Mental Health Client Action Network" that could be viewed by neighbors. As long as we were inside our created, secret, basement space, we were happy.

Although we achieved nonprofit status in August 1995, our funding was still handled through Santa Cruz Community Counseling Center. In 1996 we presented the center with a plan to gradually take over the program support functions they provided, including payroll, banking, and budget reports. We did this by having our bookkeeper begin to duplicate what the center did until we got it right. In 1997–98 the county directly funded MHCAN for the first time, and we hired an outside accountant to do our tax returns and payroll and sent out our own monthly requests to the county for reimbursement of personnel and expenses.

When we decided to train peer counselors, we put the request in our budget proposal and got a curriculum from Carol Patterson of the Center for Independent Living in San Francisco. We started what would become an annual training event of twelve classes, two hours each. If students wanted a diploma, they could miss only one class. The classes cover the following topics, with additional group practice sessions:

Figure 3.3. Drop-in Center Rules

MHCAN is a self-help program run by mental health clients for other mental health clients. We need your cooperation to keep this a SAFE Community in which all of us can recover and do our best.

Doing the following will result in eviction (1) for a week the first time, (2) for a month the second time (3) six months the third time; 4) then for a year. Ask the receptionist for a Complaint Form if you feel you are being treated unfairly.

- Name-calling, swearing, & cursing, foul language
- Borrowing without returning or asking; handling stuff on or in someone else's desk or back pack; stealing what is not yours
- Sexual innuendo that makes someone else uncomfortable; accessing pornography on MHCAN's computers
- Harassment (emotional, sexual, or physical), badgering, hounding, nagging someone to buy, borrow money, or do anything
- Failing to be quiet or leave another person alone when asked to do so
- Pushing or shoving another person
- Failing to share by taking more than your single share of food, supplies, clothes, or phone time; refusing to take turns; habitually leaving a mess for someone else to clean up
- Bad mouthing other clients behind their back
- Showing disrespect for another person's disabilities, gender, religious beliefs, interests, work
- Coming to MHCAN intoxicated by alcohol or drugs

Police will be called for the following acts, No Exceptions

- Physical or sexual assault
- Threatening another person
- Vandalism to property or parking lot.
- Fraudulent use of MHCAN's name, phone service, computers, facilities, van
- Getting into MHCAN when we are closed
- Using or dealing illegal drugs on the property or premises
- Stealing; fighting; displaying weapons
- Refusing to leave when asked to do so.

- History of the Consumer Movement
- Listening and Attending
- Mirroring and Empathy
- Boundaries and Burnout
- Suicide and Violence
- Patients Rights and Confidentiality
- Cultural Histories
- Group Facilitation Skills
- Dealing with Difficult People
- Employment and Benefits Issues

The chief lesson is that consumers, by virtue of their life experience, have resources and empathy for their peers that physicians and case managers cannot have. We have "hunches" and intuition about the meaning of the "word salads" or rage of someone considered psychotic. We make leaps of faith about another person's talents and strengths. And although we did not have money to hire the graduates from our own classes, they got jobs as community organizers and counselors for supported housing units. By the third year, we had a waiting list for our peer counselors training. Every year we slightly change the curriculum. One year we had a panel of Chinese, Vietnamese, Puerto Rican, Hispanic, and black consumers compare their families' religious beliefs about madness, how their families tried to cure them, what healing foods were in their respective cultures. Another year we paid a private therapist, who mentors our peer counselors as well as working with the AIDS project, to do a Saturday workshop on avoiding negative judgments.

Phase IV: Confirmation and Empowerment (1998 to the Present)

In March 1998, Drs. Steve Segal and Carol Silverman from the Center for Self-Help Research in Berkeley called MHCAN to tell us about a SAMHSA grant that we might apply for with other drop-in centers like ours in California. We were astonished that the government wanted to study what we do. Yet we were proud of what we had accomplished. We now had some solid conviction about our priorities. These included:

- Provide a place where consumers feel safe
- Talk to the strong, resilient part of each person
- Treat others with respect, even if you are asking them to leave because of their behavior

- Support clients in their choices even if those choices seem unwise
- Let consumers tell their stories and listen to them
- Help consumers find the services they want

In doing these things we had also observed that the consumers who volunteered or had part-time jobs at MHCAN, even for only two to four hours a week, gained stability and maturity and blossomed. Consumers who had their poetry and drawings published and displayed gained an identity other than a psychiatric diagnosis. Experience taught us that, while consumers might have some areas of cognitive or emotional disability, they also have areas of ability and talent. In reading some academic papers by Steve Segal, Carol Silverman, and Tanya Temkin (see Selected Readings) we learned that consumer services had been shown to have value. When we met with county officials and researchers about participating in the federal COSP Multi-Site Research Initiative, we felt confident and good.

We were asked to draw up a budget to cover the expense of enhancing our services to do more of what we already did. We planned to be open more days, to add a part-time driver and afternoon receptionists, to buy a computer and picnic table, and to pay our peer counselors a stipend to keep them. Although a private school was renting the former Sunday school building across the parking lot, that was the space we really wanted. It was three times bigger than the church basement and had natural light from ceiling-high windows in the main room, a full kitchen, and separate large rooms where we could have a computer lab and a peer support meeting room. We would have to wait before that space was available to us.

At the first COSP steering committee meeting in Washington, DC, we met consumer providers of other drop-in centers who had developed programs similar to what we were doing. Maine, Missouri, and Florida also had a growing homeless population served by their drop-in centers. We found that we shared personnel issues that arose when consumers worked over twenty hours and did not pace themselves. When our program expanded, and we were able to move into the larger space we wanted in January 2000, the experience of the Maine, St. Louis, and Florida drop-ins was helpful.

When the Berkeley research group dropped out of the COSP multi-site study, MHCAN was "adopted" by the PEER Center research department in Florida as part of their study site. The SAMHSA grant raised the confidence and self-esteem of our staff considerably. In 2001 we hung a sign out for the neighborhood to see. As a direct result of the COSP study, MHCAN started having regular staff meetings, learned to do Excel spread sheets, identified and paid client advisers, and turned in quarterly reports that projected future tasks not only for the research part of the project but also for the enhancement of our drop-in center. A federal officer made the suggestion that I streamline our horizontal staff by having a drop-in center manager, peer support manager, and a computer lab manager. As the consumer representative to the national Consumer Advisory Panel for the study, I learned about planning meeting agendas, note taking, and follow-up. In the national project, consumers were placed on committees with researchers, and everyone's opinion and experience seemed to be valued. Consumer researchers and consumer site directors learned to use Internet lists and discussion groups.

Because the research recruitment procedures required that traditional service providers make referrals, the county providers came to see who and what we were. Some objected to the random assignment of research participants because they wanted to refer their clients directly to MHCAN. With the extra staffing and publicity that resulted from the COSP study, our attendance increased 46 percent and continued to climb every year of the project. Because we were part of an important national study, we did not tuck our heads when asking for interviewing space or posting our recruitment flyers in the county building. The county increased our budget to $154,400 in 2001–02. With extra SAMHSA funding, in addition to extra staff, we painted and fixed up our kitchen and bathrooms and added movies, a ping-pong table, and music recording equipment. We put all our donated computers on a DSL line and bought a color printer for client artwork.

Now the church, community groups, and the county use our attractive space for meetings. Case managers meet for activities with "transition age" (17–25) clients. An interfaith homeless group puts down their bedrolls on Thursday and Saturday evenings. We have a ten-station computer lab and nine peer-led support groups. We have eighteen part-time permanent employees. We regularly write letters on consumers' behalf about landlord-tenant problems, overpayments from Social Security Administration, or complaints about services. Our input to the county and hospital quality improvement committees is respected, and we are an equal voice at county contractor meetings. We set up all the consumer satisfaction focus groups for state Medicaid reviews. When MHCAN called a meeting of contractors and occupational therapists in 2001 to create more jobs for consumers, everyone invited came.

Since we first went to the Alternatives Conference in Berkeley in 1991, we have come a long way in learning management, public relations, budgeting, group processing, and short-term and long-range planning skills. I believe that we have kept our principles intact while using government funding to provide supportive and constructive services to others. While helping someone else find a telephone number or play a game of chess or find clothes to fit or fill out a form, the persons doing the helping change their image and belief in themselves as persons with value.

High housing costs and managed care have influenced MHCAN's services. In the early 1990s MHCAN had four or five people without housing because they had chosen to live outside in a beach community. In 2002 an average of eighty mental health consumers, unable to find or afford housing, are more dependent on the drop-in as a refuge during the day. Where we used to provide four approved hospital visitors, we now have only one. Inpatients generally spend less than three days in the hospital, and so a visitor is unable to establish a relationship of support to them.

Consumers ready to transition out of long-term facilities and residents of a transition house are provided transportation to come to the drop-in several days a week. Our biggest celebrations now come when a client enrolls in community college and completes the courses, usually making A's. These clients then become ambassadors to encourage others to sign up for college classes. Although we do not have a formal speaker's bureau or any training for speakers, we give presentations to the police department on our experiences, and we tell our stories to church groups and the university's abnormal psychology class. We do not do enough public advocacy to combat the public's prejudice against people labeled mentally ill. When homeless mothers and children, seniors, and the physically disabled get together for a budget rally, it is still painfully obvious to me that mental health clients are not wanted as allies because we are not a group that the public cares about. We are so busy running MHCAN that we spend too little time in the community outside the mental health system, where personal contact might make a difference.

I do not think we have become a partner in providing services similar to those offered by the traditional system. But I do believe that the traditional system has come to see that medications alone are only a piece of regaining a good quality life. We have successfully urged the county to provide more therapists for consumers with abuse histories and treacherous family situations. We do not yet bill Medicaid for any of the services we offer to consumers because we do not want to keep progress notes on our peers for a case manager to sign. MHCAN has the time and space and patience for mental health clients to try out new ways of relating to others, to sharpen their skills without being graded or further symptomatized. We are a life laboratory for taking risks. At our December 2002 holiday lunch in MHCAN's community room, a psychiatrist observed that his patients were walking and talking and relating in a different way than they did at the county clinic. "They are not patients here," I replied. "They are just people living below the poverty line trying to help each other make it." When the medical director took early retirement in 2003, he asked his staff to contribute money to MHCAN in his honor.

One of the requirements of the COSP study was that each site produce a program manual. With MHCAN's growth spurt that brought 5,450 visitors in one year and 9,690 the next, the staff had to do a lot of problem solving without training or mentoring. We therefore needed to document how we keep attendance rolls and critical incident reports, track donations of goods and money, take care of plumbing and broken vacuum cleaners, and handle crises without calling the police. Now when our staff comes to consensus on what we want, we know how to measure our need and promise outcomes that we can deliver. I know that we now need a dedicated board of directors with skilled community members capable of doing strategic planning for our future.

Our Drop-In creates in many ways the outside world that we wish existed. As many of us reach a stage of recovery and stability, we can begin to serve on boards where policy is made and write thoughtful letters to legislators. Credible advocacy requires more than the energy of anger that PIRC had. Advocacy requires knowing providers' points of view, listening to all stakeholders, and being able to appeal to the best actions of people who can make change. Our presence supporting our peers dispels the prejudices against us. We are the agents of change—after we take the risks to practice being whole persons and not merely people with a label.

Selected Readings

Sample Reprints from the National Teleconference Packets

Chamberlin, J. 1978. *On Our Own*. New York: McGraw Hill.

Cohen, D., ed. 1990. Challenging the therapeutic state: Critical perspectives on psychiatry and the mental health system. [Special issue]. *Journal of Mind and Behavior* 11(3/4).

Frank, L. 1978. *The History of Shock Treatment*. [Self-published]. Available from *www.MindFreedom.org*

Mancuso, J. C., J. R. Adams-Webber, eds. 1982. *The Construing Person*. New York: Praeger.

Sarbin, T. R., ed. 1986. *Narrative Psychology: The Storied Nature of Human Conduct*. New York: Praeger.

Szasz, T. S. 1970. The Manufacture of Madness. New York: Harper and Row.

Articles by S. P. Segal, C. Silverman, and T. Temkin on the Value of Consumer Services

1993. Empowerment and self-help agency practice for people with mental disabilities. *Social Work* 38(6):705–12.

1994. Issues in self-help agency research. *Innovations and Research* 3(1):47–49.

1995. Characteristics and service use of long-term members of self-help agencies for mental health clients. *Psychiatric Services* 46(3):269–74.

1995. Measuring empowerment in client-run self-help agencies. *Community Mental Health Journal* 31(3):215–27.

1997. Program environments of self-help agencies. *Journal of Mental Health Administration* 24(4):456–64.

1997. Social networks and psychological disability and homeless users of SHAs. *Social Work in Health Care* 25(3):49–61.

4
The Portland Coalition for the Psychiatrically Labeled, Portland, Maine

Janine M. Elkanich

The Portland Coalition for the Psychiatrically Labeled is a consumer-run drop-in center in Portland, Maine. We are currently located in the center of downtown Portland, easily accessed by most members since we are in walking distance for them. The drop-in is a fifteen hundred square foot, one-floor building that I would have to say resembles an overly wide hallway with only one bathroom. This is a huge issue because we have between eighty and one hundred people drop in every day. Administrative offices are located in the back of the drop-in center in a small office that was specially built when we leased the space.

We here at the Coalition focus on providing peer support, education, advocacy, and systems change within our ever-changing mental health system. Our mission, vision, and values statement emphasizes client rights and personal recovery.

For over twenty years, the Coalition has maintained itself as a leading consumer-operated service agency for the psychiatrically labeled community of Maine, providing a safe haven to meet and form community, to organize around important legislative and mental health policy initiatives, to participate in the formation of statewide and national networks of consumer organizations, and to promote the individual well-being and recovery of its members.

History

The Coalition was founded in 1980 by Marty Gouzie, a member of the newly formed Alliance for the Mentally Ill of Maine. In the beginning it was a small support group for people who had experienced the stigma of psychiatric labels. Support group members met in church basements and in any other free space that they could find. Sally Clay and Dianne Côté were responsible for organizing the group into projects that brought us a place of our own and funding to conduct activities.

The Coalition gained its 501 (c)(3) status as a nonprofit organization in 1982 and Sally Clay was named executive director. The Coalition was Maine's first true consumer-run organization, as well as one of the first peer-run drop-in centers in the country. It remains the only organization in Maine that is operated completely by people with psychiatric disabilities.

Coalition members, along with other supporters of client rights, such as attorney Helen Bailey, met with the state Department of Mental Health to draft the first Rights of Recipients of Mental Health Services that were adopted by the Maine legislature in the mid 1980s. To this day, new and old members have access to these rights and are able to receive assistance from the Coalition whenever necessary.

Also in 1982, Sally Clay developed a slide show called "Stigma" that briefly described the history of attitudes toward mental illness and the experience of hospitalization from the point of view of the person hospitalized. Problems faced in the community after discharge were depicted through the experiences of two characters, played by consumers. The final portion of the show explored the role of family and consumer groups, with suggestions for future change. "Stigma" consisted of eighty slides accompanied by a synchronized taped narration with original music by the Coalition member Matt Hannigan. The presentation proved useful for publicizing the Coalition in its early days, and for involving members in public education.

In June 1983, Linda Ladew and other members of the Coalition organized a protest against the treatment of psychiatric patients in the emergency room at Maine Medical Center, where people in psychiatric crisis often waited alone for many hours in a windowless room under guard before being helped. The protest started from downtown Portland, with members marching approximately two miles to the medical center, where they confronted the waiting psychiatrists. The event was widely covered by the local media and newspapers. The result of the protest was a series of meetings between Coalition members and the Department of Psychiatry at Maine Medical Center that lasted over five years and brought improvements in the mental health system. This was the beginning of an organized consumer voice in Maine, where dialogues with mental health professionals soon were also established at the state mental hospital.

Peer advocates from the Portland Coalition were accepted at both Maine Medical Center and Augusta Mental Health Institute.

In October 1984, with fifty-five members, the Coalition opened its first office and drop-in center. The event was announced on the front page of the *Portland Evening Express.* In 1985, Dianne Côté, who has a master's degree in education, was elected as the second executive director, and under her leadership the Coalition staged its second public protest. This time it was to combat the lengthy delays, sometimes over a year, in processing Social Security disability claims based on psychiatric disability during the Reagan administration. The demonstrators protested that interminable waiting for SSI (Supplemental Security Income) benefits to be approved makes a person just give up, remain homeless, and leave services. A result of this demonstration was that disability funds were finally released to consumers who had been denied services.

Throughout the Coalition's history, the arts have been essential to our members. The Portland Coalition has published four books of poetry written by members. The first, *Take Horses for Instance,* published in 1983, contains seventy poems written by thirty-five different members. "Invitation" by Sally Clay is from that first volume.

Invitation

I know the unnatural jangle of medicated nerves,
The terminal dryness of mouth and mind,
The side effect of drugs whose sole purpose
Is the side effect itself:
The attack of a symptom as yet undefined,
The management of spirit.

I know the holocaust of solitary confinement
In a place of mercy, where mercy itself
Is defined by the cruelty
Of a door slammed on soul,
And the only escape
Is beating out brains on bare walls,
I know.

Electrodes attached to human temples
Constitute treatment of the ultimate sort:
The parental kind which says,

"I do this because I love you,"
And the blow follows
(Cold heat of destruction)
And the brain burns.

I know the years of life promised as a chalice
And given as medication. Pollution of wine
Is the final desecration, but we drink what we can
Or what we must. Stumbling to the table
We feast on a banquet of bruised peaches
And stale crusts, the crumbs themselves
the only reminder of life promised,
The soggy fruit our only taste of sweetness.

The integrity of the guest is a matter of courtesy
And pity reserved for the reluctant host.
We were invited to a table of spoils
And we accepted.

Several single-author poetry collections were published over the years by David Gilchrist, Doug Palmer, and Kit "Woody" Dana. The following is an untitled poem from *city skunks, poems by woody dana* (1995).

let's slip softly
silently away
sliding down
a narrow path
to next to nowhere
a slinky slithering
departure
a quite
unprogrammed
journey become
unplanned
uncharted
unfound
we would become
indecipherable
unforeseen and
half forgotten
no forwarding
address at all

it would be better
almost than leaving
the phone off
the hook
for a day
or more—
much more

The *Portland Coalition Advocate,* a newsletter, began publication in 1983, under a grant from the Haymarket People's Fund, and it continued to be published into the early 1990s. It contained news of interest to people with psychiatric disabilities, along with stories, poetry, and artwork prepared by Coalition members.

The visual arts have played a large role in our history. The Coalition has participated in the annual Portland Sidewalk Art Festival and put on numerous art shows at the Portland Public Library. Our members have been represented in the Matter of Perception art show since it was started in 2000. Matter of Perception is an art event for people who have physical and mental disabilities. Artwork is judged and, if chosen, is taken on tour and displayed throughout the United States. In addition, our members have contributed to other national art events, such as Pillows of Unrest, a project in which consumers depict their experience on pillowcases hung on a clothesline. The painting in Figure 4.1, by David

Figure 4.1. "Lighthouse." Painting by David Towne.

Towne, now hangs on the wall of the coalition. Karl Vertz, former Coalition executive director, commented on the artist, saying, "It took him about an hour to do this. The winter before last, the police found him passed out in the park. They propped him up next to a tree and left him. He died there in the night."

Funding

Funding for the Coalition has come from a variety of sources, including: the Maine Department of Mental Health, the Center for Mental Health Services, the Substance Abuse and Mental Health Services Administration, the National Institute for Mental Health, the Campaign for Human Development, the Presbyterian Church, the Maine Community Foundation, the Haymarket's People Fund, and private donations. The Coalition received its first federal funds for the program of Protection and Advocacy for Individuals with Mental Illness (PAIMI), which is now conducted by the Disability Rights Center in Augusta. Under that program in 1987, Portland Coalition advocates operated the first peer-run protection and advocacy program in the country.

Here at the Coalition we have many challenges to endure daily. Probably our biggest challenge is funding. There does not seem to be a year that goes by that we are not fighting to keep the same level of funding that we received the year before. Regardless of the cost-of-living increases or the influx of new people that occur each year, the Coalition has been flat funded for as long as I can remember. It is very difficult to serve people on a budget of nineteen cents a member. We have been forced to look for private funding, a challenge in itself, since many people do not understand or acknowledge the important work that we do here. Even though we live with mental illness, our inadequate funding prohibits us from being able to afford health insurance for our employees. It is very difficult for us to find enough people willing to work without benefits.

One of the other difficulties we endure is in-fighting among consumers, caused, I believe, by the frustration people feel with the way the system works and the problems that come from not having the funding to support an adequate number on staff. Sometimes the consumers who do the most damage to us are not the ones who are poverty-stricken but others on staff who do not get their way. For example, a member who wants a seat on the board but fails to get it, might respond with threats, such as "I am going to have you fired," or "I am going to go to the state and

have your funding pulled." I look at this as a childish game, which sometimes grows to be an ugly power struggle.

Organization

The Coalition currently has a membership of over eight hundred people,
and new members are joining regularly. To become a member, or to even be
an employee at the Coalition, one must have been at least self-diagnosed
with a mental illness. The membership application was put in place to
provide a "safe and welcoming place" for those diagnosed with mental
illness—it allows us to be who we are and to feel comfortable expressing
ourselves in whatever way works for us as long as it does not jeopardize
the well-being of the other members within the drop-in center.

The Coalition maintains a strict policy when it comes to alcohol or
drug intoxication. For the safety of members and any staff on duty, there
is no tolerance for such behavior. There is also no tolerance for verbal or
physical threats or abuse. Those engaging in any of these activities are
asked to leave the drop-in center for a specified period. A copy of the rules
of behavior is presented in Figure 4.2.

As a member-run nonprofit organization, the Coalition maintains a
board of directors consisting of seven members including a president, a
vice president, a treasurer, and a secretary. These members are elected for
two-year terms under a system in which four members are replaced in
one year and three are replaced in the next year. This system was put into
place to maintain some sort of consistency and seniority for board members. As a rule, the Board of Directors meets monthly and makes decisions by consensus. The agenda is formed by submissions from Coalition
members, board members, and staff and contains new business, as well
any lingering business that needs to be dealt with from the month before.
To receive time on the agenda, a member is required to fill out a board
agenda form, located at the drop-in center, and give it to the executive
director at least one week in advance of the scheduled board meeting. All
board meetings are open to the general membership, except when there
is need for an executive session. All minutes are posted.

The main responsibility of the board is to set policy for the operations at the Coalition. Organizationally, its role is to assist the executive
director in the maintenance of the programs offered by the Coalition. The
executive director in collaboration with the program director is responsible for the day-to-day operations, ensuring that staff and members are

Figure 4.2. Rules for Behavior

Purpose and Philosophy of the Portland Coalition Code of Conduct

The Coalition seeks to provide a safe and welcoming environment for all its members. The code of conduct is an agreed upon set of rules designed to keep the Drop-in Center a safe place for everyone. These rules are few and based on a person's needs for safety, respect, and dignity. By themselves, the rules cannot do this. It is by everyone following them that the Drop-in Center community stays safe and welcoming. The Drop-in Center support staff has the responsibility of enforcing these rules when situations require it. If each individual takes responsibility for their behavior and respects these rules, the need to enforce these rules by applying consequences is not necessary. Please do your part as a member to keep the Drop-in Center an enjoyable place to be by following these rules:

To keep the Drop-in Center safe and welcoming, the following are not allowed:

1. Possession of weapons of any type
2. Possession of alcohol in opened or unopened containers
3. Members are not to come into the Drop-in Center while intoxicated or if they have been drinking alcohol
4. Members are not to be verbally abusive to each other or staff of the Coalition
5. Members are not to be destructive to Coalition property
6. Members are not to assault each other or staff
7. Possession of illegal drugs, selling illegal drugs, use of illegal drugs is not allowed

getting what they need within the drop-in center and providing any necessary support or guidance outside of the drop-in center, such as helping members to sign up for programs on conflict resolution, CPR, and disability training. The board of directors oversees the executive director and program director, who in turn supervise the art coordinator, resource coordinator, and drop-in center line staff. All of these directors and staff are consumers.

The annual meeting takes place in September, when new board members are elected. Anyone interested in running for the board must have been a member for at least a year and must complete a board nomination form and have it signed by a current board member. The board as a whole then reviews the list of completed nomination forms, looking particularly at the talents a member may have to offer this community, and creates the ballot for the election. Any member who has broken a rule may be ineligible to participate in the election as a candidate. The annual meeting is also the time when changes can be made to the existing by-law policies. A copy of the Portland Coalition By-Laws is available to any member on request.

Since its incorporation in 1982, the Portland Coalition has changed its leadership several times. Claudia Anderson was hired as executive director when Dianne Côté stepped down in 1989. Altogether, there have been seven executive directors and two acting directors. It is a testimony to the strength of the Coalition's values that the organization has operated successfully for all these years.

Executive directors, 1981–present

Sally Clay	1981–85
Dianne C. Côté	1985–89
Claudia B. Anderson	1990–93
Lelia Batton	1992–97
Zahira Duvall	1997–2001
Michael Weiss	2001
Karl Vertz	2001–03
Nathan Beasley	2003–

Zahira Duvall, executive director at the beginning of the Consumer-Operated Services Programs (COSP) Multi-Site Research Initiative that was funded by the U.S. Substance Abuse and Mental Health Services Administration, became the first coordinator of the Consumer Advisory Panel of the national study. She later retired to work in the Independent Living movement for all people with disabilities. The Coalition is run by an executive director, a program director, an arts coordinator, a resource advocate, and the drop-in center staff. The Coalition has recently extended its availability to seven days a week, with Monday through Friday hours of operation from 8:30 A.M. to 4:00 P.M. and Saturday and Sunday from

9:00 A.M. to 2:00 P.M. Many members who access the services at the Coalition are considered homeless, and this schedule gives them a place to be for at least part of the day, since the shelters in Maine do not offer a place for them to be during the day.

The current staff follows and maintains a set of personnel policies that is reviewed regularly. At the Coalition, we greatly value our employees and we understand the stress that is associated with working at such a place. I find it stressful because the people who come in here tend to believe the staff are "God" in some sense, and when for whatever reason we are unable to assist them in things such as housing, we are then looked at as an organization that does not give a hoot. It seems to be hard for them to understand that there is a limited amount we can offer because our resources are so limited. Also, a lot of people who come in here have alcohol issues, and quite frequently we have to contend with someone who is drunk and very belligerent. Such incidents cause tremendous stress among the staff. For these reasons, we allot plenty of time for staff to be able to take care of themselves through generous vacation and sick time packages.

Programs and Services

Following are some of the programs and services that the Coalition currently offers its members:

- *Arts and crafts instruction and supplies.* The arts coordinator conducts an art class every Tuesday from 10:00 A.M. to 1:00 P.M. Paints and canvas, as well as other art supplies are available to the members throughout the week for use at their leisure. Members' artwork is taken home or displayed at the Coalition or put into any of various art shows in the greater Portland area. Visitors to the Coalition can see numerous paintings displayed, most of them created and donated by past and present members.
- *Free meals.* Coalition members are offered free meals on Wednesdays and Saturdays. Food for these meals is paid for with funds from the Coalition's budget and from a variety of other sources, including donations and assistance from a Portland mental health social club. The meals range from a turkey dinner with all the fixings to pizza from a local pizza shop. Although we are not equipped with the necessary appliances to cook these meals ourselves, we have access from time to time to a kitchen from the mental health social club. December is probably the Coalition's busiest time during the day, and we can expect to feed an

average of sixty to seventy people on any given day. At a Christmas party in 2003, we are proud to have been able to celebrate the holiday by feeding over a hundred people.

- *Free bus tickets.* The Coalition provides two free full-fare or four half-fare bus tickets to its members every week. Full-fare tickets are provided to those who do not receive transportation passes through Medicaid or Medicare, and half-fare tickets are provided to those who receive half-fare tickets from Medicare. This program in particular has been a huge success, since most of the members who use it have no other means for getting around Portland. Transportation is provided to York and Cumberland Counties, and tickets are available for buses that travel outside of the Portland area to places such as Westbrook, South Portland, and Old Orchard Beach. Occasionally, to get members to special functions, we have been able to borrow or rent a van.

- *Telephone access.* The Coalition provides its members with a telephone for local calls. We have placed a ten-minute time limit on the use of the telephone to help ensure that those who need to use it will be able to access it without much difficulty. Members who wish make long-distance calls must either purchase a phone card or get special permission to use the phone card the Coalition has for emergencies. This service has been of great help to our members, since many of our population are either homeless or do not have enough resources financially to maintain their own telephone at home.

- *TTY access.* The Coalition is also maintains a TTY for its members who are deaf. In recent years, more and more people who are deaf have signed up for services at the Coalition, and it was imperative for us to offer TTY access so that we could provide the same type of services for all of our members. Now at least six people who are deaf walk in our door often, and we are proud to be able to serve this community of people who live with both mental illness and deafness.

- *Resource directories.* The Coalition keeps on hand many resource directories for the use of members as well as anyone who calls to inquire about Maine resources. When necessary, we do any research necessary to locate resources outside the state of Maine.

The resources available in the state of Maine and the city of Portland range from clinics that offer medical help to food pantries that offer meals, free food, and clothing, as well as other nonperishable items. Everyday someone either by telephone or as a walk-in asks for this sort of assistance. When members need resources, we support them by verifying their homelessness or disability to other agencies by making the necessary telephone calls, or even by typing up the memo required for assistance from some agencies. Also, for our members, we print out from the Internet a free weekly calendar of recreational events in the area.

- *Free events tickets.* From time to time the Coalition receives free tickets to local events, such as hockey games, symphony concerts, and plays, which we make available to our members.
- *Video cassettes.* The Coalition has a collection of over three hundred movies that members can view here during the day. All our movies have been donated by members, and the collection continues to grow.

Advocacy

The Coalition offers a wide range of advocacy services. A staff member might attend a meeting, accompany someone to a doctor's appointment, or even sit with someone in the emergency room. Although this program is not as extensive as we would like it to be, members know that they can count on the staff at the Coalition to be in their corner when they are in need, and that knowing helps boost their sense of self-worth. It is probably one of the best feelings anyone can have to know that he or she is not alone, and it is one of the most rewarding feelings for the other person to be able to be there for someone in need. Doing so not only helps the person's feeling of self-worth but also boosts the self-esteem of the helper who knows that she is doing something good for someone else. Reciprocity is of great value and something that is seen every day at the Coalition, whether it be staff to staff, staff to member, or even member to member. It is the true belief at the Coalition that this promotes and supports the recovery process that we are all going through, even though each one of us is at a different point in our recovery. With each other's help, we create a stronger, more unified community.

Peer Support

Peer support is not recognized as much as it should be here in Maine because the Medical Model is still very dominant. There is much resistance within the mental health system to the reality that the medical model way of thinking is not always the best way for individual healing. Peer support within and outside the Coalition is tremendous. Many members come into the drop-in center for just this reason. Peer support to each of us has a different meaning. Some look at peer support as being able to come and read the paper, others look at peer support as being able to talk about things with their fellow members, and still others look at peer support as being able to talk to staff if need be. We here at the Coalition have an open door policy when it comes to peer support, and we do not try to change anyone else's view as to what this means for them. It is our belief that if it works for you, then that's what we will support.

Self-Help Groups

The Coalition has offered different types of self-help groups over the years. Some of the groups have been a Women's Group, Men's Group, Writer's Group, and AA meetings. All these groups either meet within the drop-in center or are conducted by a member who establishes an outside group that meets at their home, a coffee shop, or somewhere easily accessible to all who want to join. Although the Coalition has only one AA meeting scheduled weekly at this time, we are exploring more ways to bring self-help back into play. This is not always an easy process, since we are known to run a "low barrier" drop-in center where people can choose to do as they wish. Most who come in have been working on their recovery for a very long time and need that space to just be. It gets extremely tiring to have to continuously "perform," as one is expected to do in therapy.

Systems Change

State and local service providers, as well as local colleges regularly invite the Coalition to take part in statewide initiatives to change the way people think about consumer involvement and about the programs offered by organizations like ours. Some of these initiatives include:

- Active involvement in the establishment, implementation, and quality control measures for the Individual Support Program, a Department of Mental Health program that encourages and actually requires case managers to involve consumers in the planning of their own recovery process and to review the process every six months.
- Participation in a local-access five-part television series entitled *Breaking Down the Barriers,* which depicts all aspects of the community with respect to mental illness and the stigma that one encounters living with mental illness
- Acceptance of a seat on the board of trustees for one of the local psychiatric hospitals

- Active involvement with our local and state Office of Consumer Affairs, which keeps us abreast of upcoming issues within the mental health system and legislative bills that may need support or opposition through testimonies or written submissions
- Participation in monthly meetings on various mental health issues ranging from all-consumer initiatives to consumer-provider groups within the area.

We encourage any Coalition members interested in community issues to participate in local meetings to the extent that they are able. Sometimes we bring their views to the table or express them within the forum if they feel they are not able to do so themselves.

We have gone beyond the state level and presented consumer views and issues on the national level at such conferences as USPRA (US Psychiatric Rehabilitation Association, formerly IAPSRS) and Alternatives, an annual conference for mental health consumers. These conferences have provided wonderful opportunities for us to exchange information about successes with consumers from other states who are working and struggling with their own state issues

Education

The education we offer at the Coalition is not always traditional, but everyday people there are learning. We expect and encourage members to do for themselves, but we are there to lend a helping hand when necessary. Sometimes, for example, we help someone learn for the first time to do a task as simple as heating up a cup of coffee, for such small skills are needed to survive. Anyone who walks into the drop-in center is expected to clean up after himself, and even that can be a challenge. But we teach by example and offer encouragement and support to help members learn to be responsible for their space when there. Beyond teaching everyday skills, we offer opportunities for members to hear talks by representatives of community agencies who come to explain the services they offer.

Self-Empowerment

As individuals grow within their recovery, they slowly learn what self-empowerment means to them. Just walking through the door of the Portland Coalition is empowering, as is asking for help. .

For me, self-empowerment came a few years ago when I learned, after going in and out of hospitals for ten years, that I had the right to be treated as an individual and that I had the power and control to fight for that right. I wrote a letter to a particular hospital, simply stating the truth about their campaign of manipulation and harassment regarding a medical bill and assuring them of my determination to take the matter a step further if they persisted. To make a long story short, I never heard from the hospital again, which is exactly the goal I was trying to achieve. I never felt more empowered

Nothing is greater than the feeling of self-worth and affirmation I have, knowing I had every right to fight to be treated like an individual, not a diagnosis. To this day, whenever people come and speak to me about things they think are going wrong in their treatment, I try to instill in them confidence that they have these same rights. Everyone deserves a unique plan for recovery, one that is tailored to her needs instead of one that simply places him or her into the rigid mold of the "standard protocol."

Self-Help, Recovery, and the Coalition Library and Art Gallery

Over the years the Coalition has acquired a good collection of self-help books, video tapes, and audio tapes, which are available for members to borrow in our library. The library, like the drop-in center, is basically a wide hall, on a smaller scale and about a block away from the drop-in space. We have made this area a place where our members, who have demonstrated tremendous artistic talent, can display the artwork they do inside and outside of the Coalition. Our members have used art to express the stress and trauma they have endured over the years and to promote their own recovery. Most of the artwork on display is for sale. When pictures are sold, the artists give a small percentage to the Coalition. This contribution enhances their self-esteem by allowing them to give back something to the place they call their "second home."

The Value of the Coalition

Every year people come up to us and make statements such as, "I don't know where I would be without the Coalition," or "I would be isolated at my home if you guys weren't open," or "Thank you for giving me a place where I can be myself and not be pressured to conform to the rules of traditional mental health services." The dream for this organization, and for each of us personally, is to be able to survive the challenges that the mental health system has put before us, including lack of funding support, and to keep the Coalition open, thriving, and serving the people who need us the most—adults living with mental illness.

References

Clay, Sally, and Linda Ladew, eds. 1983. *Take horses for instance: Poems by the psychiatrically labeled.* Portland, ME: Portland Coalition for the Psychiatrically Labeled.

Dana, Woody. 1995. *city skunks: poems by woody dana.* Portland, ME: Munchko Ltd.

5

The St. Louis Empowerment Center, St. Louis, Missouri

Helen Minth

The St. Louis Empowerment Center is a peer-run drop-in center designed to meet the needs of St. Louis City residents with mental illnesses who want to take responsibility for their recovery through self-help.

The center is located in downtown St. Louis, in the basement of a mansion built in the 1890s that was originally the home of a lumber baron. The three-story brick building has interior woodwork imported from Germany and four stained glass windows. The St. Louis Mental Health Association (MHA) purchased the building in the 1980s and restored it. The Depression and Bipolar Support Alliance of St. Louis (DBSA) (formerly, the Depressive and Manic Depressive Association) now occupies the first floor and the MHA, the second. Until the 1960s, the basement was a livery stable. Now it is the home of the Empowerment Center and is the only level of the building that is handicapped accessible. It is divided into a kitchen, living room, library, office, and a large meeting room that also includes a pool table and other recreational facilities. It is comfortably furnished with couches and chairs, creating a homey environment. Up to seventy-five people can use the space at one time. Since the Empowerment Center is located in the heart of the city, participants easily reach it through one of four bus lines.

The St. Louis Empowerment Center came into being in 1996 through the hard work and advocacy of a former mental health consumer who dreamed of establishing a place for other consumers. Vicki Fox Wieselthier (now Smith), herself recovered from mental illness through self-help, worked for the City of St Louis assisting mentally ill or homeless people find housing. From that position, she wrote a grant proposal that brought funding to the Empowerment Center from the City of St. Louis Mental Health Board of Trustees. Under the contract that was awarded, the Empowerment Center is jointly operated by the DBSA and MHA.

I was hired as the first director of the Empowerment Center, becoming at the same time director of DBSA. I am a mental health consumer. I earned my master's degree in social work and worked in the mental health field for thirty years. As I assumed my new role, I was assisted by Bob Swart, another consumer who had participated in DBSA groups. Bob began working with me as a volunteer before becoming a regular staff member. Together, Bob and I put together the Empowerment Center program and created its original schedule.

The main components of the Empowerment Center are the drop-in center, the Friendship Line, peer support program, community or facility-based self-help/support groups, and advocacy and referral services.

The Drop-In Center

The drop-in center operates every day of the year, from 7:00 A.M. to 6:00 P.M. It is not intended to duplicate or replace professionally run psychosocial rehabilitation programs. Instead, it provides an option for consumers who are unable to use existing services because of the limitations funders of these agencies place on participation. For example, the St. Louis Empowerment Center is the only drop-in center in the city available to mentally ill people who are not homeless. The St. Louis Empowerment Center is clean, safe, alcohol and drug free, and intolerant of intolerance.

The Empowerment Center's philosophy is that there is no "right way" to use a peer-run drop-in center. Some consumers want companionship and the opportunity to enjoy a cup of coffee or to participate in group recreation. Still others use on-site resource materials to locate food pantries or housing. Some people use the computer equipment to develop a resume, write a letter, or learn a new software application. Some attend every day, and others come by when they are bored, lonely, or in crisis or when they have worn out their welcome at another program. Learning and growth occur because people choose to participate in activities that foster learning and personal growth. People move on because they are ready and they want to—not because their benefits are exhausted.

The Empowerment Center has become a daytime safe haven for many people with mental illness who are homeless. The center offers them a place to do their laundry or take a shower, and a place where they can meet and get help from other consumers and professionals, using the model of integrated service delivery.

We do not have case managers at the center because we do not keep "official" records on our participants. Our grants require us to keep a daily list of participants and the hours they are here. We also keep logs of meeting attendance and calls to the Friendship Line, a telephone line for peer support, staffed by program assistants from the center. Participants are not required to sign in under their legal names, so Queen Elizabeth and Elvis are regular visitors.

Volunteers come to us from other agencies, churches, and neighborhood organizations, and some are from the families of our participants. Many of our participants are living in rehab or hospital facilities and come to the Empowerment Center during our hours of operation.

This program stresses the "no wrong door" philosophy by providing people who are homeless and have a mental illness the opportunity to choose the contacts that they need though a variety of participating agencies. Representatives from public and private agencies are on site at various times to take applications for their programs and provide information and education. We expect to continue this approach throughout our program and make its benefits available to everyone, not just the homeless population.

Although we ask people who attend the St. Louis Empowerment Center to supply demographic information to help us evaluate the program by keeping track of the level of utilization, we do not require that they provide evidence that they are currently receiving mental health care. Drop-in centers like ours provide a unique service through their ability to attract and engage people who have been overlooked by "the system" or have chosen to remain outside of it. We believe it is part of our mission to serve these people. We hope that, as their level of trust in us increases, they will be open to receiving the services that they need from mental health professionals. In some instances, people are not comfortable revealing anything but the most basic information about themselves before this trust level is established. We help consumers link to the professional community right away, and we collect the data we need (emergency contact numbers and the like) only when they are ready. Requiring that consumers already be engaged in treatment, or that they provide extensive information before developing trust, is one way to "skim," or in effect to deny services, because it effectively drives away the people most in need of assistance.

The St. Louis Empowerment Center is staffed by "prosumers," or consumer workers, many of whom started out as program participants and who now receive salaries as mental health professionals. The center now employs six full-time "prosumer" workers and between sixteen and twenty part-time workers. These prosumers provide day-to-day coverage and training for other consumers who work as program assistants in entry-level paraprofessional positions throughout the program.

All employees are required to be consumers of mental health services and all are trained in their job positions, including part-time receptionists, cleaners, and peer counselors. Many part-time employees use these entry-level positions as springboards to other employment. Our full-time employees have diverse degrees from a master's degree in social work to a degree in pastoral care, although a college degree is not a necessity for employment. All employees are judged on their creativity, willingness to learn, and ability to relate to others.

Our staffing patterns are similar to the shifts at a hospital. We have openers at 7:00 A.M. and closers at 6:00 P.M. Salaried staff works 8:00 A.M. to 4:00 P.M., 12:00 noon to 8:00 P.M., 10:00 A.M. to 6:00 P.M. or 9:00 A.M. to 5:00 P.M., depending on their own needs.

The center serves as a training base for program assistants involved in the drop-in center, the Friendship Line, or individual peer support or who work as facilitators for community-based or facility-based self-help and support groups. Computers are available to St. Louis Empowerment Center participants to prepare resumés, write letters, and sharpen job skills. Our evening hours permit us to provide assistance to consumers who work during the day, including support groups, recreation, and the companionship of their peers. Twelve Step groups are welcome to use St. Louis Empowerment Center meeting rooms, and the Friendship Line operates from the drop-in center. There are a wealth of opportunities for engagement and involvement in recreation and education and for participation in self-help and mutual assistance activities. Figure 5.1 lists the goals of the Empowerment Center.

Educational and Recreational Opportunities

Professional agencies regularly provide classes at the St. Louis Empowerment Center. Participants can learn on site about Social Security disability eligibility, vocational rehabilitation services, and veterans' programs; participants and staff can learn about community resources, crisis management, group process, cultural competence, quality improvement methods, and other topics. Furthermore, our program is greatly enhanced by the

---

Figure 5.1. Goals of the Empowerment Drop-in Center

- Empower consumers to become independent and interdependent
- Complement existing community mental health resources by providing alternatives for existing programs that are not a "good fit" or that lack funding
- Expand access to recreational, social, educational, and self-help or mutual assistance activities
- Develop leadership, competency, and expertise within the St. Louis consumer community
- Foster acceptance of professional mental health services without making their use a precondition for participation in activities or opportunities
- Enhance social and interpersonal skills by providing opportunities for consumers to use those skills
- Reduce social isolation
- Provide a location for "specialty" support groups in response to program participants' interests (groups may have a mental illness or dual diagnosis focus or may reflect more general interests)
- Improve consumer access to the existing educational programs of the [St. Louis] Mental Health Association and develop richer and more varied training opportunities
- Provide around-the-job supports for working consumers
- Provide training and employment opportunities for people with serious and persistent mental illnesses
- Provide an urban location where various kinds of individual, systems, and political advocacy will flourish
- Strengthen our relationship with existing community providers of both mental health and non-mental health services

---

training sessions the MHA offers throughout the year to the professional community, and these are also open to St. Louis Empowerment Center participants. These trainings cover stress management, understanding specific mental illnesses, disaster preparedness, and other topics.

The daily activities at the center are varied, interesting, and appealing to a diverse group of mental health consumers. Recreational activities and opportunities to socialize and form friendships are primary. Every attempt is made to create a favorable alternative to isolation at home.

We have a kitchen–social area with card tables, games, a coffeepot, and snacks and a library for individuals who need and appreciate quiet space. We also provide a variety of recreational activities.

Participants and staff work together to obtain free passes to Monday evening trips to the St. Louis Municipal Opera, Cardinal baseball games, and other athletic events. The St. Louis Psychiatric Rehabilitation Center offers the use of their new gymnasium, and during the warmer months the center organizes picnics, barbecues, car washes, swimming, and softball, basketball, and volleyball games. Members and staff together make the financial decisions that determine the activities chosen, and the food and recreation budget is determined at the "community meeting." Transportation to outside recreational events is generally by public transport, although from time to time rental vehicles are donated.

The center is busiest in the cold of winter and the heat of summer. During football season, the center is one of the few places where fans can watch a Sunday football game, so on Sundays the center is packed with participants, who create tailgate parties and barbecues.

Self-Help Groups

Facility-Based Self-Help Groups

The St. Louis Empowerment Center invites all of the organizations listed in the mental health section of the MHA *Self-Help Directory* to use our meeting rooms. In addition, we are in contact with Alcoholics Anonymous (AA) Central Service so that Twelve Step groups are aware that the Center has meeting space available. Program participants have started their own groups, which now include AA, NA (Narcotics Anonymous), Men's Group, Women's Group, DBSA, Spirituality, Nicotine Anon., Emotions Anon., life skills classes, and the Brunch Bunch. Information about these and other groups is available to the community through the *Self-Help Directory*, the DBSA Quarterly newsletter, and the Empowerment Center's newsletter, *The Slant*.

Employees may be group leaders, although volunteers lead most of our self-help groups. Some of the groups focus on mental illness and mental health and its treatment, while others are organized around specific interests and needs. The Spirituality Group, for example, discusses beliefs, and the Brunch Bunch discusses employment issues. Some groups attract members who are interested in attending a group that meets every week and for an indefinite period of time. Other people may wish to attend a group that meets for a limited period of time and provides assistance in a specific area.

Community-Based Self-Help Groups

The DBSA has operated community-based consumer-run self-help groups in the St. Louis area for seventeen years. These groups assist over a thousand people a year, many of whom are St. Louis City residents who attend the self-help groups at the Empowerment Center. Although the mission of the DBSA is to provide self-help and mutual assistance only to persons with affective disorders, these groups have always been open to any mental health consumer able to participate in the group process. No one has ever been asked to leave a DBSA group because he or she did not meet diagnostic criteria. DBSA currently conducts twelve meetings a month in the City of St. Louis, including one of a self-help and mutual assistance group for people who are dually diagnosed with mental illnesses and alcohol or substance abuse. This group is one of only a handful of dual diagnosis groups in the nation with an official AA connection and full AA recognition.

It has been our experience that people who attend self-help and mutual assistance groups often need additional supports. The Empowerment Center provides those supports. Our self-help groups, for example, offer extensive contact with mental health professionals and our specially trained group leaders are able to offer referrals for other needed services. Furthermore, those who participate in self-help groups at the center may choose also to use other services at the center, which is open eleven hours a day during the week and on weekends.

We have heard often from people who attend community-based self-help groups that they wish they had known about the existence of self-help groups earlier, that they have been receiving treatment for a mental illness for years but have never been referred for self-help and mutual assistance. For this reason, we now conduct active outreach in the professional community. Our outreach is also particularly directed toward the African American community, and we attempt to recruit African Americans as group leaders.

We educate professional providers of mental health services about the value of self-help and mutual assistance. Included in these programs are professionals employed at in-patient facilities, psychosocial rehabilitation centers, and community mental health centers in the City of St. Louis.

We market our community-based self-help and mutual assistance groups so that it is clearly understood that these groups are available and open to all St. Louis city residents with any serious and persistent mental illness and to persons who are dually diagnosed.

Peer Support

The Friendship Line

The principal goal of the Friendship Line is to provide support, assistance, and friendship over the telephone to consumers who are not in crisis but who are experiencing distress because of social isolation, loneliness, or troublesome symptoms of their illness, or who require advocacy assistance and referral.

The Friendship Line has one full-time supervisor and four part-time workers. So far, this staffing pattern has worked well. All other staff, however, are also trained to answer the Friendship Line.

The line operates from 7:00 A.M. until 8:00 P.M., seven days a week. It is available both to St Louis residents who have connections with professional mental health agencies and to those who do not. We expect that, for some people, the Friendship Line may be their first contact with self-help and mutual assistance. It may also be the first step to wellness for people who in the future will benefit from professional mental health services.

Social isolation and feelings of loneliness are common denominators of the consumer experience. These feelings are often most intense in the evening and on weekends and holidays, when access to drop-in centers, psychosocial programs, and community activities is limited. Frequently, consumers who simply need to talk to someone call crisis lines and facility-based emergency numbers. These services deem such calls inappropriate. For example, an analysis of over two hundred calls made in the evening to the on-call staff at a local clinic revealed that less than 10 percent of the calls made over a six-month period needed the immediate attention of a mental health professional. The Friendship Line helps reduce the use of crisis lines and facility-based on-call systems by consumers who do not need the immediate assistance of mental health professionals.

The advocacy assistance available on site at the St. Louis Empowerment Center is also available over the telephone to Friendship Line callers. To ensure that we fully understand the concerns of our callers and respond appropriately, we keep a log of all calls. If, for example, we find that we receive frequent calls for information on a particular topic, we may decide to prepare a special brochure or plan an educational program on that topic .

The Empowerment Center provides training and part-time employment to culturally competent, racially diverse mental health consumers who exhibit the ability to listen empathetically and understand fully the nonclinical, nonprofessional nature of their responsibilities as program assistants on the Friendship Line. The center staff meets regularly with the program assistants to make sure that they are comfortable with their role and that they are not attempting to provide crisis services. Program assistants also receive on-the-job and around-the-job assistance and support. In particular, we attempt to establish links with institutions that offer vocational rehabilitation and educational opportunities so that program assistants can move on to other jobs or further education. Many Empowerment Center participants have used their job as a stepping-stone to employment or education in the larger community. Theresa is a sterling example of this process. She was one of the first persons hired in 1996, and after becoming empowered by her job at the center, she returned to graduate school. She has now completed her doctorate at Washington University and works in publishing.

Individual Peer Support

Not everyone who would benefit from self-help and mutual assistance chooses to receive that assistance in group settings or at fixed sites in a mental health environment. For some, a one-to-one relationship, such as that offered by the St. Louis Empowerment Center through the individual peer support (IPS) program, works better. The IPS program provides opportunities for consumers to form one-to-one relationships with other consumers who can help ease their way into activities in integrated community settings. IPS workers are matched with consumers who would like a "buddy" willing to spend about four hours a week with them. Together they may explore the city and participate in activities in the community. IPS helps people as they attempt to make the transition from facility-based mental health daytime activities to activities in integrated community settings, and it reduces reliance on mental health professionals to meet consumers' needs for recreation, social support, and companionship. It also promotes effective partnerships between mental health professionals and the practitioners of self-help.

The Empowerment Center engages, trains, supports, and supervises consumers who function as IPS workers, providing them with pre-service and ongoing in-service training. Central to the successful operation of this program is the development of a respectful, comfortable, working relationship with the community mental health centers in St. Louis, which work together with the Empowerment Center to match clients with an IPS worker to make a "buddy pair.." The Empowerment Center's IPS coordinator and the referring agency staff help the "buddy pair" as they establish and develop their relationship.

The Empowerment Center organizes group meetings for all of the people working in this program and social events for the buddy pairs take place both at the St. Louis Empowerment Center and in the community.

Some people who become part of a buddy pair are receiving professional services from other programs in the area, as well as from the Empowerment Center.

One early participant who benefited from peer support was Brian. When he first came to the center, he could not get his medication and required our assistance to access treatment and peer support. Now Brian volunteers at the Empowerment Center in the daytime, and in the evening works as *maître d'* at an upscale St. Louis restaurant.

Advocacy and Referral

Advocacy is a natural part of self-help and mutual assistance. The Empowerment Center library contains reference materials that assist consumers interested in their legal rights and responsibilities. The program collects and provides information to consumers, professionals, family members, and other interested parties in the community in the areas of benefit acquisition assistance; individual professional agencies provide information and education to center participants at regular intervals. The center also collaborates with Paraquad, a local disability rights organization, in providing cross-disability training for staff and participants.

In its advocacy efforts, our program works with other community organizations, such as Community Alternatives, neighborhood churches and organizations, the St. Louis Police Department, NAMI (National Alliance for the Mentally Ill), the Salvation Army, and homeless shelters. Working side by side with these organizations helps us improving our own skills and knowledge and allows us to provide more productive advocacy. At the same time, it educates the other organizations in mental health issues and the needs of mental health consumers.

Benefit Acquisition Assistance

Program staff, together with program participants, provide assistance to persons with mental illness and their family members who are
attempting to receive social welfare benefits. These benefits include, but
are not limited to, Social Security Disability Insurance, Supplemental Security Income, food stamps, general relief, vocational rehabilitation services, inpatient or outpatient treatment at public health facilities (not
limited to psychiatric services), services from traditional day treatment
facilities, and housing and habitation services.

Frequently, mental health consumers, because of illness and medications, their position in society, or lack of self-esteem are unable to take a
strong stand in providing for their own welfare. The consumers most in
need of information and assistance are often the least able to negotiate a
system that is complex, fragmented, and always changing.

Prosumer staff are available to intervene with agencies to insure re-
ceipt of services and may accompany consumers to service providers for
interviews, appeals, and other efforts to get public assistance. Program
participants who have themselves successfully negotiated the various entitlement systems act as mentors to their peers and even qualify as "prosumer" staff themselves. An Empowerment Center prosumer can assist
in the following ways:

- Provide consumers with eligibility information on programs that might
  offer benefits
- Educate consumers about application processes, administrative appeals processes, benefit waiting lists, and the like
- When appropriate, accompany consumers who need support to interviews or hearings
- Act as ombudsmen between other consumers and appropriate agencies, when needed

Individual Advocacy and Legal Referrals

People with mental illness often find they need legal assistance.
Sometimes that assistance is directly related to their mental health status
and needs. At other times it involves more routine matters unrelated to
their consumer status. The Empowerment Center consults Legal Services
of Eastern Missouri, the Law Clinic at St. Louis University, and Protection
and Advocacy Services, Inc., when appropriate and refers people to attorneys who have proven themselves to be consumer friendly. The center

also makes resource materials, such as the Legal Services pamphlet on tenant responsibilities and rights, available to program participants. .

Both DBSA and MHA support these referrals to ensure that mental health consumers have a legal resource to whom they can submit legal grievances or accomplish preparation of wills and divorce proceedings and that consumers who feel they have been wronged by the system, discriminated against, or inappropriately denied services have an opportunity to learn what the law is and what their rights are. Although a consumer may find that he or she has no legal standing in the issue at hand, the knowledge gained makes it easier to move on to other issues and concerns.

The St. Louis Empowerment Center maintains a library of information on eligibility, application, and appeals processes in the areas of housing, social welfare programs, insurance, in-kind programs, vocational services, managed care, and clinical treatment. A list of contact persons within applicable agencies is maintained. Much of this information is also available in the DBSA and MHA libraries.

Systems Advocacy

The St. Louis Empowerment Center promotes primary consumer involvement in mental health policy planning. We encourage and help program participants to seek involvement in regional advisory and state advisory councils, boards of directors of not-for-profit mental health agencies, and the Protection and Advocacy system. Information is shared with local, state, and national self-help and mutual assistance groups. Access to national advocacy information is available through subscriptions to advocacy-related journals and through the Internet.

A major arena for systems advocacy is legislation. Mental health policy and legislation are entwined in ways one does not find in other areas of health care. Changes in services and systems almost always require legislative action. In Missouri, the organized consumer movement has not been very strong, despite the presence of several influential consumer leaders within the state. The DBSA has long held that it would not devote its resources to legislative and political advocacy. While it has always distributed advocacy materials to its members and maintains a library of such materials, including current legislation and action alerts, the organization maintains the policy that no person should feel unwelcome or threatened because he or she does not share the organization's political viewpoint. Much of the Empowerment Center's information on current legislation comes from the resources of the Mental Health Association of Greater St. Louis, which currently maintains an active legislative component.

Civil Rights

The St. Louis Empowerment Center staff and members disseminate information that pertains to the rights of people with mental illness in the St. Louis metropolitan area, such as:

- Commitment laws and legal rights within the commitment process (e.g., right to an attorney, right to a speedy hearing, right to be present at hearings)
- Rights of inpatients under Missouri law (including the right to a telephone, privacy, safety, privileged communication, visitors, involvement in treatment planning, petitioning the court for release, and presenting administrative grievances)
- Aspects of guardianship, outpatient civil commitment, and conditional release
- Information on civil rights and other advocacy issues, available both on site and through the Friendship Line.

Administration and Partnerships

When the Empowerment Center was founded, DBSA and MHA entered into a partnership to insure the continuation of the program. The MHA is fiscally responsible for the running of the center, and DBSA has program control.

The Depression Bi-Polar Alliance of St. Louis has an excellent reputation in local mental health circles. DBSA itself is a consumer-operated organization. Its board of directors, with up to thirty-one members, of whom at least 51 percent are consumers of mental health services, is also the Empowerment Center's board of directors. All board members are volunteers, and many are center participants. The Empowerment Center is considered to be a program of DBSA which, as a non-profit organization, manages the center's contract.

The MHA had strong financial backing and an excellent reputation in financial management. Thus it was designated as the pass-through agency for Empowerment Center funding. However, although the center must be financially accountable to the MHA, participants themselves decide how to spend the money, and the Empowerment Center director, who is also the director of DBSA and accountable to the board of directors, develops the budget. Some of the major expenses now in the budget are bus tickets for participants and help for new participants in paying for prescriptions while they are in the process of applying for benefits or work.

The Empowerment Center is funded by a city mill tax—a portion of the sales tax—that is specifically earmarked for self-help. It is administered through the City of St. Louis Mental Health Board. We are on a three-year grant cycle. Our first grant was awarded in 1996, and in 2001 we were again funded. The Empowerment Center also receives funds from the Missouri Department of Mental Health for expansion of our peer support programs and the Friendship Line.

Accomplishments and Plans for the Future

The St. Louis Empowerment Center provides opportunities for consumers to create an empowering, nonhierarchical environment of their own design in which self-help and mutual assistance flourish. Consumers develop skills and competencies through exposure to their peers. Support groups and educational programs are formed in response to the needs of those who use them. Leadership skills develop because of the need for leadership. Decision making is participatory, and rules and standards of behavior are self-imposed and self-enforced.

During an average six-month period, the Empowerment Center provides services to nearly 7,000 mental health consumers through the drop-in center. In fiscal 2004, the Friendship Line received 3,030 calls; 4,185 persons attended 340 self-help groups; 504 people received 5,987 hours of services through the Peer Support Program; and 775 volunteers provided 4,106 hours of service to our participants.

The Empowerment Center continues to grow rapidly. When the center was opened, the founders thought they would serve about eight to ten persons a day. Just five years later, an average of fifty to seventy-five persons attended daily. The center offers eleven self-help support groups a week on site and hosts several agencies that use the facility to meet with consumers. Since 1996, the topics for support groups have evolved from being entirely selected by the staff to being based entirely on the ideas of participants. Empowerment Center participants are 47 percent African American and 46 percent Caucasian. They are 27 percent female and 73 percent male and include 24 percent who are veterans. Almost all of the participants (99 percent) are residents of St. Louis, and 51 percent of these are considered homeless as defined by the U.S. government. This figure includes all ethnic groups.

The St. Louis Empowerment Center has built a reputation for excellence in service and for collaboration with other social service agencies in the area. Before the center opened, neighborhood churches and organizations protested the establishment of a mental health program. Now these same organizations are partners in our work. Groups from the drop-in center are now asked to speak in educational institutions, the state legislature, and other public forums. In 2001, the Empowerment Center received the Vanguard Award from the city for its partnering agreement with the DBSA.

The most substantial achievements of the Empowerment Center, however, are the daily successes enjoyed by regular participants. One of these successes—that now adds up to years of success—is the achievement of Lionel, a longtime Empowerment Center participant. Lionel first came to the center in 1997, shortly it opened. He was one of those mental health consumers who seem to fall through the cracks of conventional mental health services. He had been expelled from every mental health service in city, and he was drinking heavily and not receiving or taking his medications. He spent his first days at the drop-in begging other consumers for money to buy cigarettes or liquor. As one staff member said, "He was a mess." But after a few months at the center, Lionel sobered up and, with the help of center staff, was able to find the treatment that he needed. He is now a staff member at the center, and he runs two dual-diagnosis self-help groups. He fills in wherever he is needed and is the shopping partner for the director. According to the staff, "He's a fixture."

The St. Louis Empowerment Center is currently the only funded self-help program in St. Louis and the only consumer-operated drop-in center in the state of Missouri. Despite the center's demonstrable success, Empowerment Center staff worry that funding for continued operation remains uncertain, as government mental health programs are continually cut and funds for mental health programs are fragmented into specialized areas that prevent large numbers of persons with mental illness from receiving the help they need.

6
PEER Center, Inc., Oakland Park, Florida

Compiled by Bonnie Schell and Nancy Erwin from material supplied by PEER Center directors and staff

The PEER Center in Oakland Park, Florida, is a thriving consumer-operated drop-in center with an active membership of over one thousand consumers, a mailing list of three thousand, and a staff of forty. It is the largest consumer-operated drop-in center in the state of Florida and one of the largest in the country. While many consumer-run programs, such as MHCAN in California (see Chapter 3) and Advocacy Unlimited in Connecticut (see Chapter 9), are the product of one person's devotion, the PEER Center has enjoyed the contribution of many service organizations in the community and a continual influx of consumer leaders.

Mission

When the PEER Center was incorporated in 1993 under 501 (c)(3), its mission was "to improve the quality of life of members through peer support groups, advocacy groups, educational and social projects, and programs for public information and education." The name PEER stands for the goals of personal empowerment, education, and recreation. The original facility welcomed all mental health consumers, survivors, and ex-patients seeking a place where they could be free of the stigma and pressure they experienced as consumers in today's society. In Broward County, with a population of 1.9 million, the transience that characterizes the Florida populace extends into the consumer community as well: some PEER Center members spend the winter in Florida and return to northeastern states in the summer, and many members and staff move to Broward County from other parts of the United States. Bonita, a nurse from Maryland, for example, found herself stranded after being attacked and robbed. She says, "I would have starved to death because I did not even know what a soup kitchen was. I had some of the most loving workers helping me here. That's why I volunteer now as much as possible—to say thank you." With the help of the PEER Center staff, Bonita transferred her bank account to Florida and found housing.

The first PEER Center had a staff of four consumers who believed in the self-help empowerment philosophy that enables consumers to return to the community as confident, productive citizens. The purpose of the PEER Center was to offer consumers a place of respite, a place where they could feel safe and meet with their peers without pressure and without stress. Consumers found a place where they could feel comfortable and interact freely with others, and where they could receive support and advocacy when they most needed it. These original goals of the PEER Center, despite three changes in location and many program additions, are still the primary reason the PEER Center exists.

Brief History

The PEER Center was the product of consumer needs voiced by a group called M.I.A.M.I. (Most Important Advocates for the Mentally Ill) of Broward County, and the influx of funds for community services developed through the Sanbourne v. Chiles class action lawsuit. The M.I.A.M.I. group initially refused government funding, choosing the philosophy "On Our Own" espoused in the book by Judi Chamberlin of the same title. The M.I.A.M.I. group attended the conference "Alternatives 1990" in Pittsburgh and returned with information about programs from across the country.

Ed and Patty Cooper, recent arrivals from North Carolina, had been working with the Mental Health Association of Broward. Ed put together a proposal to study the feasibility of a drop-in center, which he presented to Florida's state social service agency, Health and Rehabilitation Services (HRS). The M.I.A.M.I. submitted a request for ninety thousand dollars to fund the drop-in center itself, rather than the twenty thousand dollars for the feasibility study. The proposal was approved by the Alcohol Drug Abuse Mental Health Planning Council of HRS.

Patty Cooper was running a group at the Mental Health Association called "Project Return" that was similar to MHA programs in Los Angeles. This group began the process of determining what consumers wanted.

A steering committee was formed with members from M.I.A.M.I, Project Return, and the DMDA (Depression and Manic Depression Association). At the same time, members of that committee worked with HRS on a contract spearheaded by Ann Loder from M.I.A.M.I. and Jay Steinberg from HRS. Focus groups, facilitated by Steve Ferrante, were set up to gather consumer input in the community as well as from all the units at South Florida State Hospital. The mandates from the focus groups shaped what the PEER Center was to become. Prior to incorporation, the PEER Center was a collaborative project between the MHA and the consumer leaders. The contract specified timelines for the establishment of an independent 501 (c)(3).

In 1992 the PEER Center opened a drop-in center in a small two-story building with a kitchen and courtyard for barbecues in downtown Fort Lauderdale (see Figure 6.1). Attendance in the first year averaged thirty consumers a day, but it was not long before the membership began to outgrow the building, and it became evident that new, larger quarters were needed. Marti Foreman, the PEER Center's first executive director, led the center through these early years and its move in 1993 to Shoppes of Oakland Forest, a suburban shopping mall. There the PEER Center operations expanded to include a consumer-run desktop publishing and print shop, a housing assistance program, a cafeteria-style meals program, and an employment assistance service, as well as peer support. Two one-thousand-square-foot bays were rented originally at the Shoppes, but within a year,

Figure 6.1. The First PEER Center

the center expanded to three adjacent bays. Walls were dismantled to create one large three-thousand-square-foot facility with a staff of approximately twenty consumers.

The PEER Center at this time began a program of issuing "medic alert" bracelets to members who were at risk of being apprehended by the police for irrational behavior in the community. The bracelets were engraved on the backside with the crisis telephone number for the PEER Center's Crisis Intervention Team. It was hoped that the bracelets would prevent undue use of the Florida Baker Act for involuntary commitment, and that members who wore them would be brought to the center for intervention. Unfortunately the authorities did not honor them.

In April 1996 Marti Foreman left the PEER Center to become the director of the Cooperative Feeding Program of Fort Lauderdale. In June 1996, the PEER Center Board of Directors hired Dianne Côté as executive director. She had previously been contracted as a consultant for drop-in staff training during the initial stages of the center's development, and she had experience as director of two other peer organizations, including the Portland Coalition for the Psychiatrically Labeled in Maine. The expanding activities of the PEER Center took an even broader direction in 1998. Dianne Côté, with the board's support, gathered together a team to apply for a large federal grant, part of the multi-site research project funded by the U.S. Substance Abuse and Mental Health Services Administration (SAMHSA) to measure the effectiveness of consumer-operated services programs(COSPs). Of the eight sites selected, the PEER Center was the only nonuniversity site, as well as the only site with a consumer as project director. To provide the same level of academic expertise as the other locations, the center contracted with two state universities, the

Figure 6.2. New PEER Center, 2002.

University of South Florida and Florida International University. Dianne Côté acted as the original principal investigator for the project, and other research staff was developed from PEER Center members. In 1998, before the COSP research began, the corporation purchased a building with seven bays on Powerline Road in Oakland Park (see Figure 6.2).

This Oakland Park building was purchased with a substantial down payment, including funds from the sale of Alan's Alcove, a crisis and respite house. Owning a building freed up funds previously used for rent and provided more space. A ten-by-forty-foot awning was added at the back door to shade tables and chairs so members could relax outside. The drop-in included a games area, a board meeting room, a television and meeting room, and staff offices.

After four and a half years as leader of the PEER Center, Dianne Côté was succeeded by Edward Pazicky, who became the third executive director. Roger O'Mara is now serving as the sixth executive director.

Executive directors, 1991–present

Marti Foreman	1992–Apr. 1996
Dianne C. Côté	June 1996–Feb. 2001
Edward Pazicky	Feb. 2001–Aug. 2002
Norman Tetrault	(Interim)
Mark Moening	(Acting) Aug.–Dec. 2002
Sandy Lange	Dec. 2002–Sept. 2003
Roger O'Mara	Sept. 2003–present

Governance and Structure

The PEER Center is above all a membership organization. Potential members fill out a confidential application with the help of drop-in or peer support staff. To provide members with a sense of belonging, a fee of one dollar a year is charged to applicants for a membership card. Applicants may perform two hours of voluntary service in lieu of the fee. To be an active member, one must have a valid card and show the card when entering. Most members find the center by word of mouth, but others are referred by provider agencies or come on a visit from their residential programs. A typical member is a person who has been diagnosed with a "severe and persistent" mental illness, has been hospitalized at least once, and is typically on social security disability or SSI (Supplemental Security Income).

The center operates as an independent entity, with no affiliation to any local or national organization. The members are at the heart of all governance functions. Monthly membership meetings are led by an advisory committee and at each meeting, the center's staff present reports and answer individuals' questions. Any member can bring a topic of interest to the group's attention. The president of the advisory committee sets the agenda and runs the meeting. A secretary takes notes with the aid of a tape recorder.

The monthly Board of Directors meeting is also open to all members. Transportation is provided for any member who needs it in order to attend the board meetings. While attending members cannot actively join in board discussions, the president of their advisory committee sits on the board. Whenever the agenda allows, the chairman of the board makes time at the end of the meeting for open discussion with all those present.

Every February at the annual meeting, the PEER Center holds two well-publicized elections, one to fill vacant seats on the Board of Directors, and the other to elect officers of the Members Advisory Committee. Election announcements are prominently displayed in the center's monthly activity calendars mailed out earlier. Any member with a valid membership card can attend, nominate candidates, and vote. The staff prepares for a "full house" at every February meeting. A nominating committee normally presents a slate for the directors' positions. Additional candidates can be nominated from the floor. Candidates who are present speak briefly, presenting their qualifications and their visions for the future direction of the organization. While votes from the first election are being tallied from printed ballots, the outgoing president of the Members Advisory Committee sums up the past year's activities and makes some farewell comments. The floor is then opened to nominations for president, vice-president, and secretary for the upcoming year. The second election follows and is much like the first but without any slate. These positions are very important to membership governance because the Membership Advisory Committee handles general membership affairs and submits grievances and suggestions for programs or projects to the board through its president. Although most PEER Center employees are also members, full-time staff are ineligible for Members Advisory Committee positions.

The current Board of Directors consists of fifteen persons. The by-laws require that the board be composed of at least two-thirds consumers. The positions are structured with overlapping terms so there will always be directors with experience as well as new directors following each annual election. The board has evolved over the years into one that is very involved in center affairs and includes various professionals as well as active PEER Center members. PEER Center staff cannot hold a director's seat.

The administration of the center is vested in the executive director and managers of the departments. Historically, staff learned their duties on the job, with commitment and caring the most important qualifications. The increasing size and complexity of the services available, however, and the requirements of the funding sources and corporate compliance have presented the need for a more professional staff. The executive director must of course have a personal history with, and sensitivity and insight into, the consumer experience but must also understand contracts, grants, fiscal operations, personnel management, and plant operations. The print shop requires experience with complex equipment as well as business practices, and the computer department, with its responsibility for the center's network, needs a manager with specialist training.

Consumers with these qualifications have the opportunity to use them in a productive manner. Yet individual and group vigilance and support are required to prevent the stress of great responsibility from endangering the stability of all the employees. Managers step in to help each other and a rotating team of volunteers assumes substantial parts of the workload.

Physical Plant

The center is equipped with restrooms and a shower facility that are handicapped accessible, a ramp for wheelchairs at the drop-in front door, and a laundry. Situated in a business office strip center within a commercial and light industrial area, the PEER Center with its seven bays offers the consumer a wide choice of activities and services (see Figure 6.3). Each bay has a front door, and the drop-in, which occupies two and one-half bays in which interior walls have been removed, opens to the back area with awning-covered benches, tables, and chairs for smoking. The drop-in section has comfortable furnishings for pool, ping-pong, television, and table games and a piano and organ. Members also come to the drop-in for food baskets, parties, organized day trips, and support group meetings.

The PEER Center faces a busy six-lane street with a bus stop in front of the building. The back area is fenced to safeguard three vehicles, to prevent theft of lawn furniture, and to keep homeless persons from camping out in the evening. The police ask people trying to sleep in their cars in the front to move on. Both the PEER Center and its neighbors have

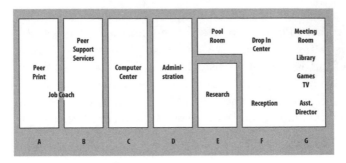

Figure 6.3. PEER Center Layout

a problem with homeless people who are not members but come from encampments near a railroad. To maintain a good relationship with the neighborhood, PEER Center volunteers help neighbors cut back vegetation and dispose of trash.

Having front and back doors for each program poses special security needs. Every bay has an alarm system with a unique code. The bay manager sets the code at night and deactivates it in the morning. The perimeter fence that surrounds the backyard is locked every evening. To provide extra security, the Research Bay has a permanent interior wall and access only by the front door.

PEER Center Programs

The PEER Center is now open every day of the week and remains open until 8 P.M. on weeknights. The drop-in center is open 360 days every year, with snacks, coffee, and soft drinks available at all times. The daily average attendance is between 100 and 110 during the week and 65 a day on weekends. The programs of the PEER Center express the needs of adults diagnosed with major mental illness. They are the same basic needs that existed when community organizations collaborated to create the PEER Center, the need for:

- An accepting place for socialization and recreation
- Employment and job training
- Affordable supported housing
- Food and clothes
- An alternative to hospitalization when people are experiencing crisis

An Accepting Place for Socialization,
Recreation, and Peer Support

At the drop-in center, members can sign up for weekend camping trips to local state parks or for excursions to tourist attractions in Broward County and in the adjacent counties of Miami-Dade and Palm Beach. Other events may include entertainment programs provided by community groups, fishing trips, picnics, and beach outings at local parks. Numerous support groups meet regularly in the drop-in center. The center has a television room with satellite reception and VCR and DVD equipment. Every Friday evening a full-length movie is shown.

The PEER Center has been instrumental in the founding of other drop-in centers in Broward County. For example, Silver Impact, a consumer-run support group for elderly consumers, began meeting casually in 1992 under the guidance of Virginia Frey. In 1997, volunteer consumer leaders conducted activities on weekends in the bay used for the weekday lunch program at the PEER center. This became known as the Silver Center, and a part-time staff of two employees worked from an office in the PEER Center. Within one year, Silver Impact became independent of the PEER Center and moved into a new space in adjacent Lauderhill, Florida.

Along with the other dynamic consumer projects in the early 1990s, a drop-in center was set up at South Florida State Hospital by two members of Project Dream Again, who ran the center for its first year in an old doctor's house on the grounds of the state hospital. It was one of the first drop-ins in the country at a state hospital; the hospital patients named the center Forest Park and established its rules and purpose. In 1993 Mark Moening was hired by the hospital as director, and he ran the center with consumer staff, including patients at the hospital. Later South Florida State Hospital became the nation's first privately operated state psychiatric facility when Florida's Department of Children and Families turned the management of the hospital over to Atlantic Shores Healthcare, Inc., a subsidiary of a corporation for privatized correctional and detention management. The new management subcontracted with the PEER center to run the drop-in center, and this arrangement continued for four years, with consumer staff hired as PEER Center Employees. In September 2002, amid restructuring of the PEER Center, the administration and control of Forest Park Drop-In Center were relinquished to Atlantic Shores.

Employment and Job Training

Employment is one of the greatest concerns of consumers. To address this need, the young PEER Center obtained funds in 1994 from the State of Florida Vocational Rehabilitation Agency to begin a job placement program. Getting commitments from local companies to hire consumers proved difficult. After a year of persistence, without a reasonable expansion of the job base, the program was cancelled. On a smaller scale, a program called Peer Employee Leasing found job slots with the landlord of the shopping mall where the center was then located.

Another ambitious attempt for employment of consumers was "Eyes for Humanity." Local optometrists wanted to provide eyeglasses to the poor and the center agreed to provide space and trainees who were to learn the skills of lens grinding and eyeglass assembly. During the months the business operated, many eyeglasses were distributed, but only one consumer member was trained. Again, the amount of effort required to maintain the program exceeded the results realized.

Although these innovative ideas failed, the PEER Center itself has been successful in employing dozens of its members to run the organization and help their peers. Jobs have ranged from general maintenance up to management with skilled technical positions especially in the print shop and computer lab. The center provides the experience and support needed for its employees to move into the public sector. As Nancy Erwin, a longtime PEER Center employee and current principal investigator for the Florida COSP site, writes:

> My illness had prevented me from continuing my professional employment and I became homeless. The PEER Center not only rescued me from the streets but also aided my recovery by giving me a job in the print shop. It was my very own work therapy and I rose from volunteer to manager and editor of the center's periodical publication. Finally when the COSP grant opened up research positions, I was able to return to familiar employment using my academic training.

In addition to regular permanent jobs needed to run all the PEER Center programs, the center has sought funding by the state of Florida as a sheltered workshop site in the print shop, where between seven and ten employees produce professional printing jobs. This employment program requires minimal cost for labor and services.

The Print Shop is a business offering print services to other mental health agencies, commercial businesses, and the public at large while earning income for the PEER Center. It has the capacity to do general layout, books, programs, business cards, and posters with Risograph printers and a full range of adjunct equipment. It trains members and staff and employs general volunteers from the drop-in center to meet the requirements of large, rush jobs. The Print Shop handles the internal needs of the center, which involves creating stationery, making up membership cards, and printing the board election ballots as well as an eleven-by-seventeen-inch monthly calendar of events and a periodic newsletter, called *Transitions*. The calendar and the newsletter are made available to all members and other agencies and professional providers. *Transitions* contains articles about consumer affairs and current events at the PEER Center, columns from each department and the board chairman, letters from members, and poetry and other items of interest by members.

As a part of the ongoing commitment to helping consumers help themselves, executive director Dianne Côté, with the board's approval, converted a section of the old center into a computer lab. Computer services now fill an entire bay in the present center. Members can learn keyboarding, programming, and researching topics on the Internet, as well as play games. Some consumers use the computers to study for GED tests, practice reading and typing skills, and research their own disorder and medications on mental health Web sites. In addition, the Computer Center supports the administration. When research funding allowed the expansion of the system, the center tapped Paul Collins, one of its talented members, to develop an in-house network server. He became the manager of information systems, as well as department manager and Web master. Now the center has computerized its administrative functions in accord with other local and state agencies.

Included in the Computer Center operations is a computer assembly and repair shop called PEER Computer Care, where a consumer technician builds new computers from donated and purchased parts and sells them at reasonable prices. A webmaster maintains the Web site *www.peercenter.org*.

Basic Clothing, Food, and Housewares

When Marti Foreman decided to organize a Thrift Shop, she secured donations of clothing and household items that were either sold to the general public or given to needy PEER Center members. Florence Merson, the director of volunteers, started a new thrift shop. Excess clothing was placed in the Members' Clothes Closet to be given to those in need.

For several years the Thrift Shop was able to generate profit that helped support the cost of the Computer Center. The Thrift Shop operated until 2002, when revenues declined and its space was needed for an expanding program.

The PEER Center distributes food boxes to members from food obtained at the local food bank. Food is paid for by cash and by vouchers earned by center volunteers at ten pounds of food per person per hour. Several bakery outlets also make regular donations.

Affordable Housing

Marti Foreman organized a housing assistance program in 1995. The program was designed to locate reasonable, suitable housing for homeless members who were capable of maintaining independent living. Local landlords were contacted to provide one- and two-bedroom apartments, and the PEER Center provided the initial move-in expenses for the occupants.

In many instances, the PEER Center was able to negotiate reduced move-in expenses. But the center also purchased a large box truck to be used as a moving van. Funds for Project Take Me Home came from a state grant and from the Broward Community Development Corporation (CDC), a nonprofit community housing assistance agency.

During the period when there was a separate housing department at the center, housing staff provided regular visitation to those members occupying supported apartments to ensure that they were complying with the requirements of independent living. Initially, two-bedroom apartments were provided and roommate selection was arranged through the PEER Center support specialists with the agreement of both parties. Because many problems arose from conflicts between roommates, the CDC has changed their policy to provide single-occupancy apartments only.

In 2002, the PEER Center initiated a program to rent apartments on its own and sublease them to members who were homeless. There are two two-bedroom apartments, which have been changed from transitional to permanent housing. The members who occupy PEER Center apartments may rent or work at the center in lieu of part of the rent. These members pay their expenses but may be supplemented by food baskets. The staff provides peer support and ascertains that members living in the apartments remain stable and continue to progress in their goals of independence. One staff member stated:

We are truly "Making a Difference" for the mentally ill homeless, hungry persons. Most of all, the comfort and emotional support the members provide as we counsel each other gives us a sense of hope for our future as we work on our recovery together. I remember saying in a treatment center twenty years ago, that I was sailing out of a Sea of Pain into a Sea of Serenity.

Crisis Support

In early 1993 the PEER Center applied to Broward County Health and Human Services for a $110,000 grant. This grant was awarded later that year and the program called Reach Out/Reach In was established. This grant created official "PEER support specialists" at the PEER Center to provide peer counseling. The grant also funded a crisis team of three workers for members in crisis. The members in crisis could stay at Alan's Alcove, a respite house for members, while they recovered emotional stability. This program proved its value when there were no occurrences of suicide among members during the three years the safe house was maintained.

As one crisis client testified:

I only spent two nights at the safe house, but what an important time that was for me. The authorities had threatened to Baker Act [involuntarily commit] me and I had nowhere else to go. I thought I was just getting a place to sleep. Instead I found a lovely home with a well-stocked kitchen, but most of all lots of PEER support. One counselor stayed up with me the entire first night. He didn't try to fix anything. First, he just listened and then he led me into a general conversation. It was just what I needed. The night passed quickly.

The county grant evolved over the years to establish the center as an alternative provider of services in Broward County. In mid 2002, however, the county restructured its funding of services, bringing the grant to an end. PEER Support Services in 2003 were funded by a $90,608 local match grant added to the center's contract with HRS, which was now renamed Department of Children and Families (DCF), A program was developed in 2002 to provide individual peer support and assistance. Restrictions on certification, liabilities, and the desire to provide independently controlled support services prevent the PEER Center from providing "case management," which is why the alternate classification of "peer support specialist" is used. Two consumers—a medical doctor and a consumer with extensive past experience in peer counseling—currently staff the department. A clerical worker has been employed to handle the client files and to screen members for qualification for housing and peer support.

Recently the need has increased considerably, and the PEER Center has had to establish a policy to provide support for only those members who are not receiving case management from other agencies.

Unfortunately, in 1997 DCF reassigned one hundred thousand dollars in funding from the PEER Center to a local community mental health agency to train consumer crisis specialists for eventual assignment to a re-organized PEER Center Crisis Intervention Department. This plan, however, never materialized. Sadly, the present caseload of existing community mental health service providers has grown to a point where case management cannot be immediately provided to all consumers in need of the services.

Police officers frequently intervene when consumers experience a crisis. To their credit, the Fort Lauderdale Police were the first officers to organize a crisis intervention team (CIT) in Broward County, and the PEER Center was selected to assist in training them. Officers are taught to stabilize a situation by taking a calm approach. Once stabilized, the prospective offender is then taken to a safe place. Sometimes police bring people to the PEER Center if their condition is not severe. There they are introduced to the center's services and are provided with regular follow-up by the support staff.

The PEER Center has maintained its original goals and objectives under energetic leadership and wide-ranging innovations in its programming by executive directors and dedicated community volunteers. Always the needs of its members drive the changes. Consumers who have experienced a lengthy stay in the hospital or incarceration or homelessness are usually at a loss to find services in the community. Getting connected with community mental health services or obtaining medication or finding a case manager can be overwhelming. As a consumer-operated service program, the PEER Center helps bridge gaps in the community mental health system, advocating for each person, as his or her needs require.

In the past, consumer-operated programs have experienced a stigma in society similar to that suffered by individuals with mental illness. The programs were not taken seriously, and many agencies were reluctant to work hand in hand with consumers. But now with the breakdown in the formal system and a nationwide budget crisis involving health and hu-

man services, traditional providers of services have perhaps come to realize the importance of peer support and services.

In its twelve-year history, the PEER Center has had many successes,
but it has also encountered painful obstacles and periods of acrimony and
anarchy. There are several factors involved in the growth of consumer-
operated programs, not the least of which is adequate, continual fund-
raising. Traditional services mandated by federal and state government
regulations can depend on a base of reimbursement for services delivered. Consumer-run services by unlicensed providers cannot. An effective and strong board of directors is essential. A bridge must be built
between private foundations and benefactors, and this can be done only
through education. Community involvement, outreach, and support are
other important factors in building successful programs. Consumer-run
programs need influential community leaders and people able to provide
technical assistance.

In the October 2001 issue of *Transitions,* members wrote about how
they felt about the center. One of these, "PEER Center Anthem" by Brad
Robertshaw, was written in the form of a song to be sung to the tune of
"Auld Lang Syne."

Welcome to the PEER Center
Come in and have a seat
Pour yourself a cup o' joe
And have a snack to eat

Karaoke, BBQ's
And camping once a year
A quarter for a lemon lime,
A cola or root beer.

There's fun and games,
And talent shows
Something for everyone
There's raffles free
From time to time
Neat prizes can be won

The staff is helpful, smart and fun
Their job is never done
They teach you how to help yourself
You never have to run

Personal Empowerment
Is what we're all about
Education, Recreation
Are included in this route

There are group discussions all day long
And self-help groups abound
So join us at the PEER Center
Where once lost now you're found.

PART III

Peer Support and Mentoring Services

7
GROW in Illinois

Lorraine Keck and Carol Mussey

Mental illness is no respecter of persons—it can happen to anyone. The GROW mental health movement was born out of a creative response by ordinary people to their own mental and emotional suffering. It did not matter when, why, or even how the early founders of GROW became sick and tormented by inner demons, obsessions, or delusions. What did matter was that these tenacious and dedicated individuals did something about it. They conquered the giant within—through a proven method of mutual help, shared learning, and friendship—and then passed on to others the good news that there is a way to recovery.

GROW is an international mental health organization run by its members. It is based on a network of structured mutual help groups and a "caring and sharing community" and is guided by the written GROW Program of Recovery and Personal Growth.

The organization that became GROW was founded in Australia in 1957 by Con Keogh, a Catholic priest who had suffered from mental illness himself. He was searching for a way to help himself and others like him and initially attended Alcoholics Anonymous (AA) for friendly support. In AA, Con and his fellow mental sufferers discovered something essential—people recovering together by sharing personal resources and finding their way back to full and lasting mental health. Inspired by his AA experience, Con brought together other recovering patients to form their own mutual help group. Soon this one group grew into a network of groups and became know as RECOVERY, which eventually spread throughout Australia and then to other countries.

Severe mental illness brought the original RECOVERY members together. In time, however, many long-time members had fully recovered but wanted to stay involved to help build the organization and serve as leaders and helpers to others. They wondered, "Where do we go from here?" So, to reflect the evolving diversity in membership, they changed the name of the organization in 1971 to the more inclusive name GROW. Today the GROW program encompasses not just goals for recovery but also practical ideals for personal growth.

GROW has almost one thousand groups throughout the English-speaking world. In North America, one of the organization's successes has been in Illinois, where its development now includes more than one hundred groups across the state. GROW came to Illinois thanks to seeding money from W. Clement Stone, a business entrepreneur and philanthropist from Chicago (and the first international patron of the Australian RECOVERY program, the forerunner of GROW), and at the invitation of O. Hobart Mowrer, professor emeritus of psychology at the University of Illinois in Champaign-Urbana.

In October 1964, while Clem Stone was in Australia working on a personal project of prisoner rehabilitation, he met Con Keogh and Albert Lacey, an Australian lawyer and RECOVERY promoter. Stone was impressed by what he heard about RECOVERY and offered to help with organizational promotion and development. To that end, he funded the first salaried RECOVERY fieldworker (program staff person) in Australia. He also promised that when the time came to transplant the program to the United States, he would provide start-up money for the expansion. That time came in 1978.

With Stone's funding in hand, Con Keogh and Joan Baynes, another recovered international leader, came to Illinois and stayed at the home of Hobart Mowrer in Urbana. Mowrer was interested in the mutual-help concept guiding member-run services such as GROW (as it was called by then) and was impressed by the organization's rapid expansion. With Hobart's help, the Urbana Baptist Students' Union basement was secured for use as a temporary GROW Center and, in addition, Mowrer allowed his home to be used as a base for the initial development of groups in central Illinois. Hobart's support gave Con and "Joannie" the opportunity to establish the first ten Illinois groups in the Champaign-Urbana area.

By 1981 there was a network of twelve groups operating in central Illinois, and this GROW development became the subject of a four-year evaluation co-designed by Julian Rappaport and Edward Seidman, professors in the Department of Psychology at the University of Illinois, and funded by the National Institute of Mental Health. Of particular interest to Rappaport and Seidman was the alternative nature of our member-run organization and also its phenomenal growth—from eighteen to ninety-nine groups in eighteen months. Since the initial University of Illinois evaluation, which has proved extremely effective in promoting GROW as an alternative mental health program, several other teams of researchers have conducted studies of our organization. (See, e.g., Young and Williams 1989.)

In January 1998, GROW in Illinois participated again in a significant research project—the Consumer-Operated Services Program, a multi-site research initiative. Patrick Corrigan of the University of Chicago invited GROW to participate in this four-year federally funded study. After serious deliberation, we agreed to become a part of the project, which presented both a challenge and an opportunity for us. The challenge was to find common ground with a very diverse group of project collaborators, while also working within the constraints of the grant guidelines. And the opportunity was the chance to participate in a study that could potentially demonstrate the impact of GROW on the lives of persons with serious mental illness.

This $20 million project, funded by the Substance Abuse and Mental Health Services Administration (SAMHSA), had two phases—a multi-state study and a site-specific study. Project collaborators at the Illinois site included our own "consumer-operated" service (GROW), a team of researchers from the University of Chicago Center for Psychiatric Rehabilitation, and two professional mental agencies in Illinois (Janet Wattles Center in Rockford and Provena Behavioral Health in Champaign-Urbana). Pat Corrigan was the principal investigator, and his colleague, Sarah Diwan, was the project director. Carol Mussey, long-time GROW member and leader, served as the "consumer investigator," and Lorraine Keck, program coordinator for GROW In America and president of GROW In Illinois, coordinated GROW's participation in the project.

Three major research questions were asked: First, what is the impact of a complex research project on the collaborators, including the consumer-operated services, the traditional service providers, and the research teams? Second, do people with severe mental illness benefit from attending consumer-operated services such as GROW, in addition to receiving traditional mental health services? And if so, how do they benefit? And third, if consumers benefit from attending member-run services, in what specific ways do they benefit?

To answer these questions, four substudies were conducted in Illinois:

a study of consumer outcomes associated with GROW participation, a study of the keys to success in GROW, a fidelity study of the processes at work in the GROW organization, and a study of consumer service usage and its associated costs.

Today, emotionally troubled people continue to benefit from any one of the one hundred GROW groups meeting throughout Illinois. Since 1990, when we began keeping official records of attendance, 21,678 different individuals have participated in GROW. Annual attendance at weekly GROW groups has averaged between 1,200 and 1,500 people. And in 1990, with a $450,000 grant from the Robert Wood Johnson Foundation, GROW was able to expand to three additional states: Delaware, New Jersey, and Rhode Island. Today, twenty groups continue to flourish in New Jersey.

Where GROW Happens

GROW is not confined to a particular space or place. General GROW groups meet in public buildings, churches, and other locations in the community, and special groups meet in hospitals and professional agencies. GROW In Illinois has a branch office that houses the administration and serves the staff. It also rents houses throughout the state, called GROW Centers, for informal get-togethers, GROW group meetings, and other organized social, educational, and leadership events.

GROW owns a large house in Kankakee, Illinois, where it operates a twenty-four-hour residential rehabilitation program. This small residential community is based on a family environment, where both residents and staff participate in a structured, intensive program of mutual help and leadership.

Who Is a Member of GROW?

GROW is open to everyone, regardless of need, but our overarching goal is to serve those who most need help and can least afford it. In keeping with this goal, we charge no fees or dues. And because we value inclusiveness, we aim to provide reasonable accommodation to those with disabilities.

Our membership is diverse. Most of us have come to GROW because of mental illness and are working toward recovery. Others have already recovered through GROW and are contributing leadership to recovering members and to the organization. Still others come to GROW to prevent a threatening breakdown or to gain support while in a crisis.

Since GROW is for people with diverse needs, it calls itself a program of recovery and of personal growth. However, while GROW is open to everyone, we never claim that GROW is "a good fit" for everyone. When we say that the organization is strictly voluntary, this statement implies a personal challenge to members. We believe when a "perspective" member chooses to become a "committed Grower"—thereby identifying consistently with GROW's aims and methods—he or she may confidently expect to recover and ultimately progress to full and lasting mental health. "Perspective members" become "committed" Growers by voluntarily reciting with other group members the final two clauses of the GROW "Commitment," whereby they freely choose to identify fully with the GROW program and to cooperate with its methods.

Laurie, a member of one central Illinois GROW group, is a good example of a "prospective" member who remained undecided about committing to full membership. Laurie had been attending GROW for several months and was making real progress in her life by practicing the program attitudes and problem-solving methods. Week after week, however, she continued to declare herself a "prospective" Grower, signifying that she was not ready to "commit" to full membership. Initially, group members explained to her that pledging the "Commitment" should not be taken lightly. One night, however, a group member pointed out to Laurie that "living out the program" and "giving back to others" would surely signify that she was ready to commit to membership. Laurie thought about this comment for a few weeks and then announced that she was dedicated to recovery by using GROW's program and method. And even if she slipped a little along the way, she could "resume quickly" and get back on track. Laurie never looked back. Today she is a GROW leader, serving as organizer of a GROW group and as a program team member.

GROW's Essential Nature and Operation

GROW has a written program based on twelve practical steps (see Figure 7.1). The organization should not, however, be characterized merely as a twelve-step program. We describe GROW more specifically as a mental health organization with four essential, interconnected features: the written GROW Program of Recovery and Personal Growth; a structured method for its weekly mutual-help groups, known as the group method; a "caring and sharing community," based on a network of friendship; and an organizational and legal structure.

Figure 7.1. The Twelve Steps of Recovery and Personal Growth

1. We admitted we were inadequate or maladjusted to life.
2. We firmly resolved to get well and co-operated with the help that we needed.
3. We surrendered to the healing power of a wise and loving God.
4. We made personal inventory and accepted ourselves.
5. We made moral inventory and cleaned out our hearts.
6. We endured until cured.
7. We took care and control of our bodies.
8. We learned to think by reason rather than by feelings and imagination.
9. We trained our wills to govern our feelings.
10 We took our responsible and caring place in society.
11. We grew daily closer to maturity.
12. We carried GROW's hopeful, healing, and transforming message to others in need.

The GROW Program

GROW groups, their leaders, and the "caring and sharing community" are all informed and guided by the GROW program, which is, in the words of Con Keogh, a written, organized "philosophy of life and psychology of mental health." The program has evolved as a result of our founding members' resolve to share their common experiences and try to make sense of the disruptive events in their lives. Through this process, they discovered and wrote down, in an organized fashion, the attitudes and problem-solving methods they found effective in rebuilding their broken lives. The basic GROW program, known by members as "the Blue Book," or formally as "The Program of Growth to Maturity," has been slowly and carefully developed and refined by GROW leaders.

The Group Method

Members of each group elect an organizer and recorder, who are responsible for the administration and general welfare of the group, but any GROW group member can learn to lead the weekly meeting by following a uniform meeting format called the group method. Adherence to this format ensures that important work is accomplished at every meeting and that certain essential ingredients are always included. Each group meeting includes a personal testimony, problem solving, assignment of practical tasks, reports on progress, and an educational section with a group reading of a selection from GROW literature followed by an "attempted objective" discussion of its contents.

At the GROW meeting we invite a member, whether general group member, leader, or staff, to share his or her story. Telling our stories (or "personal testimonies"), we believe, helps us come together as ordinary persons and find our common humanity. We recognize that no one is exempt from life's suffering—or, as G. K. Chesterton wisely put it, "We're all in the same boat and we're all seasick." By telling our testimonies we help dissolve artificial dividing lines between persons and prevent unnatural boundaries from developing between members, leaders, and staff.

A "personal testimony" tells the story of how a person came to GROW and reveals how he or she has been successful in making significant life changes by participating fully in all aspects of the organization. For example, Tim shared his testimony one evening with the Monday night group, first by describing in detail how he had suffered from hearing voices for many years, and then by explaining how he was helped by participating in the GROW group and "practicing the GROW program."

Tim's personal testimony inspired Alice, another group member, and gave her hope that she too might overcome her own problems. Later, during the "problem solving" time, Alice described the fears that had tormented her for years. The group listened attentively and assigned her a "practical task" from the Blue Book that was directed at "control[ing] unhealthy thoughts." By following the principles from the program, Alice worked hard to overcome her fears and was soon able to "give a progress report" to the group by describing her success in "crowding out" her troubled thinking by "cultivating positive thoughts and talk, and wholesome interests and habits."

The Caring and Sharing Community

The third essential feature of GROW is its "caring and sharing community," the true heart and spirit of the organization. Much of the real work of GROW is done informally, outside of the weekly meeting, when members give one another friendly support and help and build healing friendships. For example, Tina, Mandy, Jen, and Terry from the Tuesday night group met at the GROW Center for pizza one Friday evening and rented the movie *A Beautiful Mind*. This gathering grew into an occasional night out with Growers, and soon other members joined in. Ultimately, one informal evening gathering of a few GROW friends became a regular community event.

Not all of the work of the GROW community is informal. Community activities also include structured events, such as live-in community weekends, leadership meetings, monthly socials, and workshops and training courses.

Community weekends are annual events, usually held at a centrally located campsite. At these weekends, we offer something for everyone, including families of Growers. The event will most likely begin on a Friday evening with recreation, such as a dance and social, followed by singing and roasting marshmallows around a campfire. Saturday events will include an educational session in the morning, with the focus on a topic such as "Laugh and Be Healthy." Then Bingo, softball, volleyball or other indoor games follow. The evening is topped off with the ever-popular Saturday night GROW Social, which includes the creative practice and sharing of our talents. The weekend concludes on Sunday morning with another educational discussion on a topic of general interest. These annual community weekends bring 90 to 175 Growers and family members together and help animate and promote the spirit of the "caring and sharing community."

Structured *leadership meetings* are held every other month. At these meetings, GROW leaders discuss topics related to authentic leadership and the use and development of the written program, which has being refined and improved through the years to its present depth and stability. Members eligible to attend leaders' meetings must have been "committed Growers" for at least three months and have led a minimum of three weekly GROW meetings.

Monthly socials are also organized events which are part of the "caring and sharing community." These are informal gatherings where Growers and their families have fun and get to know one another better in a relaxed and friendly atmosphere. At these get-togethers we enjoy community singing, socializing, dancing, and games, and during the summer we may go swimming or on picnics or perhaps on an outing to the zoo.

The GROW community is as much educational as it is social. In fact, we describe GROW as "a school for living." Participation in community means joining a mutual education process, which includes essential structured learning events. Among these are organized training workshops and courses, where group and organizational leaders and program staff learn about the GROW philosophy, group method, and organizational structures. Topics at training courses include "The Essential Features of GROW," "The Roles of the Organizer and Recorder," and "The GROW Philosophy of Friendship, Leadership, and Community."

Through community, both formal and informal, we strive to develop as reflective persons. When it comes to education and learning in GROW, there are no privileged classes. We are all students of life, and with adequate development, we can become leaders and teachers to others.

The bedrock of the caring and sharing community is friendship, which we identify as "the special key to mental health." We believe recovery is not possible without true friends—those who become our "kindred spirits" and our "other selves." Our friends in GROW reach out to us when we are in despair; they ignite in us a sense of hope, illuminate the way out of our misery, and share a common journey with us. Our GROW friends know the way because they have been there too.

Organizational and Legal Structure

As GROW developed, the leaders built an organizational and legal structure through which the other three essential features of GROW are administered and protected. This fourth essential feature is like the shell of an oyster that protects the live pearl inside. Our network of groups, the GROW program, and the caring and sharing community represent the pearl, and the organizational structure functions as the shell to protect the valued ingredients. This organizational structure includes teams for group development, leadership training, and administration. In any formed GROW area, there are leadership meetings, organizers' and recorders' meetings, and training events to protect, administer, and develop the GROW groups, program, and community; and there are administrative teams to execute and serve the practical needs of the organization as a whole. All members of program-related teams are GROW leaders, as are most members of the administrative teams.

Any of the four essential features can be changed, but not easily or carelessly. Changes must be based on sound reasons, accuracy of thought, and truth. GROW's program and method have evolved through sharing and reflection and can be altered only through a similar means. The systematic processes of change are laid out in a definitive document titled "Procedures for Change" (published in Australia by GROW International).

Change in GROW is deliberate and systematic and so is organizational growth. Before we expand to a new area (or into a new state or country), we first consider that area's need for, and receptiveness to, the GROW program, with its alternative philosophy of mental health service delivery. Furthermore, we take into account the commitment of funding authorities to help support a full GROW community development, along with a GROW Center. Necessary staff will include a fieldworker and the supportive help of a receptionist, a program secretary, and an administrative assistant, as well as an automobile for program activities. We know from experience that GROW can be effective only when this whole package is accepted and adequately funded.

A recent situation in a state into which GROW was hoping to expand reveals how a new GROW development can fail through lack of adequate funding and official acceptance. Dan, an employee of a drug and alcohol program in that state, persuaded the executive director to provide some funding to develop GROW groups at two sites—one in a short-term residential program for drug and alcohol rehabilitation and the other in a homeless shelter. This funding, however, was not sufficient to cover the program and operational costs required to insure an authentic GROW development in the wider community. As a consequence, when GROW participants left the sheltered programs, they found no GROW groups or community activities for follow-up support and friendship. This attempted expansion into another state taught us that GROW has little chance of success without adequate commitment of official support and funding.

Leadership

GROW is run by its own members, but the quality of the organization and its development is sustained by its leaders. We are all invited and encouraged to offer leadership—by, for example, leading a meeting, helping someone else recover, or giving a personal testimony. But, ultimately, we become true leaders when we choose to identify with GROW's aims and methods, to work fully toward our own recovery and growth, and to be dedicated to showing the way to others. In the words of the GROW document "The 8 Characteristics of Leadership," published in Australia in September 1992, a GROW leader is "a living example" of authentic GROW, one "who is going the way we need to go, who knows the way and can show the way." Leaders uphold and protect the four essential features of GROW; they govern GROW, train new leaders, promote GROW's development, and advocate for GROW in the wider community.

Project C.O.P.E. (Community Outreach Program for Education): An Example of Organizational Leadership

From the GROW program, we have learned the following, as stated in the Blue Book: "The reality test of how much you value anything is how much you are prepared to sacrifice, when necessary, to secure it." In early 2002, we were put to this very test when we learned that the mental health budget in Illinois was being dramatically reduced and that our own organization was targeted for a whopping 66 percent cut. Such a reduction would have resulted in loss of financial support for all Illinois groups, leaving only the GROW residential community with funding. Rather than "hunkering down" in our local areas and hoping for some miracle, we launched Project C.O.P.E., designed to pull together GROW members and leaders throughout Illinois to advocate for the mentally ill and the legitimacy of member-run services. We Growers decided it was time to "step outside our comfort zone" by speaking to our legislators, both in the state capital of Springfield and in our local areas, thereby demonstrating leadership and doing what was necessary to keep GROW alive and well. On a few occasions we also joined efforts with other coalitions in protesting the cuts to mental health services. The ultimate result of our advocacy efforts was the restoration of our state funding for the fiscal year 2003.

The Nature of Staff Leadership

We stress the voluntary nature of GROW and emphasize that much of our real work is done by members strictly on a voluntary basis. But because we aim to make GROW available to many people in need, and because we need to insure authentic GROW development, we also hire fieldworkers. It is the fieldworker's job to oversee the groups and GROW community, facilitate leadership training, and organize outreach efforts. GROW staff may or may not have had experience as members and leaders in GROW when they are hired. Nevertheless, they are expected to make the same commitment to GROW's aims and methods that any volunteer GROW leader does. Like other leaders, staff commit to full participation in the whole GROW process. They are expected to join a GROW group, learn to understand and practice the program, and learn to appreciate the role they play as living examples of GROW's goals and values.

Spirituality in GROW

We are able to come together in community and find our common humanity because we share one essential, unifying belief—we believe in one another and in our unique personal value. We believe in the value of each individual, irrespective of appearance, behavior, or achievement. This unwavering belief in persons is characterized as *horizontal spirituality*. Belief in one another links us solidly with others in the GROW community, and it is often through these human connections that we first find spiritual meaning.

There is a second spiritual dimension open to GROW members that we call *vertical spirituality*. This refers to a spiritual connection with God. Some members already believe in God when they join GROW. Others become believers and experience this second spiritual dimension after they have formed meaningful bonds in community. "We surrendered to the healing power of a wise and loving God" is the third of our "Twelve Steps of Recovery and Personal Growth." It is included in the program because many GROW members have testified that their maturing belief in God has made a significant difference in their recovery.

GROW is open to everyone, believers and unbelievers alike, and it is nondenominational. Talk of God and participation in the two GROW prayers recited in our weekly group meetings is optional. But, to repeat, we include the concept of God (the vertical spiritual dimension) in our program because, from the very start, the overwhelming majority of members have found it meaningful.

Self-Activation through Mutual Help Paves the Way to Empowerment and Recovery

We come together in GROW with two mutually inclusive goals: we aim to help ourselves and, at the same time, to help others. We describe this work as self-activation through mutual help. In other words, we believe, "You alone can do it, but you can't do it alone."

We believe that what matters most about help is *what kind* we receive and *how much.* We need different kinds of help at different stages in our recovery. When we are in crisis, out of control, or incapable of communicating with others, we may well need professional help, which could involve hospitalization and other medical intervention, such as medication. Counseling may also be necessary. But, ultimately, to recover fully we also need other, more personal kinds of help, such as support from an understanding family member or friend. In the art of friendly, supportive help, we believe there are no experts. In fact, when it comes to prevention and rehabilitation, we have found that the best helper is the ordinary person, the one who knows firsthand about life's struggles.

Help from others, however, is not enough. In fact, too much help and especially too much of the wrong kind of help ("disabling help") will weaken our resources for living and keep us stuck in the role of "permanent emotional invalid." For this reason, we must contribute to our own recovery and growth by patiently practicing the GROW program and systematically developing our own personal resources.

We cite an example of the GROW concept of "self-activation through mutual help" from an occurrence in a Monday night GROW group meeting in Urbana. Group members noticed Carrie had been lacking in motivation for a few weeks. In fact, she was falling asleep during meetings. A couple of Growers contacted Carrie during the week and invited her to go out for coffee, but she declined, which was not typical of Carrie. At the following weekly meeting, Carrie told the group that her medication had been increased and consequently she was feeling sleepy all the time. She was talking about discontinuing the medication because it made her feel "lousy." The group advised Carrie against this action and, instead, assigned her the practical task of talking with her doctor about the problem. Carrie acknowledged she was nervous about talking with her doctor, so Jack, another group member, offered to go along with Carrie to the doctor's office. Through Jack's support, Carrie gained the courage to talk with her doctor, who reduced her medication dosage. Soon she became more alert and focused and was able to report to the group the following week that she felt empowered through their support.

When we speak of *empowerment,* we mean learning to believe in ourselves and becoming effective through the expectation and realization of success. In GROW problems become opportunities. We say, "You've got a problem? That's good!" The GROW message is, "We need you." We don't hear, as we did from some professional helpers, "You need us and always will." Through GROW, we find new meaning and purpose in life. There are others who need our help, there are meaningful jobs for us to do, and there are leadership roles to fill. We grow from "problem person" to solution person." With the encouragement of our weekly groups and GROW friends, we become successful in making step-by-step changes in our lives. We gain a sense of security through belonging and confidence by doing. We learn personal responsibility and gain our true freedom when we are no longer enslaved to destructive habits. And, ultimately, we become positively glad we had a breakdown because it has become a breakthrough to a new, more successful way of living.

We believe empowerment contributes to recovery, and recovery includes empowerment. In GROW we believe full recovery from mental illness (that is, complete rehabilitation) is possible, not just theoretical. It is a reality for us, based on our own experiences and the experiences of many of our friends and leaders. Our written program describes the step-by-step process of recovery, and these writings reflect our actual experience.

It is important to note that our understanding of recovery may differ from beliefs held by others. We respect the diversity of individual beliefs and experience and appreciate the opportunity to express our own views on the important mental health question of recovery.

We have specific ways of recognizing our recovery. For example, we know we have recovered when we have become "a person rather than an emotional reaction" and have learned "to do the ordinary thing despite strong contrary feelings of fear." We know we have recovered when we can "control the sequence of events in our minds and in our lives," meaning we have control over our thoughts and actions (rather than their having control over us). We know we have recovered when we have learned to live with (or even above) a certain amount of anxiety, boredom, confusion, disability, discord, guilt, and loneliness, and when we can put up with the usual daily disorder, for the sake of the bigger issues in our lives.

Once we have recovered, we find that the quality of our relationships has improved, and mainly we feel at home and know we have "friends for living." In fact, we have a real sense of belonging and recognize that we are a connecting link with others. Having recovered, we have learned to accept ourselves and others, with all our strengths and weaknesses. We have also learned to accept our past, including the wrongs we have done and the wrongs others have done to us. We now have a better understanding of ourselves, other people, and the causes in our lives. And we have found a heightened sense of purpose and a deepened spiritual life.

Recovery requires *responsible personal action*. We must do the part that depends on us, not others. Therefore we need to outgrow excessive dependence on others and on certain kinds of help. As we recover we require less and less professional help, such as medical intervention and counseling, and we depend increasingly on the help of friends and our GROW groups. After recovery, "to keep order in our minds and lives," we depend on personal, friendly, and spiritual resources, and we no longer require medical intervention or treatment.

Remember Carrie, who became empowered by approaching her doctor and requesting a reduction of her medication? Well, thanks to the support of her GROW group and the persistent use of her own personal resources, Carrie was eventually able to become completely well and was released from her doctor's care. As Carrie worked on her own recovery and growth, she was also serving as a leader to other Growers and to the organization. She was first a group recorder and then an organizer, and she served on both the regional and the branch program teams. In time, she no longer depended on Social Security disability benefits and eventually became a proud wage-earner when she was hired by GROW as a fieldworker. Carrie has now been working for GROW for several years, and her staff responsibilities include supporting and developing groups and conducting training workshops. When she gives her personal testimony at this point in her life, Carrie acknowledges confidently that she no longer fears another breakdown. In fact, she considers her breakdown to be an actual breakthrough to a happy, healthier life.

The Four Causes in Our Lives

We believe the human processes of breakdown, recovery, and growth are complex because the causes in our lives are complex. A person should never be defined merely in terms of diagnosis, treatment, and prognosis. To understand and label people chiefly in medical terms is to put them down to something less than human. Understanding the causes in a person's life requires us to begin with a deep respect for the uniqueness of that individual and the forces of growth and ultimate mystery at work in his or her life.

In GROW we explain personal breakdown, recovery, and growth in terms of four causes: nature, nurture, personal action, and God (or the Overall Cause). We believe we have become the persons we are today because of inherited characteristics, such as temperament, personality, and disposition; the influence of parents, peers, opportunities, and education; the consequences of our personal choices and actions; and our spiritual experiences.

Although we acknowledge the effect of all four causes on our lives, we realize that at this point in our development we have direct control over only two of these causes: personal action—doing the part we must do for ourselves and with others—and our unique spiritual development.

The GROW "Blue Book" and "Brown Book"

As noted above, the GROW groups, its leaders, and the caring and sharing community are all informed and guided by the GROW program, an organized, written philosophy of life and psychology of mental health . The program includes an extensive body of literature developed systematically over the years by GROW leaders. The most frequently used program materials are the Blue Book, entitled "The Program of Growth to Maturity," and the Brown Book, entitled "Readings for Mental Health." Both books are organized around the "Twelve Steps of Recovery and Personal Growth" and are used as educational and practical tools in weekly GROW meetings, and by Growers as problem-solving tools in their daily lives.

The Blue Book measures only five inches by three inches, so it is easy to carry with us at all times. Its everyday wisdom serves as a guide for our GROW groups and is referred to frequently throughout the meetings—during testimonies, problem solving, and reports on progress, and during the educational "middle routine." Newer members are inspired by the example of other members who report success in using the Blue Book guidelines, and these newer Growers learn by example and encouragement to put the program into practice themselves.

The longer readings in the Brown Book provide a further understanding of the GROW program, expand on each of the "Twelve Steps" and illustrate specific attitudes described in the Blue Book. Brown Book readings include writings by our founder, Con Keogh, selections by other authors that illustrate one of the Twelve Steps, and other "Program Commentary" written by GROW leaders and approved through a systematic process at leadership meetings. A selection from the Brown Book, chosen by the organizer, is read aloud and discussed at each weekly meeting.

As noted above, the GROW program is organized around the Twelve Steps, beginning with the Step 1: "We admitted we were inadequate or maladjusted to life." Originally, the first step read, "We admitted we were mentally sick." This wording reflected the initial influence of AA and our early members' insight that, as a first step to recovery, they needed to admit they were sick. This wording was challenged several years later, however, by several inmates of Long Bay Prison in Australia, who were attending a group facilitated by our founder, Con Keogh. The inmates explained they could not relate to this first step because, as they put it, "It's bad enough to admit we're bad, let alone to admit to madness too." As a result, the GROW leaders searched for wording of the first step that could reflect both human conditions—the state of being sick and the state of being in the wrong, and they eventually settled on: "We admitted we were maladjusted." Still later, as the focus of GROW expanded from recovery alone to include prevention, the wording of the first step was changed again to its current form, allowing those members who have never suffered mental illness to "take the first step" comfortably by admitting they are "inadequate to life."

Our program literature, including the Blue Book and the Brown Book, has been updated over the years, with a store of "program commentary" emerging from our worldwide leadership meetings. Some of these writings have been assembled in a workbook and distributed and welcomed throughout the movement. Their contents will contribute to a final and definitive Blue Book, as well as additional volumes of the Brown Book.

Several other books and articles are available from GROW. For example, the Red Book, entitled "Reading for Recovery" was printed in Sydney in 1964 and is the predecessor to the Brown Book. Also available is "Joannie's Story," an inspirational testimony of one member's recovery from paranoid schizophrenia. And highly recommended is Con Keogh's work, entitled *GROW Comes of Age*, which is GROW In Australia's twenty-first birthday book, published in Sydney in 1978. This anniversary edition includes personal testimonies by early members, writings by Con Keogh on our history and philosophy, and short biographies of friends and promoters of the organization known then as RECOVERY.

Grow Is a Program of Recovery and Personal Growth to Maturity

Our long-time leaders dedicated their lives to their personal recovery and to defining the necessary steps leading to this end. These steps—the embodiment of a practical ideal—came about through the resolve of our early leaders to discover the practical guidelines leading to health and wholeness and to record them for posterity. The tangible results of our early members' dedication are our formulated GROW "Program of Recovery and Personal Growth," our group method, and our caring and sharing community. We are profoundly convinced of the effectiveness of our philosophy and methods, because we have been putting them to work successfully in our lives for years. With approximately one thousand mutual-help groups, spread over Australia, the United States, New Zealand, and Ireland—and their accompanying leadership teams, organized training, and organizational structures—we have, after nearly fifty years of growth, become one of the most fully developed, viable organizations in consumer-operated mental health care. And as individual members, through our commitment to full GROW involvement, we have been able to break through to renewed and more meaningful lives and are becoming the whole persons we were always meant to be.

Reference

Young, J. and C. L. Williams (1989). Group process and social climate of GROW, a community mental health organization. *Australian and New Zealand Journal of Psychiatry.* 23 (1): 117-123.

8

The Friends Connection, Philadelphia, Pennsylvania

Jeanie Whitecraft, James Scott,
Joseph Rogers, Bill Burns-Lynch,
Terrance Means, and Mark S. Salzer

> Keep coming back, keep trying a new way.
> —Juntos Podemos, *Together We Can*

The Friends Connection is a consumer-operated peer support program started in 1989 that promotes recovery among people with significant mental health and substance abuse problems (i.e., co-occurring disorders). The name of the program is a takeoff on the title of the 1980's film *The French Connection*, about a major drug bust in France. We help people make a Friends Connection to become clean and sober. We believe friendship and peer support are critical elements in recovery.

A division of the Mental Health Association of Southeastern Pennsylvania, the Friends Connection is based on the notion that recovery requires building a new set of behaviors, cognitions, social networks, and interests, essentially a new life that abstains from substances and enhances mental health. It was born out of consumer advocacy efforts to secure funding for community-based services following the closing of the Philadelphia State Hospital and the long-term commitment of the Office of Mental Health in Philadelphia to consumer-run services. The closing of the Philadelphia State Hospital (also known as Byberry) in the late 1980s provided an opportunity to build appropriate community resources to support the needs of people coming out of the hospital and to provide "diversion" programs using funds that normally would have been used to operate the hospital.

A consumer-led assessment of the needs of the Byberry residents was conducted using funds from the Pennsylvania Office of Mental Health. Consumers developed a questionnaire to assess the needs of residents, interviewed residents, and made themselves available to advocate around those needs. It was noted that a large number of the people who were due to be released from the state hospital upon its closing were unlikely to make successful transitions into the community given the lack of services to address the joint problems of substance abuse and its impact on mental illnesses. Little was known at that time about the scope of co-occurring substance use and mental illness, the impact of substance use, including "recreational" use, on persons with severe mental illnesses, or how to treat these individuals. Moreover, very little thought was given to the possibility of recovery from either disorder; "chronicity," or long-lasting and continuing illness, was viewed as a natural, unrelenting progression, and very few drug-and-alcohol rehabilitation programs dealt with this issue.

Through the efforts of the Coalition for the Responsible Closing of Philadelphia State Hospital, which advocated for state hospital dollars to follow patients into the community, approximately $60 million was allocated to create new community mental health services. The Friends Connection was one of the programs developed to serve the needs of former Philadelphia State Hospital residents. The program now serves former state hospital residents and a group of persons who would have likely been hospitalized there, as well as forensic clients—persons who have committed a crime and are referred directly from jail by Philadelphia's Community Treatment Team.

Funding for Friends Connection is maintained through advocacy efforts that led to the creation in Philadelphia of a behavioral health system through which Medicaid dollars for substance abuse and mental health services are co-mingled. This is a great step forward, since these issues have historically been kept separate and people with co-occurring disorders previously obtained fragmented services from two separate systems. Continued funding and possible expansion of Friends Connection is strengthened as a result of this important coordination of mental health and substance abuse resources.

Jeanie Whitecraft developed the Friends Connection in 1989 in Philadelphia and has directed the program since its inception. She significantly expanded on the ideas underlying a program in Ohio developed by Estelle Richman, secretary of public welfare in Pennsylvania; Marti Knisley, director of mental health, Washington, DC; and Phyllis Solomon, professor of social work at the University of Pennsylvania. The Ohio program linked people in recovery from mental illness and substance abuse with people who were seeking to get into recovery. Similarly, the Friends Connection program is designed to help the participant achieve his or her vision for successful recovery and independent living through support provided by others successfully recovering from similar problems. From personal experience, peers understand the pervasive effects of a disabling condition that often leads to social isolation, withdrawal from the community, and ongoing substance abuse. The Friends Connection staff serve as role models and bring practical experience to assist others with options to support recovery.

The specific goals of the Friends Connection are:

1. Help program participants decrease their substance use.
2. Help program participants increase their community living days by decreasing the number of days spent in inpatient treatment facilities, both psychiatric and drug and alcohol.
3. Increase consumer satisfaction with services by providing a community-based peer support program that integrates rehabilitation interventions for both mental health and substance disorders.

These goals are achieved through skills development in four areas: instrumental, social-emotional, leisure, and recovery skills (see Table 8.1) and are exemplified in the stories told later in this chapter. The development of proficiency in these areas is crucial to the maintenance of psychiatric and residential stability for individuals with co-occurring disorders. Specific program operations are described in the following section.

Program Model

The Friends Connection consists of three components: one-to-one peer support services, sponsorship of group activities, and an alumni program. The program is provided as an adjunct to traditional mental health services (i.e., case management) and has historically targeted those who have had significant recent treatment histories involving hospitalizations for mental health and substance abuse problems. Formal referrals to the Friends Connection are made from traditional mental health services providers. All people admitted into the one-to-one peer support program are screened by supervisory staff and reviewed by the clinical manager, although group activities are open to everyone in the community. Acceptance to the program is contingent on a few eligibility factors, but most important, the person must freely choose to participate. Unlike in many programs, the goal of being clean and sober is not required to partici-

Table 8.1. Skills Targeted by the Friends Connection

Skills	Examples
Instrumental skills enable the consumer to meet basic needs (e.g., food, clothing, shelter, self-maintenance).	1. Activities of daily living 2. Community living skills 3. Money management and budgeting 4. Medication adherence 5. Travel and community orientation 6. Self-monitoring 7. Problem solving
Social-emotional skills help to provide a sense of belonging to a group or community, of well-being, and of family and friendship.	1. Conversation skills 2. Conflict management 3. Problem solving 4. Assertiveness 5. Developing friendships
Leisure skills enhance community integration through participation in recreation activities that are substance free.	1. Recreation and leisure development 2. Knowledge of community recreation resources 3. Travel and community orientation
Recovery skills help to provide the cognitive and behavioral resources necessary to maintain psychiatric stability and substance reduction and abstinence.	1. Utilizing recovery community resources (12-Step fellowships) 2. Finding a "home group" 3. Finding a sponsor 4. Saying "no" to offers to use drugs/alcohol 5. Relapse prevention 6. Medication adherence 7. Problem solving 8. Conflict resolution 9. Self-monitoring 10. Identification of relapse triggers 11. Mental health education 12. Drug and alcohol education

pate in the Friends Connection. Moreover, those who use drugs or alcohol while in the program are not automatically discharged. Program staff, who themselves have personal experience trying to recover from substance abuse, attempt to facilitate any participant's move toward sobriety, understanding that the path to sobriety is not always straight and narrow for those who attempt it and is fraught with bumps and stumbles.

Upon entering the program, the individual is matched with a peer support staff person who is viewed as being most compatible in terms of experience, demeanor, and skills. Matching this peer support staff person with a program participant also requires connecting the person with someone who has a similar drug and alcohol background and, when possible, similar mental health issues. For example, it is better to connect someone whose drug of choice is alcohol with a peer staffer who is in recovery from alcohol abuse, or to connect a participant who has issues of depression or schizophrenia with a peer staffer who has had the same issues. This policy also applies to narcotics or poly-substance use where, whenever possible, similar mental health issues or experience are matched. Often similar experiences between the program participant and the peer support staff person will result in the development of faster and more solid relationships and inspires the first glimmer of hope for recovery.

Choice is a major value of the Friends Connection, and program participants design their own individualized personal plan, setting goals and objectives for themselves and determining specific steps needed to achieve the goal and objective. Goals are updated every three months. For example, participants might indicate that they feel isolated and alone much of the time. They might choose a goal of learning how to increase their social activities and networks and identify steps aimed at enhancing their skills in this area with the assistance of their peer support staff person. A specific step might be, "I will attend the Valentines Day Dance." A second step might be, "At the dance, I will introduce myself to someone I have never met before," and a third step might be, "I will stay late and help clean up." As we support every participant to help them achieve their goals, we work with them on social skills related to these goals.

In setting and meeting goals, the peer support staff person always works with the participant to identify intrinsic motivations that facilitate the promotion of mental health and recovery. An example of this is the case of WR, who was in his fifties and had spent several years in Philadelphia State Hospital. WR had difficulties with alcohol abuse for many years and, upon discharge from the hospital, returned to his old neighborhood and the only friends he knew—his drinking buddies. Soon he spent every day with them, getting intoxicated. Program staff persisted in helping WR learn about alternatives to drinking, while managing his mental health symptoms. After a year of engaging him in various activities, the peer support staff person learned that as a young man WR was a boxing coach in his neighborhood gym and had a passion for boxing. The peer staffer started going to the boxing gym with him and attending matches. Before long, WR found a community center that taught boxing to children and became involved as an assistant coach and support person to the children. WR was thrilled to reconnect with his former passion and to expand that interest into helping children to learn the sport. Over the years, through his addiction and mental illness, WR had given up and forgotten about the flame that once burned within. Once that flame was reignited, he became motivated to stay sober. He began attending Twelve-Step meetings and a day program for his mental health while spending every afternoon training and coaching underprivileged children in the art and sport he loved. At present, with the exception of one relapse, he has been sober for eight years.

The Friends Connection assists the participant to achieve goals and develop skills by emphasizing three program levels. The peer support staff person, in consultation with his or her supervisor, decides which level to emphasize, depending on the needs of the person when entering the program and during involvement in it. A peer support staff person may emphasize Level 1 issues with one person and then begin transitioning to Level 2 in a few months after the relationship is more solid. With other participants the peer staffer may emphasize Level 2 from the beginning while continuing to monitor Level 1 issues.

Level 1

1. We begin with development of rapport and relationship between the peer support counselor and program participant, focusing on one-to-one interaction.
2. We focus on relationship building and identify the person's recreation preferences, and we follow up by participation in the recreational preferences of the participant.
3. While engaging in activities and casual talks about recovery, we begin to identify the person's level of recovery support, and from there begin to identify recovery supports in the community such as the Twelve-Step meetings.

4. As time continues, and based on the individual's progress and level of comfort, we move forward with expansion of recreational options and encourage trying new and different things.
5. By the end of this period, we focus on attending weekly group activities sponsored by the Friends Connection.

An example of moving through Level 1 involves one Friends Connection participant, SJ, who was having a difficult time developing and adjusting to new people in her life, including new supports from the Friends Connection. She was at such a basic level in her trust that, in the beginning, she would not answer her door. So we began to make telephone calls to her a couple of times a week, just to say, "Hi, hope you are well, look forward to talking with you soon." Sometimes we were able to speak with her, and at other times we would just leave a message on her answering machine. Slowly, we were able to have longer conversations on the telephone, and we moved to the point of meeting her just long enough to have a cup of coffee. While gradually spending longer periods of time with SJ, we began to learn more about her interests, and our relationship grew slowly from there.

Once the peer support staff person and the program participant have spent a significant amount of time getting to know each other and learning about the participant's likes and dislikes, they make plans for a greater variety of activities. Participating in activities helps participants achieve goals, such as introducing themselves to new people, to the next step of getting the new friends' telephone numbers, to the third step of calling them. Each new experience builds on the next until participants begin attending group activities. The length of time spent on Level 1 varies with each individual.

Level 2

1. We expand the recovery support network and continue to develop social and leisure skills through participation in Friends Connection group activities.
2. The participant develops peer relationships with other program participants by taking part in group activities planned by Friends Connection peer counselors and staff.
3. We focus on involvement in group activities.

At this level we make plans to engage in social activities with other peer staff and program participants. This is a good way for people to develop friendships and ongoing support as they move through Levels 1 and 2 and prepare for Level 3. During Level 2, participants become familiar enough with each other that they begin to feel comfortable in the social settings and become more motivated to attend group activities in the community. Activities might consist of a small field trip with two or three other peer staffers and their program participants, or perhaps a simple picnic lunch and walk in the park. As reported by one peer support staff person, when he, another staff, and their program participants spent time walking and sitting in the park together on several different occasions, the dynamic of the group began to change from the staff people initiating conversations to the participants initiating conversation and taking the lead. From this point, they began joking with each other and started to make plans to meet each other apart from the peer program staff.

Our philosophy is that people become involved with illicit drugs out of boredom, isolation, and stigmatization. We encourage active community participation to decrease boredom and help people begin to feel better while having something to look forward to in place of using drugs and alcohol. For some, this means reconnecting after a long lost contact with a family member and for others it could be a hobby, poetry, art, or sports. One way we pursue discovering a person's interests is by encouraging program participants to find one new and different kind of activity, place, or thing a month that they have never experienced. Some of the things that program participants enjoy the most are activities they have never experienced and thought they would not like but that produce great joy and happiness when they do try them. This point is important because many people would not pursue new and different things without encouragement or support of a friend or peer. Our experience indicates that those who have been using drugs or alcohol and have struggled with mental illness most of their lives may never have had an opportunity to pursue such activities or potential interests. Learning to recover means learning a whole new way of being in the world. The length of time spent on Level 2 can vary greatly, because it requires the acquisition of new skills and the development of new recovery community social networks.

Level 3

This level is designed to support and encourage participants to increase independence in using supports and activities with others that they have met during Levels 1 and 2. Friends Connection peer support is the catalyst for personal development during this level. The participant

1. is encouraged to independently access community recovery supports;
2. continues participation in ongoing Friends Connection group activities while face-to-face contact with the peer counselor decreases;
3. is introduced to the alumni program and encouraged to attend meetings before discharge to begin to develop friendships and support from the alumni group;
4. focuses on participating more independently in recovery support and recreational activities, while face-to-face contact with the peer support counselor gradually decreases; and
5. attends Friends Connection group activities independently and occasionally meets the peer staffer at a meeting rather than being accompanied. During this time, the peer counselor encourages the participant to call on new supports so that the program is phased out. Participants are encouraged to engage in group activities after they are discharged

During Level 3 a peer support staff person meets participants at a destination, day, and time away from the program rather than picking them up. As time goes on, a plan is made for two program participants to meet each other for an activity at a place of their choice without the presence of a peer support staff person. Gradually, the peer staff see the participants less frequently on a one-to-one basis and transition into seeing them in the larger group activities that are provided by the program every week. By this time, participants know where they can go on any given day of the week and be confident that their friends and other familiar people will be there. Participants at this stage feel more comfortable going out to places on their own.

Recovery Communities and Group Activities

Joining recovery communities of others seeking to make and maintain changes in their lives and to live substance free is a major part of the Friends Connection. The peer support staff teach participants how to find Twelve-Step programs, such as Alcoholics Anonymous, Narcotics Anonymous, or Double-Trouble (co-occurring disorders) that meet their needs, personality, or culture independent of the Friends Connection. We have found that program participants sometimes stop attending meetings because they did not mesh with a particular group; therefore, we make it a point to go with participants to try several different meetings until they find the right place for themselves. The peer support staff person will show program participants how to meet people, get telephone numbers of others in recovery whom they can call for support, and find a "sponsor" who is a person that people in the Twelve-Step meeting rooms buddy with and call to help implement the program when the going gets tough.

In addition to encouraging participation in Twelve-Step groups and other community activities, the Friends Connection sponsors weekly, monthly, and annual group outings. Recovery from both mental illness and substance abuse does not occur in isolation, and the Friends Connection actively works to engage participants in group activities and to develop and maintain a social support network. By sponsoring several of these activities the Friends Connection creates a structured environment where a participant's skill level can be assessed in the natural community setting and where participants can practice the skills they have identified on their rehabilitation plans. These activities include monthly dances attended by as many as 150 to 200 people and weekly group activities such as bowling, billiards, field trips, and skating and swimming parties, along with community activities offered by the city and other public facilities.

Over the years the Friends Connection has traveled south to Baltimore to enjoy the Inner Harbor, sailed on the Hudson River to visit the Statue of Liberty, and taken the elevator to the top of the Empire State Building in New York City. We have listened to the brilliance of an orchestra; been awed by the magic of the circus big top; danced to the rhythms of jazz, pop, blues, and rock at concerts; and rooted for our favorite Philadelphia sports teams. All of these experiences, and many other social, cultural, and educational activities, expand our participants' horizons, encourage their sobriety, and engage them in the communities where they live.

The group activities are available to everyone in the community, even if they do not receive one-to-one peer support in the Friends Connection. These activities continue to be a support and resource for people who graduate from the program and have established a support network in the natural community. They may continue to take part in program activities as they choose, even if they do not want more formal involvement with Friends Connection.

For the many graduates who do want to maintain a strong bond with the Friends Connection, we have the Alumni Program. Those who choose to be alumni continue to receive support from and feel a sense of belonging with each other. The Alumni Program holds fundraisers, trips, and activities of its own, and alumni act as role models for other program participants by attending the regular Friends Connection weekly group activities in the community.

Impact on Program Participants

The Friends Connection has been interested in participating in research to document the success of our efforts and promote greater general acceptance of consumer-operated programs. A small-scale study of the Friends Connection was conducted in the mid-1990s (Klein, Cnaan, and Whitecraft 1998). Ten participants in our program were compared to twenty people with co-occurring disorders from the same case management agency that did not participate in the program. The people involved in the Friends Connection were found to have fewer crisis events and hospitalizations, improved social functioning, greater reduction in substance use, and improvements in quality of life compared with the nonmatched comparison group over a six-month period. The Friends Connection, along with the other programs described in this book, is currently involved in a more rigorous randomized, controlled trial examining its effectiveness. The multi-site study of consumer-operated services programs funded by the U.S. Substance Abuse and Mental Health Services Administration that began in 1998 has ended, but results of the study are still being tallied.

Participant stories are another way to see the impact of this program. The story of JP is one example: after sixteen years living in what he describes as "literal hell," JP is picking up the pieces of his life. JP was a talented musician and athlete who dropped out of college when he first became ill with schizophrenia. He spent years bouncing in and out of almost every psychiatric facility and detoxification center in Philadelphia, fighting both his mental illness and problems with alcohol and drugs. He heard voices, had violent episodes, tried to kill himself several times, and endured periods of great loneliness while living in rented rooms. Despite his years of dogged attendance at Alcoholics Anonymous (AA) meetings, sobriety remained elusive.

He was introduced to the Friends Connection in 1997 after becoming stabilized on a medication that helped control the debilitating symptoms of his illness. Together he and his peer support staff person took walks, ate dinner, shot pool, went to jazz concerts and the theater, and attended recovery meetings. With this support, JP got back in touch with activities he liked, and he started to develop a healthy social network. When he was ready to work, the Friends Connection introduced him to Mainstream, a consumer-run vocational and life-skills training program also administered by the Mental Health Association of Southeastern Pennsylvania, which works with homeless people who have mental illness. Most also have a drug or alcohol addiction.

Mainstream staff helped JP move out of his rented room into one of the program's one-bedroom apartments, enrolled him in its three-month job-readiness program, and provided intensive job counseling. An internship for JP led to a permanent part-time position as a transit clerk and a handyman. Stable on his medication and sober, JP now plans to attend college. He is also president of the Friends Connection Alumni Program and serves on the Friends Connection Advisory Board. AC's story demonstrates one of the Friends Connection's mottos, "Keep coming back, and keep trying a new way."

When people leave substance use for recovery programs, the hardest thing for them to do is to learn what there is to do besides getting "high." All the people they have known and things they have done up until this time have been about drugs and alcohol. Once they give these up, they are often lost, unable to find new people, places, and things to do that are clean and sober. Friends Connection offers the link for people to make that community transition to successful recovery. Most people had given up hope for AC and concluded that it was just a matter of time before he perished from drugs and alcohol. He was often found in the streets or at police stations, barefoot, with foot infections and barely able to walk. He would disappear for days at a time, delusional and on drug binges. Since he was a Latino, we connected him with a Latino peer at Friends Connection. For the first year in the program it was "catch as catch can" with AC. Sometimes we would connect with him by happenstance on the street or just by checking out the police stations where he would go to sleep. AC had traditional treatment services but did not connect with them for very long at any given time. Sometimes he would come in off the streets and be fine for a few days, but then the cycle would start again. There were times when his physical condition was so poor he would need to be hospitalized.

Slowly he began to connect with a peer support staff person and started going to Twelve-Step meetings. Still struggling with his mental health and addiction issues, and periodically lost to the streets, AC met with his peer, who persisted in taking him in like family, escorting him to Latino cultural events, and just doing simple things, such as working on the engine of a car. One day AC's peer staffer felt that if he could get AC to a national AA convention it might make a difference. Sure enough, AC went to the convention and was astounded to see more than a thousand people struggling for recovery. When he told his story, he received a standing ovation and was transformed by the caring warmth and support he felt from so many people also in recovery. From that day forward he began to grow. He attended regular meetings and continued to go to AA conventions. AC has been in recovery for six years and, with the exception of one setback, has been working at the same job for four years. He lives independently, has a son that he supports, is an officer in the Friends Connection Alumni Program, and facilitates the Spanish Speaking Double Trouble meeting for the Friends Connection.

Impact on Peer Staff

Often ignored in evaluations of consumer-run programs are the benefits that mutual support has on staff who are themselves in recovery. Salzer and Liptzin Shear (2002) studied the benefits to peer staff of the Friends Connection. Interviews were conducted with fourteen peer staff, who unanimously pointed to facilitating another's recovery as the principal benefit of the program for them. Such a response has special meaning in the context of those involved in Twelve-Step-oriented programs, since Step 12 advocates for helping others as part of one's own recovery. "When I go home at night, that's the rewarding part," one staff member said, "knowing that I made a difference in somebody else's life." Another noted, "It wasn't the pay, I can tell you that. . . . [It was] being here with someone who would normally not get out and actually watch them get out or take a chance."

Peer staff also reported that they were able to practice their own recovery. They mentioned specific features that helped them do so, including building their own positive support networks, improving their ability to behave responsibly, dealing with personal problems through self-discovery and skill development, and learning about things to do when bored other than using drugs or alcohol, such as becoming active in the community. One peer support staff person reported that his position taught him to "embrace life and enjoy things," while another reported that his role helped him to really "enjoy" recovery. A third peer staffer said, "It helps me with my own recovery, you know, because I take my consumers to meetings—so therefore, I'm getting a meeting also." Another staffer noted that, in other jobs, that kind of benefit "is something that you rarely get."

Finally, working in a recovery-oriented, supportive work environment was also viewed as important, where struggles with mental health and substance abuse problems were an asset rather than a liability. The Friends Connection staff indicated that they felt that they were allowed to be themselves and not hide their problems: "With other jobs . . . you have to do this, you have to do that. I mean . . . you know what you have to do, but you're allowed to be you." Staff also said that they obtained support from co-workers, including supervisors, who came from similar backgrounds. "Here, people understand what the disease of addiction is (and mental health problems)—we understand some of these things because we been through it." Two others reported that they liked getting paid for things they would do anyway, like attending Twelve-Step group meetings and helping others.

Administrative and Staffing Structure

The Friends Connection is a program of the Mental Health Association of Southeastern Pennsylvania whose president and CEO, Joseph Rogers, is an internationally known consumer advocate, and at least half of whose board of directors are people who self-identify as mental health consumers. The program comprises a manager, three supervisors, a field coach, an administrative coordinator, and twelve paid peer support staff who each support six to eight participants. The program manager oversees the successful implementation of the program, working closely with supervisory staff, updating policies and procedures, and recommending new hires and terminations.

The three supervisors each supervise several peer support staff persons, and each of the supervisors reports to the program manager. The senior supervisor is responsible for the smooth functioning of daily operations and is the person in charge when the program manager is absent. The supervisor who is also the continuous quality-improvement coordinator supervises intake assessment and goal updates for each of the program participants and coordinates staff schedules and documentation. The supervisor who is also the alumni coordinator provides staff with education and skill building and coordinates the Alumni Program.

The field coach implements a structured field orientation program for new peer support staff and works directly in the field with them, solving problems with senior staff and manages crises that occur in the field as well as unplanned schedule changes. The activities coordinator plans program and community trips and activities and facilitates outreach (advertisement) of these events. The administrative coordinator electronically computes program units of service and keeps records in compliance with funding regulations.

Peer Support Staff

Peer support staff are required to be in recovery and stable with their mental health issues, which generally means that they are living satisfying lives in the community and have not been recently hospitalized for psychiatric reasons, have a minimum of three years of abstinence from an addiction to substances, and actively work a recovery program (e.g., as a member of a Twelve-Step community or other recovery-oriented supportive community). Also required is a minimum of two years of work experience in direct services in the behavioral health care field. Staff are recruited through job postings at consumer-operated programs, word of mouth through various recovery and rehabilitation agencies, and at times, newspaper listings. Peer support staff report to their supervisor once a week for individual supervision and informally throughout the week as needed. Peer support staff also participate in two full staff meetings a week to receive mutual support and process the successes and challenges they experience in their work.

Staff Training and Supports

The program provides special field trips and activities for staff. These field trips and activities help staff build on their individual skills, confidence, and self-introspection. One example is our annual outward-bound trip; staff are taken to an undisclosed location to engage in individual skill and team-building exercises. We have climbed the hills of the Pocono Mountains and hiked on wilderness trails, floated on tubes and rafts down the Delaware River, and visited the New Jersey shore to fly kites and go bird watching. We have gone on hunting and gathering excursions, taken walks on the cliffs of Jerico Mountain, climbed Bowmen's Tower, explored the history of the Revolutionary and Civil Wars in various historical parks, including Washington Crossing and Valley Forge, learned first hand about the Amish tradition in Lancaster, Pennsylvania, and just sat in the quiet of the woods to experience the silence and nature.

Many activities for the staff are organized simply for the experience or sheer enjoyment of it; others are organized to build skills and provide training. Some staff report that at the beginning of each trip that because they are not told where they are going, they feel some anxiety; others are exhilarated by a sense of adventure. Either way, the outings help staff to empathize with program participants when we teach them to engage in something they have never done before.

Growth of the Friends Connection

After many years of successful outcomes, the Friends Connection began to build a positive reputation. We made presentations at hundreds of conferences and in other counties in the surrounding areas as well as in other states that expressed interest in this model as a way to expand their service provision.

In 1989, the Friends Connection program faced several challenges. One of them was earning status as an equal player in the Philadelphia mental health care system among many professionals. But we persisted, maintaining confidence in ourselves and knowing that, as recovering people, we had valuable information that could benefit others. And finally we were granted status as an equal player in the system, with a place in treatment team meetings and clinical reviews.

At these meetings, when case managers and clinical professionals heard us during case conferences, they began to value what we had to say. They had often been at a loss for how to deal with some of the issues that people with co-occurring disorders struggle with. At times we would use self-disclosure to help them understand how to work with a person who displays certain behaviors. It was a rewarding process for the non-consumer-provider community and us; eventually Friends Connection came to be considered a valuable resource and member of the support team.

Another challenge was finding consumers who were living successfully in the community and interested in working as staff in the program. Over the years we have developed a pipeline for identifying and recruiting successful staff, including referrals from mental health and substance abuse agencies and other consumer-run agencies. Also, we have learned that to retain staff and allow them to work effectively, we must teach them how to provide support without crossing boundaries as a provider and to how to find low-cost community resources and activities. Most important, however, we must provide them intensive individual and group support, with weekly individual supervision and twice-weekly staff meetings. Staff meetings are especially valuable because each person has an opportunity to report on personal challenges and successes and receive support from the others. They also receive support during staff meetings from the program manager and other program staff. Additionally, staff needed a lot of support to learn how to provide support without crossing boundaries as a provider, and how to find low-cost community recourses and activities.

Since 1989 more than four hundred people in Philadelphia have participated in Friends Connection one-to-one peer support, and several thousand have participated in the numerous community activities promoting fellowship and recovery. In 1994 the Friends Connection received a Proclamation from Mayor Ed Rendell for their contribution to dual-diagnosis in the city of Philadelphia. The program received an Honorable Mention in 2000 from the Thomas M. Wernert Award for Innovation in Community Behavioral Health by the David and Laurel Lovell Foundation in collaboration with the National Association of Community Behavioral Health Directors. The award gives national recognition to programs that demonstrate innovation and creativity while ensuring community and consumer participation.

Finally, in fall 2000, Montgomery County, which borders Philadelphia County, became the first of the five surrounding counties of Philadelphia to implement the Friends Connection program. In 2000 the Friends Connection was included among a select few programs in Pennsylvania to take part in a demonstration to examine the feasibility of funding such programs, defined as "mobile psychosocial," through Medicaid. Medicaid payments would be made on a fee-for-service basis and such funding would also allow the program to expand its services to those with less extensive histories of intensive service use. While the Friends Connection has taken steps to meet funding requirements, the status of this demonstration program is unclear. The Friends Connection continues to receive strong support from the Philadelphia Office of Mental Health and the behavioral health service community in general and continued support is expected well into the future.

Friends Connection in Philadelphia County is funded with county dollars as well but the Connection is also prepared to meet Psychiatric Rehabilitation regulations for Medicaid funding in the future. Since Friends Connection has been an urban model for more than a decade we have made some minor adjustments in the program to adapt to a suburban environment. The challenges are mostly geographic. Public transportation runs less frequently in the suburbs than in Philadelphia, it takes longer for travel, and there are fewer community resources.

It is an honor that the Friendship Connection is recognized as an important adjunct to traditional services for people in recovery. In the future we plan to disseminate the program throughout Pennsylvania and hope ultimately to be recognized as a national model for addressing the recovery needs of people with co-occurring disorders.

Conclusion

Peer support staff persons are indeed a unique group of people. They know from firsthand experience what it takes to recover from drug and alcohol addiction and mental illness. The result of staff success in their recovery is a desire to support others in their own quest to achieve similar goals. The willingness to offer a hand up to someone who is considering a new way of life is the very basis of who staff are and what they do. Staff themselves have taken many paths to reach this point in their own lives where they walk alongside others just beginning a journey to recovery. Together as consumers and professionals in the field of behavioral health, consumer staff and participants weave a common tapestry to promote and honor recovery. It is wholeheartedly believed that recovery from addiction and mental illness is possible because staff have lived it.

References

Klein, A., R. Cnaan, and J. Whitecraft. 1998. The significance of peer social support with dually diagnosed clients: Findings from a pilot study. *Research on Social Work Practice* 8:529–51.

Salzer, M. S., and S. Liptzin Shear. 2002. Identifying consumer-provider benefits in evaluations of consumer-delivered services. *Psychiatric Rehabilitation Journal* 25:281–88.

PART IV
Educational Programs

9
Advocacy Unlimited, Inc., Connecticut

Yvette Sangster

Advocacy Unlimited, Inc. (AU) is one of the largest statewide not-for-profit advocacy-training organizations in the country, operated by and for people in recovery with psychiatric disabilities. AU educates and creates a network of peer advocates, strategically placed throughout the state of Connecticut. Our headquarters are located in Wethersfield, just seven miles from the state capital of Hartford. Permanent staff work out of this central office, but advocate volunteers and educators are available state-wide, working out of the social clubs, drop-in centers, and clubhouses where people in recovery with psychiatric disabilities congregate. Our advocates provide individual advocacy and support, and they conduct workshops to educate the members of the consumer community in self, systems, and legislative advocacy, among other skills. The advocates also join local provider boards, councils, and task forces of funding organizations to ensure that the consumer voice is heard.

With this network, we are able to produce a clear and unified voice to reform the mental health system and to build the grassroots consumer movement in our state. AU promotes self-determination and works to put an end to "parallel communities," where persons with psychiatric disabilities are housed, employed, and offered medical services separate from persons who have not been labeled with a psychiatric diagnosis. My earliest work as an advocate began after my son was severely injured in

I want to thank and give credit to all the people who have given their time and talent to this chapter, editing or writing: Sally Clay, Robert Slate, Nancy Covell, Linda Dunakin, and the Advocacy Unlimited, Inc., advocates whose words are quoted throughout this chapter.

a car accident in 1984. I was told that the extent of his traumatic brain injury would prevent him from ever leaving an institutional setting. I was further told that there were no services in place and no funding available to help my son move beyond this pessimistic vision. I immediately understood that to ensure that my son had a future, I would have to act as an advocate for him. I worked hard to see that he received the proper treatment and services. Through this work, I became keenly aware of the need for organized advocacy for people with disabilities. I saw that the social welfare and medical systems were woefully unresponsive to the expressed needs of persons with disabilities. They created bureaucracies and organizations that fostered sick roles and dependency, disregarded personal choice and self-determination, and ignored individuals' strengths and abilities—while instead focusing on deficits and limitations.

Some years before my son's accident, I myself had been diagnosed with a mental illness and had experienced firsthand how persons with mental health disabilities are told to set their sights lower and to aban-

Figure 9.1. AU Logo

don many of their dreams. Like my son, I, too, had once been told that I could not do certain things because of my disability. Since the age of ten, however, I had learned to set tasks for myself as a way to cope with my disability, and when I was confronted with imposed limitations, I took them on as a challenge.

After I joined the physical disability movement in an effort to create the supports that would eventually help my son walk freely into his future, I became more aware of the horrific barriers that confront all people with disabilities. I saw that many of my peers continued to experience the abuses and prejudices that batter people with psychiatric diagnoses, causing them to believe that they are "less than" other people. I saw, too, a lack of belief in recovery, and a lack of organized advocacy to foster self-determination and a healing environment.

In 1990, I chose to focus my energy in the mental health arena. Most mental health service providers, I discovered, embraced a medical model that viewed mental illness as a defect to "cure," without regard to the individual's choices or abilities. Too often providers believed that people with mental health disabilities just needed to be medicated and cared for: "Do *for* them because they cannot do for themselves."

From the physical disability movement, I brought with me the Independent Living philosophy of "doing *with*" a person rather than "doing *for*" the person. Accepting this philosophy required a huge culture change for the mental health system, which was accustomed to "doing for." My personal experience of feeling disempowered qualified me to speak out with, and on behalf of, my brothers and sisters with psychiatric disabilities. I founded AU in 1994. At the time, I was working as a legal rights advocate for Connecticut Legal Rights Project, Inc. (CLRP), and I designed and implemented a new division of consumer education of CLRP. We set up AU under the umbrella of CLRP, which provided us with office space and technical assistance until we could set out on our own. Although the idea for the new organization was mine, I was able to use contacts that I had made with advocates and officials around the state, all of whom gave me invaluable advice and support. These contacts, as well as experts within the mental health and legal systems, worked with me to develop the curriculum that we now use to train advocates. In 1998, the Division of Consumer Education became independently incorporated as Advocacy Unlimited, Inc.

While working at CLRP, I assisted in reactivating an often-discounted grievance procedure in state mental health facilities. That this procedure was seldom used pointed to a mental health system that was both nonresponsive and stagnant. The grievance form was posted in a glass case in the hallway of the Fairfield Hills Hospital, a long-stay psychiatric hospital. But it was never used. The patients did not know that they could file a grievance, and neither the head nurse nor even the affirmative action officer knew what the grievance procedure was. When I pointed this out to the nurse, she took the form out of the glass case and made copies, and CLRP staff began to use it. At first, hospital staff dismissed the grievances and blamed the patients who submitted them. To counter this response, we started tracking the complaints, and CLRP took the results to the Freedom of Information Commission of the State of Connecticut.

As a result, CLRP and the Department of Mental Health, in settlement of the complaint, entered into an agreement that included the stipulation that grievances must be addressed within a timeline and acknowledged the right to appeal and the right to a fair hearing process. (See *www.state. ct.us/FOI/1993FD/19931110/FIC1993–163.htm* for a record that the matter was resolved.)

This agreement set the stage for several future consumer rights victories, including a standard grievance process and rights regulations for clients of the state mental health system and those funded by the department. AU worked with the addiction advocacy organization Connecticut Communities for Addiction Recovery for three years to get into place a recovery policy and core values that were adopted by the Department of Mental Health and Addiction Services September 16, 2002 as "Commissioner's Policy Statement No. 83." "The purpose of this policy," according to the statement, "is to formally designate the concept of 'recovery' as the overarching goal of the service system operated and funded by the Department of Mental Health and Addiction Services" (see *www.dmhas. state.ct.us/policies/policies83.htm*). This case proves once again that with patience and hard work we can change the system and be heard.

Many factors have to be considered when starting a peer-run advocacy organization. Success depends on the consumers who do the organizing, the funding available, the state's receptiveness to the program, and appropriate connections within the state. In the beginning one of our biggest problems was to find funding. The search took a little over a year. Not many people want to support a consumer advocacy organization because advocates are thought to be troublemakers. Furthermore, state and federal grants do not allow lobbying, and legislative advocacy is difficult to accomplish within some funding criteria. For these reasons AU is called an educational program, and we teach people to represent themselves in areas of system and legislative change. As an educational program, we qualify for funding from the Department of Mental Health and Addiction Services and other government agencies.

I founded AU for the primary purpose of educating others with psychiatric disabilities about how to advocate for themselves and for their peers. In the belief that advocacy begins with the "self," with my advisers and experts I developed a curriculum that allows people to recognize their individual paths to recovery.

AU's Advocacy Education program teaches that people in recovery with psychiatric disabilities are allowed the same rights and opportunities for the meaningful and personally satisfying life all members of society expect. People with psychiatric disabilities learn the skills necessary to play a central role in the planning and delivery of mental health services that directly affect their lives. AU educates individuals in self, systems, and legislative advocacy skills. AU's students empower themselves to make informed choices about their own care and to chart their own recoveries and futures. The most important attainment for consumer advocates is empowerment. Their anger is a motivation to gain life skills, and they become role models to show other consumers that they can do it, too. The work that advocates do takes time and effort and patience. The rewards are a full and satisfying life with all doors opened for their future. AU is successful because we help people look at both their abilities and their areas for improvement, turning their disappointments and what they think as failures into positive ways to move forward.

Administration and Staffing

By mandate of our by-laws, people in recovery with psychiatric disabilities constitute the majority of the board of directors and staff of AU. The very nature of our mission requires that our officers serve as role models and mentors, and thus the board president and executive director are always people in recovery.

Anyone involved in developing an organization needs to have patience and the ability to think creatively, along with basic business skills, supervisory expertise, and expertise in concept development and in networking, negotiating, fund raising, creating budgets, building infrastructure, and developing management and personnel. I was fortunate enough to have a great many mentors, including an experienced accountant and board members who had these skills and were willing to assist me in learning them. I would have found it most helpful, however, to have had these skills before starting. AU's paid staff comprises an executive director, two educators, an advanced education coordinator, an Internet technology coordinator, and an administrative assistant. The executive director is the chief executive officer responsible for all administrative activities. Among other duties, the director is charged with setting the budget and hiring and supervising all staff to meet the mission and the goals of the organization. The educators coordinate field activities and teach classes, and the Internet technology coordinator maintains the Web page *www.mindlink.org* and other communications.

While job descriptions of most staff call for a bachelor's degree in a related field and minimum of two years of public relations, consideration is given to a combination of life experience and education, if these demonstrate equivalence to formal education and the capacity to perform the requirements of the position.

Personnel issues are one of the biggest hurdles to cross. As a consumer organization, our priority is to hire people in recovery whenever possible. One of the obstacles is that many people in recovery have not worked for many years. So training and education are very important, especially cross training to allow personnel to fill in other jobs when necessary. But most important is flexibility and a good support system to encourage the efforts of the people in recovery when things are not going well. In a small organization like AU, however, with a limited number of people (six) to do a lot of work, covering for anyone who does not come to work is difficult. Others in the office feel an enormous amount of pressure, and someone has to pick up the slack.

An important task is to teach the responsibilities of employment to persons in recovery. People who come out of supported employment, in a system that asks them to buy into their illness, sometimes find it difficult to make the change to the idea that they are capable and competent and that they have a responsibility to their employer. Persons in recovery often must be taught to take responsibility to maintain their wellness. Professional ethics is a big issue when hiring people from within one's own ranks. It is hard to draw the line between friendship and business, and it is hard to adopt a professional relationship with people who are one's peers, while still keeping that peer-to-peer quality that is necessary. When intense personal relationships develop and then dissolve, the organization itself can suffer.

The egos of people who have been disenfranchised for most of their lives and then achieve a position of some power sometimes get in the way of their doing their jobs. When dealing with others on a peer-to-peer level they might try to take a position of superiority, rather than working from a position of equality. Constant awareness is necessary for the employee and volunteer advocates to grow in the ability to serve people in recovery. Senior staff can help in this situation by acting as role models of appropriate behavior. When a situation arises at AU in which people get too full of themselves, the peer advocates and peer staff help to bring them back to earth with the rest of us. One of our sayings at AU is, "You can't lead from the horse but from the ground with the rest of us."

Funding

AU received its initial funding was from the Connecticut Department of Mental Health and Addiction Services (DMHAS), under Commissioner Albert Solnit. We were fortunate to have a department in this state that was forward thinking and that believed that advocacy was a key factor in the management of a high quality service system. Commissioner Solnit, who called us his "eyes and ears," counted on us to let him know whether he was doing a good job. Sometimes he did not like what he heard, but he always listened.

If an advocacy education program is to be effective with system and policy change it must maintain its integrity. Fear of losing funding should never be part of the equation when taking stands or making statements to improve the services and lives of people you serve. Many people have asked me how AU can do advocacy work and still keep its funding from the DMHAS. My answer is that I never think of telling anything but the truth, and when the truth changes, I change what I have to say. I tell both the good and the bad about the program and needs of the people we serve, and in doing so I have gained the trust of the people we serve and the respect of the funding organizations we deal with.

AU currently receives funds from the Connecticut DMHAS, from federal grants, and from a modest number of private donors. We maintain these funding sources by virtue of our demonstrable record of performance in training and nurturing effective peer advocates. Agencies fund AU because the program works. Nevertheless, one of the biggest problems for all consumer-run services is finding funds to continue. And finding funds requires skill in research, grant writing, and problem solving.

The Advocacy Education Course

AU's core service is the rigorous Advocacy Education program, which offers individuals with psychiatric disabilities the skills and education they need to become leaders in their communities. The topics covered in these classes are listed on the AU Web site at *www.mindlink.org/ed_course.html* (see Figure 9.2).

Classes are taught by experts in each subject area: advocacy by the Connecticut Legal Rights and the Office of Protection and Advocacy, the structure of the mental health system and issues by the DMHAS, and SSI (Supplemental Security Income) entitlements by a staff person from the Social Security Administration. There are several reasons for having ex-

Figure 9.2. Advocacy Education Program

Advocacy Education Course Outline
The following are some but not all of the topics and skills that
our students learn. Each class is designed to meet the needs of
the particular group of students, and additional topics may be
included:

Informational Topics
General information about advocacy
History of the Consumer Movement
Americans with Disabilities Act
Legislative process, talking with legislators, and testifying
        at legislative hearings
Fair Housing Act
Catchment Area Councils
Social Security Benefits/Title 19 (Medicaid)
Stigma
Rehabilitation Act
Dept. of Mental Health and Addiction Svcs.
— DMHAS Grievance Process
— Advisory structure of DMHAS
Hope and Recovery

Skill Building Topics
Stress and Time Management
Organization and Prioritization
Networking Skills
Goal Setting
Body Language
Public Speaking
Participating on boards
Negotiation and Documentation
Researching Skills
Team Building
How to use the media
Getting your voice heard

perts in each area do the teaching. The students can get quick, accurate, and up-to-date answers to their questions, and they can start networking with the instructors, who have knowledge and skills they can call on later when they are in the field. Also, the students can feel confidence in the education they receive and they feel a sense of pride that they are important enough to be taught by these experts. Classes are presented in a lecture format with concluding questions and answers.

People who take the course can get three college credits, a source of motivation for them to go back to college for still more credit. Students receive modest stipends as reimbursement for course-related expenses, and scholarships are available for graduates to attend conferences. The intensive fourteen-week course is offered approximately twice a year at various locations around Connecticut. Each class is limited to ten students so that each student gets individual attention in an environment that is conducive to learning. A tremendous commitment is required of the students. Besides attendance at fourteen seven-hour classes, the course requires the completion of challenging reading and other homework assignments related to advocacy, as well as weekly public speaking activities.

The Advocacy Education program provides individuals with all the practical information and training they need to become successful advocates and leaders in their communities. Four themes run through the program and are reinforced in every session.

- *Work with people, not for people, as they find their path to self-empowerment.* We believe in the strength and the ability of individuals to control their own lives, accomplish their own goals, and shape their own destinies. Our objective is not to take charge of other people's lives and make them dependent on us but to help them find their own light and strength, master their abilities, and achieve their goals.
- *Follow through all individual and group advocacy.* Many people with psychiatric disabilities have experienced the mental health system as uncaring, unresponsive, and unreliable. We set high standards for professionalism and honor our responsibility to the people we work with.
- *Document all activities as a key element of the work.* Advocacy work frequently involves disputes, disagreements, and contradictory versions of events and facts. It is imperative that actions and conversations be clearly documented so that credibility and accountability can be clearly established. Each advocate submits a monthly report documenting individual advocacy; from these reports systems issues or problem providers are identified.

- *Believe in recovery and self-determination.* We believe that faith in the possibilities of recovery and self-determination is a necessary precursor to actual recovery and self-determination in ourselves and in those we work with. We are all born with the power of self-determination!

Since effective communication is essential to an advocate's success, students devote several hours each week to public speaking. They are videotaped weekly giving their speeches, and they receive constructive feedback from the instructor and the other students in the class. Critical thinking and discussion is encouraged, including questions about AU and the education program itself. At the end of every session, students submit written evaluations of all presenters, the AU course, and their teacher. During the class, participants discuss their spiritual or religious beliefs and recount personal experiences. Rules of etiquette and professionalism, including showing respect for one another, are observed at all times.

Students are recruited for classes in a variety of ways. AU educators and former graduates of the program often recruit new students through presentations conducted in areas of the state where additional advocates are needed. Consumers also apply at AU's Web site *www.mindlink.org,* in response to advertisements in newsletters, and through applications that are distributed at AU graduations, clubhouses, drop-in centers, social clubs, and other locations where consumers assemble.

Those participating in the Advocacy Education program come from all communities, including white and African American and Hispanic, gay and straight. The majority of members are white, reflecting the population that most often joins mental health programs and consumer groups. However, AU conducts outreach to minorities through churches and other locations and is currently creating an Hispanic advocacy class. To participate in the Advocacy Education program, interested persons must be willing to be public about their experiences with mental illness and have a strong desire to make changes in the mental health system for themselves and others. They must also be registered voters. Before applicants are accepted, they are interviewed by three people—the teacher ("educator") of the class, a graduate of the program, and the AU executive director. Applicants are rated according to the interviewers' perception of the applicant's readiness for the program. Those applicants who are not selected the first time they apply are encouraged to assist an advocate in the field and to participate in advocacy efforts. Their applications are put back into the pool to be considered for the next class interviews.

Despite differences in personal experiences, AU members share a common philosophy and determination to succeed. AU looks for people who genuinely believe that they can make a difference in their own and others' lives. AU believes that recovery is possible, that recovery is a positive process unique for each individual, and that well-educated and committed peers acting as advocates and support can be critical to an individual's recovery.

A cardinal requirement is that potential advocates be willing to support others' individual choices, even when that choice is in conflict with the advocate's own belief about what would be best for that person. Further, program participants must complete an internship and commit to attending bimonthly meetings, at which they recount their experiences, brainstorm on the direction of advocacy efforts statewide, and make comments and suggestions about AU programming and development. Graduates of the Advocacy Education program become advocate volunteers who then provide individual advocacy by helping consumers assess their full range of options and achieve personal goals in psychiatric treatment, health care, work, housing, and all other aspects of their lives.

At AU, there is never any threat of commitment to an institution, clinical diagnosis, or unwanted treatment. Such threats would be antithetical to AU's entire philosophy and very purpose for existence. All AU educational classes and events are voluntary and free of charge, although students are expected to make a serious commitment to their Advocacy Education program.

AU believes that many of the skills necessary to become a successful advocate also are important for pursuing a successful recovery. We believe that advocacy and recovery are two processes that go hand in hand. Students' self-esteem is increased as they overcome the challenges associated with learning complex skills and information needed for advocacy, discover that they can help others in addition to themselves, and begin to recognize their own strengths, worth, and capabilities.

Advocate Placement

Program graduates fulfill their internship by devoting six hours a week for six months to volunteer advocacy in their communities. In this way, AU reaches into local communities throughout Connecticut and teaches other consumers the skills they need to advocate for themselves.

The volunteer community commitment is detailed below.

- *Two hours of individual and systems advocacy.* The advocates post office hours at their local drop-in center, social club, or clubhouse, indicating that they are available at the same time and location every week to help individual consumers or groups of consumers resolve problems pertaining to mental health issues. For example, to help consumers who have problems with medications, they teach effective ways to negotiate with providers and encourage record keeping. They assists the individual in gathering information and making informed choices through the proper channels. In this role advocates can serve as mentors as they model their skills.
- *Two hours of community education.* Advocates serve their fellow consumers by inviting guest speakers to the drop-in, social club, or clubhouse and developing and presenting workshops designed to promote recovery through knowledge, improved decision making, and ever-increasing self-confidence. Members at the consumer organization suggest topics of special interest to them. Two such presentations must be offered monthly, and the advocate is responsible for publicizing as well as planning the events.
- *Two hours of community mobilization.* The first of two separate but interrelated components of this requirement is network building, which involves inviting other consumers and interested parties to become part of the Action Alert Fax Network (see below). The second component involves starting and chairing a committee to explore transportation options, such as bus lines, car pools, and van pools, and running fundraisers to have monies available when there is a need to move people to Hartford or wherever else advocacy efforts are needed.

Graduates are also expected to make follow-up telephone calls to advise AU of their progress. While they are actively working within their community placement, they call their educator at least once a week for support, advice, and consultation. AU also provides answers to questions arising out of the individual advocate's work, as well as the support of AU resources, such as systems advocacy work, workshops, mobilization, and networking. Thus, the Advocacy Education program through its graduates, adds to the number of consumers equipped to make informed choices and take action to shape mental health policy and advocate for change. They move from an "I want, I need" thinking process to a "We want, we need" way of thinking and acting and come to understand the power of numbers in making a real difference. This change in their thinking is reflected in their advocate monthly reports about the work they do during their internship. For sample statements from these reports, see Figure 9.3.

Figure 9.3. Samples from Individual Advocacy Reports

- Individual has been treated rudely at a local pharmacy. Advocate assisted person to get the district managers phone number to file a complaint. Manager apologized and said he would take care of the situation. No further problems reported.
- Person felt that they were mistreated in emergency room. Advocate assisted person to file grievance at hospital.
- Person feels that their treatment plan does not meet their needs. Advocate assisted person to get copy of treatment plan, reviewed it with person, and helped the person to develop a treatment plan that they felt met their needs to present to treatment team.
- Assisted a person to file a change of address card at post office.
- Person wants a less restrictive treatment in nursing home. Advocate assisted person to list issues and concerns to present to treatment team.
- Assisted person to apply for assistance from the Department of Rehabilitation Services for work support.
- Assisted person to get legal assistance with recent arrest.
- Assisted person to negotiate with landlord about repairs, connected person with legal services in regards to Fair Housing Act.

Graduates of the program also become involved with legislative advocacy and networking, testifying before the legislature, working with the Connecticut DMHAS, and joining various committees and councils to ensure that consumers have a voice everywhere in making decisions about mental health services and policy. Those forums include but are not limited to the state-mandated Catchment Area Councils, the Connecticut Valley and Cedarcrest Hospital advisory boards, the Office of Protection and Advocacy for Persons with Mental Illness Advisory Board, special task forces at the DMHAS, local service provider boards, and local Mental Health Authority advisory councils. Again, advocates' reports reflect the work they do (see Figure 9.4.)

At the time of this writing AU has graduated 200 advocates. These advocate-graduates have offered supportive advocacy services on more than 3,500 occasions; they have conducted 3,000 workshops and trainings to 18,000 people; and they have expanded the network to include 3,100 people who currently subscribe to the AU newsletter.

Supports and Continuing Education

To support advocates and enhance and encourage continued growth of advocacy skills, AU offers advanced education classes and seminars. Topics, based on suggestions from graduates of the Advocacy Education program, range from grievance procedures to the state legislative process. The advanced education coordinator arranges these classes, which are given two or three times a year and generally attract about twenty students.

Bimonthly meetings of the advocates across the state provide fellowship and support, as well as an opportunity for old and new advocate graduates to exchange knowledge, experiences, and concerns. The meetings, open to all graduates, are held at the central office in Wethersfield.

The *AU Web site* (*www.mindlink.org*) offers graduates of the training program a password-protected Advocate's Connection section where they can find help, resources, and information provided just for program graduates. Public transportation to the Wethersfield office is available through the state's Dial-A-Ride program, though AU staff encourage students and advocates with cars to approach others in their area to offer rides. Graduate advocates can also arrange rides through the AU *Ride Share program* posted on the secure section of the AU Web site This program is another way that advocates can support each other and build unity.

Acknowledging the "digital divide" between those who can and cannot afford the latest computer technology, AU accepts donated computers, updates them, and provides them (along with the appropriate training) to advocates. Advocates earn the computer by participating in meetings and legislative efforts.

Other ways that fellowship and education are continually nurtured at AU include annual advocate retreats, annual holiday get-togethers, annual leadership conferences, and monthly newsletters. The *Action Alert Fax Network* is maintained by the AU administrative assistant, who faxes information to advocates at their community placements, letting them know about key public policy events, hearings, meetings, votes, plans, and actions. The advocates in their field placements receive the messages and then spread the word throughout their communities and networks. Thus the "grassroots" are mobilized for action. Through its executive director

Figure 9.4. Samples from Legislative Advocacy Reports

- Attended legislative task force meeting to plan for budget rally.
- Visited with my legislator to talk about upcoming bill in regards to zoning issue.
- Contacted numerous clubhouses to inform them of budget rally.
- Testified at Medicare hearing at the capital.

and advocates, AU helps educate the general public about the myths and realities of people with mental illness. AU also keeps both the public and the advocate network apprised of the latest developments in the mental health arena, including legislative and budgetary proposals that could have an impact on their lives.

In addition to the section for advocates, the AU website offers information and resources, directly and through links, for persons with mental health disabilities and their families. Consumers of mental health services can keep up-to-date on pertinent events and activities. They can learn about employment opportunities for persons with disabilities and find information about resumé writing, interviewing, and job search skills. They can interact with AU and other consumers online through several means, including discussion boards. AU publishes a monthly newsletter, *Your Source for Help and Hope,* for consumers, family members, and service providers that includes personal experiences contributed by AU's advocates and others on the mailing list. It is distributed by mail throughout Connecticut as well as to many other states and countries, in response to the growing number of requests. In addition, AU staff make frequent phone referrals to other mental-health-related offices and organizations.

Accomplishments

AU has changed the status quo for people with mental illness in Connecticut. "I will take the lead on my treatment choices" is now a viable, respected position. To get to this point, AU achieved some important successes.

We have developed one of the largest grassroots peer-advocacy organizations in the country. This movement is now a significant force that is well respected within the state's political, legal, and administrative systems.

Our organization reduces isolation and feelings of powerlessness by educating and supporting consumers to make a difference in their own lives and the lives of others as they influence social institutions that control access to and the quality of mental health services. Now people who are hospitalized can be present at their own medication hearings, can have an advocate of their choosing with them, and can take part in choosing their own hearing officers. AU provides highly visible role models for other mental health consumers, both statewide and nationally, showing a way for persons in recovery with a psychiatric disability to seek treatment while retaining their personal dignity and independence, and thus increasing the likelihood of continued recovery.

AU graduates voted and worked with the state legislature as never before, serving on several legislative task forces and meeting with their legislators regularly. Gaby Litchner, Paul Gilbo, and Yvette Sangster sat on the Study for Outpatient Commitment; Gaby, Yvette, and Marc Jacques sat on the Blue Ribbon Commission for Mental Health; other members sat on the Advisory Council of the Office of Protection and Advocacy, catchment area councils for state mental health funding, hospital advisory boards, such as Cedarcrest Hospital in Newington, Connecticut, the Anti-Stigma Campaign for the state of Connecticut, the Work Incentive Focus Group, the Ethics Committee for the DMHAS, the Federal Block Grant Council, local clubhouse boards, and Common Ground (a local social club).

AU provides the legislature, state agencies, and other mental health organizations with information about what consumers need and what types of services are likely to make spending more cost- and person-effective. We teach consumers the skills necessary to mobilize and give testimony to influence important legislative decisions, such as those regarding outpatient commitment and the amount and allocation of funds for mental health services. These activities increase the visibility and participation of persons with psychiatric disabilities at the tables where decisions are made about development and delivery of their services and policies.

In 1997 AU challenged the Connecticut governor's decision to cancel work furloughs for persons receiving services in state-funded vocational programs. The outcry was swift and powerful: within three days, the ban was lifted. AU coordinated efforts to repeal legislation that imposed a co-payment for prescription medications on the persons who could least afford them, that is, persons receiving Title XIX benefits. The AU staff assembled a team that included activists and advocates working on behalf of such diverse groups as the elderly, persons with physical disabilities, and persons with AIDS. AU's campaign was successful, and the proposal was defeated.

AU was instrumental in defeating a strong legislative effort to institute forced outpatient commitment in the state. More than 150 people testified against the measure at public hearings in 2000. No one expected such a show of strength. AU also succeeded in mobilizing enough people to restore millions of threatened dollars to a past DMHAS budget proposal, and AU advocates turned out in record numbers in 2001 at public hearings in support of the recommendations of the Governor's Blue Ribbon Commission on Mental Health. AU contributed substantially to the report, which describes the state's current mental health service crisis and makes key recommendations for the future direction of services in Connecticut. The full report can be found at *www.dmhas.state.ct.us/blue ribbonreport.htm*.

AU helps to decrease the stigma associated with mental illness through role modeling and participation in public forums and by becoming a resource for councils and boards looking for members. AU graduates have become equal and valued partners with DMHAS, the legislature, and other mental health organizations, which often request AU's suggestion about and endorsement of decisions regarding mental health service development and delivery. AU works in coalition with other organizations who have overlapping concerns and interests—such as the Connecticut Legal Rights Project, the Office of Protection and Advocacy for Persons with Mental Illness, the Mental Health Association, the Department of Families and Children, the Department of Social Services, the AIDS Coalition, and NAMI-CT (formerly the Connecticut Alliance for the Mentally Ill).

AU believes that, in general, state mental health departments should buy into the education of people in self-advocacy and systems advocacy, and they should adopt the recovery model of service provision. The Connecticut DMHAS has recently adopted a recovery model throughout its delivery and development network of services. The core values of this network were developed by AU and Connecticut Community of Addictions Recovery over a period of three years.

AU believes people have the ability to take charge of their own lives and to make a difference in the lives of others. Graduates leave AU with skills they can apply to their own recovery process as well as the skills necessary to speak out on behalf of other consumers. Testimonials from

---

Figure 9.5. Testimonials from AU Graduates

- When I went to AU classes, we had to focus. It was hard. I wanted to quit, but my friend pushed me. That program was hard. It taught me to fight, to see right, to not act like sheep, and to question. — *Suzanne Silva*

- Hope is an essential part of self-discovery, recovery, and empowerment. It is what we dispense as mental health advocates. — *Marcia Smith*

- Not everyone can identify with the problems we have. We can truly say to people that we have been there and we have beaten the odds. —*Al Harris, Sr.*

---

some of our graduates appear in Figure 9.5. Unlike clients in some traditional programs, our advocates use their full name rather than stigmatizing themselves with initials.

Now, nearly a decade after we started, AU classes continue and our students, graduates, presenters, and staff constantly update the teaching curriculum. The impact of our efforts can be seen in the students who now apply and are accepted into AU classes. Compared with most of the first students, many students who now come to AU already know a lot about their rights as mental health consumers. Thanks to AU, they have already had role models and opportunities for learning before participating in advocacy classes.

From the roots of our self-advocacy has grown a tree called AU. This tree boasts a strong foundation of empowerment and the "working with, not for" philosophy. Its limbs spread throughout Connecticut. Its advocates, the leaves and branches of the tree, grow each year as more students work to become new advocates. The multiplying leaves of the AU tree ensure that there will always be a consumer voice in the places where decisions are made about people in recovery with psychiatric disabilities.

10
BRIDGES in Tennessee: Building Recovery of Individual Dreams and Goals through Education and Support

Louetta Hix

Consumers often ask, "How do you run an education and support program that helps mental health consumers progress toward a more fulfilling life?" The BRIDGES Education and Support program is an answer to that question. The original BRIDGES program was started in Tennessee in 1995, and within five years had expanded to eight other states and one Canadian province. The program consists of two parts. The first provides a fifteen-week course on mental illness, mental health treatment, and recovery, taught by consumers to consumers. The second offers ongoing support groups facilitated by consumers who have been trained in the BRIDGES method. With the BRIDGES program, consumers find that we are not alone in our struggles. BRIDGES offers us hope, state-of-the-art information, and a chance to help others and to be helped in return. The program empowers us to make changes that we desire in our lives, particularly in respect to mental health treatment and discovery of meaning and purpose. These are powerful themes, for they strike deep in the hearts of many who participate in the program.

History of BRIDGES in Tennessee

BRIDGES was formed in response to constant requests from consumers across Tennessee for accurate information on the causes and treatments of mental illnesses as well as strategies on coping with their effects and a way of connecting with others who would understand. In 1994, three groups joined in a collaborative effort to respond to these requests for help. These groups were the Tennessee Mental Health Consumers' Association, NAMI-Tennessee, and the Tennessee Department of Mental Health and Developmental Disabilities, who, respectively, represented consumers, families, and mental health providers. The state agency obtained a grant from the federal Center for Mental Health Services to develop a peer-run consumer education and support program modeled on the Journey of Hope, an education and support program piloted in Tennessee that targeted family members of persons with mental illnesses. Some of this process is described in the book *Back from Wherever I've Been* by Sita Diehl and Beth Baxter (2000), two of the founders of the new BRIDGES program. Other founders who worked in this collaborative process were Cynthia Barker, Darryl Hubbard, Irene Russell, and Christy Talley. Soon many others signed on to help form this program, making it a creative product of many contributors.

Based on information obtained through face-to-face interviews and focus groups with 140 consumers statewide, we learned that consumers want basic facts about psychiatric diagnosis and medications and information about how to identify their own needs and how to access mental health resources, and about dimensions of recovery.

Armed with the information about what consumers want to know, we recruited individual consumer experts to contribute to the BRIDGES curriculum. The BRIDGES classes were piloted in 1995 in three communities of diverse sizes from East, Middle, and West Tennessee. Responses from teachers, students, service providers, and family members were enthusiastic. The curriculum was then revised in response to feedback from piloting and reviewers, and from course and teacher evaluations. The following were excerpts from evaluations:

- BRIDGES gave me more information and encouragement in one course about mental illness and recovery than [I have learned] in thirty years of attempting to learn through the mental health system.

- With BRIDGES, we finally know we are not alone, that we can get clear information and we can help each other.

- This course addresses the isolation that our illness forces upon us with a level of social bonding that I never expected to find, and do not find in any other area of my life.

As the program got started, the demand for classes was tremendous. People were eager to participate in classes and equally eager to assume the meaningful work of teaching (Diehl and Baxter 2000). As of spring 2000, BRIDGES had held sixty-eight classes in twenty-nine Tennessee communities and had expanded to nine states and provinces.

The support group component of BRIDGES was initiated in the spring of 1996 and has likewise enjoyed an enthusiastic response. The BRIDGES method provides a clear, concise structure for facilitating support groups. This structure includes techniques for opening and closing meetings, tools for encouraging discussion among participants, and common procedures and philosophies, such as meeting guidelines, principles of support, and a philosophy of recovery. It is flexible, yet responsive to the needs of facilitators and members alike. A member who attends a BRIDGES support group in one city would find commonalities at a BRIDGES support group in another city. Support group facilitators are well trained in their role. They have well-defined expectations and resources to turn to for guidance. The BRIDGES administrative staff is available for problem solving when questions or challenges arise. As we often quote in BRIDGES circles, "With BRIDGES you are not alone."

The history of BRIDGES does not end with the expansion of the courses and support groups throughout Tennessee and other states and provinces. The BRIDGES story is being made every day in the lives of people who are touched by one another in the program. Many of us hold our heads higher because we have found that others could identify with the courage we have practiced in our own lives through our darkest moments. Many of us have taken the first steps of returning to work by taking a job as a BRIDGES teacher or facilitator or volunteer. Many of us have found our voice to speak to a treatment provider about issues and concerns long kept silent. Many have found life-long friends; some have found life-long partners. All have found the opportunity to meet and know others who have felt the sting of stigma and the indescribable relief of talking to someone who understands and has been there. And we carry from that connection a flame, sometimes a torch, to illuminate the way for others who have had similar experiences. This is where the history of BRIDGES becomes its present and future.

Mission and Goals

The BRIDGES program is based on a philosophy of recovery. The letters in the acronym BRIDGES represent "Building Recovery of Individual Dreams and Goals through Education and Support." It is the BRIDGES philosophy that a person can pursue his or her dreams and goals even while experiencing symptoms of mental illness. Thus our mission statement:

> The mission of BRIDGES is to empower people with psychiatric disabilities to take an active and informed role in their treatment and to recover a new sense of purpose in life.

As they acquire knowledge about psychiatric disorders, medications, and best practices in mental health treatment, course participants become skilled in self-advocacy and in advocating for one another. A related outcome is that people feel encouraged to face their fears. The primary goals of BRIDGES are to initiate outreach and provide emotional support to those in pain, to provide insight into mental illnesses and share knowledge and skills that help us progress in our recovery, and to reduce the stigma of mental illness.

With the strength of peer support and role modeling in classes and support groups, we learn to overcome barriers that were overwhelming before we took these courageous steps to deal with them. BRIDGES provides the tools and the milieu. It is a goal of BRIDGES that everyone has access to the latest information on mental health treatment, although it is not expected that everyone will come away from the course with the same knowledge gained. People are encouraged to take what works for them and leave what they are not interested in.

BRIDGES owes its success to the support and caring of the group members and to its recognition of the importance of one's feeling safe in talking openly about one's own experiences with others who can affirm them. In an atmosphere of dignity and respect toward members, toward staff, toward the mental health community, and toward the community at large, BRIDGES encourages frank examination of the subject of mental illness. Its goal is to provide state-of-the-art information to participants, by teachers who are also consumers of mental health services. An attitude of "If they can do it, I can too!" pervades the program and is encouraged by the staff.

Location and Membership

Most BRIDGES classes and support groups meet at consumer-run drop-in centers, settings in which consumers are in charge and self-help is emphasized. Some classes and support groups meet in other neutral settings, such as churches, libraries and hospitals. BRIDGES encourages classes and groups to meet in neutral settings, though many are held at mental health facilities. Classes and support groups are almost always held in handicapped-accessible locations and, in cities offering bus transportation, on bus lines. In addition, teachers and support group coordinators work with members to coordinate ride sharing when possible.

BRIDGES seeks to reach people in both rural and urban communities. The collaboration with Journey of Hope has proven advantageous especially in rural areas where transportation is limited. Specifically, in some communities, the BRIDGES consumer program and the Journey of Hope family member program offer meetings at the same time so that family members can share transportation and simultaneously participate in their respective programs. This cooperative effort has allowed several people to engage in BRIDGES who would not otherwise have had the chance. BRIDGES seeks to build networks of support by requesting collaborative invitations from various stakeholder groups in other states to bring the BRIDGES program to their states.

There are several criteria for eligibility to participate in a BRIDGES class or support group. First, one must qualify as a mental health services consumer by being a current or former recipient of mental health services. Second, one must acknowledge that one has been diagnosed with a mental illness. Third, one must participate of one's own accord (not as a requirement from service provider, relative, or other, although in some communities exceptions have been where participation in the course has been made as part of a probation agreement). Finally, one must agree to come for the entire course. An exception is made for support groups, however, where people come and go as their need arises and according to their sense of commitment.

Administrative and Staffing Structure

The BRIDGES program is administered, taught, and facilitated entirely by consumers. The BRIDGES program director reports to the executive director of the Tennessee Mental Health Consumers' Association (TMHCA). The program director supervises the teacher and facilitator trainers, an inventory clerk and shipping clerk, and two van drivers. Additionally, the program director supervises the regional coordinators (see below).

The executive director reports to the volunteer board of directors of

TMHCA, all of whom are consumers. TMHCA is a 501(c) 3 nonprofit organization. The BRIDGES program has seen growth of administrative staff from one person in 1996 to nine people in 2000.

Tennessee is divided into seven mental health-planning regions. In each region a part-time BRIDGES coordinator supervises the support-group facilitator teams, teaching teams, and monitors for that region. The inventory clerk distributes program materials to the teams as needed.

Trainers, current or former teachers and facilitators who have participated in additional training, train the teaching and facilitator teams. Trainers, teachers, and facilitators work on a contract basis. They are paid to attend training sessions and are also paid a stipend for each class or support group session they conduct. Monitors are teachers and facilitators who have received additional training and also work on a contract basis, observing classes and support groups for quality assurance.

Funding for the BRIDGES Program

BRIDGES was initially funded as a pilot project through a grant from the Center for Mental Health Services. Subsequently, funding has been obtained through a variety of sources. The Tennessee Department of Mental Health and Developmental Disabilities has provided financial support, as have the TennCare Partners managed care companies, Premier Behavioral HealthCare Systems, and the former Tennessee Behavioral Health. BRIDGES has also received grants from Janssen Pharmaceutica and the Eli Lilly Company and in-kind support from various mental health programs, hospitals, agencies, and churches in the state, such as space for holding classes and trainings, meals and refreshments, overnight accommodations, and transportation to training and classes. Currently BRIDGES receives capacity-building funds from the Substance Abuse and Mental Health Services Administration (SAMHSA) Consumer-Operated Services Program research grant in addition to other sources of funding.

Programs

The two components of the BRIDGES program are the classes and the support groups.

Education

In the education program, BRIDGES seeks to provide a safe place, that is, a place for validation, where you can gain understanding and acceptance, learn and practice real life skills, exchange information about mental illness—a place to learn strategies for recovery and to build recovery skills. (Nelson 2001)

The primary goal of a BRIDGES course is to help consumers understand mental illness and recovery from mental illness. The courses provide a safe place to discuss feelings and are designed to help consumers understand mental health treatment and how to make it work for us and to give consumers the tools we need to move toward recovery. The course also helps us deal with stigma, both the way we feel about ourselves (internalized sigma) and the attitudes and biases of others.

BRIDGES classes are led by two co-teachers with the support of a resource person. With job-sharing and cross training the program can continue even if someone on the team needs to take a break from his or her role. The co-teachers lecture from manuals especially prepared for their role. The students have corresponding student manuals, which contain all class handouts and additional readings, and they are encouraged to read along and often to take turns reading aloud to the class. The manuals are provided to students at no charge. In addition, co-teachers guide group discussions.

The BRIDGES curriculum is developed with the idea that even people with no previous teaching experience will be able to lead the class comfortably. Teacher training consists of a four-day workshop on group facilitation, on the philosophy of BRIDGES, on the process for teaching the class, and on the curriculum itself. Included in review of the curriculum are ample opportunities for practicing exercises and discussions. Teachers receive a complete curriculum guide that includes all charts, handouts, and supplies. .

In response to the suggestions of the focus groups conducted during the development of the BRIDGES curriculum, in which consumers said they prefer short classes with frequent breaks and that they want to have fun while learning, the BRIDGES classes are two hours long and include songs, games, biographies, and crossword puzzles, as well as lecture and discussion. Most BRIDGES classes are held once a week, although some choose to meet more often. All courses meet for fifteen classes (see Figure 10.1). Each class includes a five-minute period in which a member is asked to tell his or her story. (For an example of such a story, "Voice from the Region," see Figure 10.2.)

Support

In the support group program, BRIDGES seeks to provide a place where individuals can confront their fears, share feelings/experiences and find they are not alone. They find a place to learn and practice skills related to real-life issues and gain understanding through exchange of information about mental illnesses and strategies for recovery. (Nelson 2001)

BRIDGES support groups have several goals. Their first goal is to let people know they are not alone. Other goals are to offer hope, to provide information, and to give people a chance to help themselves and an opportunity to help others.

Two co-facilitators, along with a crisis and information responder, all of whom have participated in a three-day experiential training in group facilitation, facilitate the BRIDGES support groups. The responder provides information about resources in the community and helps any members who come to the meeting in a crisis obtain appropriate support. Just as with the teaching team, job-sharing and cross training are emphasized within the support group facilitation team. If one of the three cannot attend, the other two cover. Other members of the support group are recruited for volunteer roles, such as the buddy, who helps with newcomers or assists the co-facilitators or responder. The job of the co-facilitators, who are taught facilitation techniques and communication skills, is to elicit group participation rather than take the lead, allowing the group eventually to take charge of itself. The co-facilitators always make sure that the meeting is started and concluded according to the BRIDGES formats. At times, the co-facilitators may lead a structured process such as a problem-solving technique. However, even this process engages the group as a whole in supporting the person whose problem is being addressed.

BRIDGES support groups meet on a variable schedule, with each group deciding how often it will meet. Most meet twice a month, but some meet once a week or every other week. Support group meetings typically last for one and one-half to two hours.

All BRIDGES staff and members of the teaching and facilitator teams are expected to respect fellow BRIDGES participants as equals. In addition, there is a "Pass" rule throughout the BRIDGES program. Any time anyone is called on or is next in a circle of speakers, he or she may choose to be bypassed without question simply by saying "pass." This rule is

---

Figure 10.1. The BRIDGES Course

Class 1:   Introductions: Emotional Stages of Recovery,
           BRIDGES course outline
Class 2:   Thought Disorders: Schizophrenia
Class 3:   Mood Disorders: Depression, Bipolar Disorder,
           Schizoaffective Disorder, Suicide Prevention
Class 4:   Anxiety Disorders, Personality Disorders, the Recovered
           Memory Debate, Use and Misuse of Diagnosis
Class 5:   Exploring and Understanding Dual Diagnosis
Class 6:   Building Support: Principles of Support, Circle of
           Support, Crisis Planning, Recuperation
Class 7:   Biology, the Environment, and Major Mental Illness
Class 8:   Medication: What It Is Supposed to Do, Side Effects,
           How to Talk to Your Doctor about Medication Problems
Class 9:   Mental Health Services: Part 1
Class 10: Mental Health Services: Part 2
           Recovery and Working: How Does Work Affect Benefits
           and Insurance?
Class 11: Tools for Recovery: Wellness, Problem-Solving
Class 12: Tools for Recovery: Communication . . . Supportive
           Listening and Assertiveness
Class 13: Religion and Spirituality: Developing Healthy
           Spirituality . . . Finding a Supportive Church or Spiritual
           Community
Class 14: Advocacy: Let's Gripe about the System, How
           Advocacy Works, Consumer/Patient Rights, Changing
           the System!
Class 15: Review, Sharing, Evaluation. Certification Ceremony;
           Party!

---

clearly and frequently stated in meetings and classes so that all participants know they have the right and option to use it at any time.

Regional coordinators supervise teachers and facilitators at the local level to provide general support, to make sure the program is implemented as designed, to help solve problems, and to provide quality assurance. Classes and support groups are monitored periodically by trained

Figure 10.2. A Voice from the Region

by Sam Viar

Several months ago I had sunk to a point where I was getting frighteningly close to suicide. I had lost contact with people who were closest to me, and the combination of a couple of ongoing traumas and sleeping two hours a night for the past year was crushing me. I felt as if I had nothing left to give, and I was at the point of total collapse physically. The telephone rang.

It was a woman who said she was in her mid-fifties. She said she did not remember how she got my number, but she had heard of BRIDGES at a mental health center. She never gave me her first name and would only say that she lived way out in the middle of nowhere by the Tennessee River. I explained briefly what BRIDGES stands for and what we try to do, and the woman liked the fact that the entire organization is consumers and are peers, no matter what their position or role is. The agitated voice I heard at the beginning of our conversation lost its edge, and she told me of her situation and the hopelessness she felt and revealed some wild exploits of late that indicated to me she was in dire straits. She seemed fascinated that I had been blessed with the opportunity to change so many people's lives through BRIDGES and volunteer service, when I for so many years had lived such a precarious, perilous existence similar to her own.

consumers who also provide feedback and quality assurance. Students are asked to complete consumer satisfaction evaluations four times during the fifteen-week course. Revisions in the curriculum and program design are based on feedback from these consumer evaluations.

BRIDGES teachers, facilitators, and administrative staff receive in-service training at two annual conferences. The fall BRIDGES Empowerment Conference consists of training workshops providing updates on changes in the program, as well as training in ways to improve various aspects of program implementation. The annual TMHCA conference held every May includes BRIDGES workshops as well as the BRIDGES Awards Banquet, a big celebration of accomplishments that includes accolades, music, and poetry.

This beautiful yet faceless woman who felt so comfortable talking to me was unaware that I was applying a few basic facilitator techniques to help her feel that way, such as self-disclosure to establish common ground and reflective responses to let her continue to talk it out. What she *was* aware of was that I had respect and love for her as a human being, whether stranger or best friend. This sincerity reached her and touched her and transformed her right before my ears. It was at this point I made some gentle suggestions.

Before we hung up I told her to remember that, no matter what happened, there was a person in the world who was her friend from this moment on. I also let her know that she had helped me as much as I had helped her, and I explained how our common ground made this possible. All during our talk she had never cried, but after hearing this she wept softly, and I heard an object fall to the floor in the background. She shocked me by revealing she had been holding a shotgun under her chin while we had been talking and was barefoot so she could pull the trigger with her toe. No one had ever told her she had helped them, nor had she ever known that through such means her life and spirit could be redirected.

I later got a call from a tech at a private hospital, who told me my friend had checked in for help. More often than not, empowerment is a two-way street. It was through my sincere giving to her and the dramatic result of this true story that I began to rediscover the limitless beauty and power of my simple gifts.

All training and support group participation through BRIDGES is free to participants. Sponsoring organizations are required to raise the necessary funds from public and private sources, not from course participants.

The education program does, however, pay course teachers and support group facilitators for both training and program implementation. BRIDGES offers work opportunities and people earn the compensation for their contribution as teachers and facilitators. Some of us use these roles as stepping-stones to other work. BRIDGES participants and leaders often receive invitations to become advocates, spokespersons, and public speakers in the community as well, although this work is not a formal part of the BRIDGES program.

Accomplishments and Plans for the Future

Each year since its inception, BRIDGES has offered new initiatives and continually improved its programs. The BRIDGES education curriculum has added psychotherapy, managed care, new medications, advanced directives, advocacy and dual diagnosis, with optional short modules on attention deficit disorder and dissociative identity disorder. To allow an easier commitment of time by both teachers and students, BRIDGES revised the original fifteen-week course to make it a ten-week course. The classes are now more flexible in that course participants can choose topics of particular interest to them. As of 2004, fewer classes and support groups are being offered in Tennessee than at the time of this study; however, the program continues to flourish and thrive.

BRIDGES staff has collaborated with Journey of Hope staff on joint presentations throughout Tennessee and at national conferences to demonstrate the importance of communication between mental health consumers and family members.

New programs have been implemented in Louisiana, South Carolina, Mississippi, Ohio, Wisconsin, Utah, Minnesota, Hawaii, and other states, as well as in British Columbia, Canada. Initially, the BRIDGES staff from Tennessee go into other states to train their new staff on implementation of the BRIDGES curriculum and support group method. Thereafter states can send their delegates to Tennessee to participate in the annual Train-the-Trainers workshop, where they can learn the skills to develop their own training staff in their own state.

In its first four years, BRIDGES conducted 68 classes and trained 157 teachers. By December 1999, 672 students in Tennessee had graduated from BRIDGES classes, and 613 consumers attended 78 support groups led by 114 facilitators. Other goals of the BRIDGES program in Tennessee include the implementation of the annual BRIDGES Empowerment Conference, implementation of a program monitoring process and participation in the SAMHSA multisite Consumer-Operated Service Program research project. Future goals are to expand the BRIDGES program farther into the more rural areas of Tennessee, as well as into other countries.

BRIDGES plans to follow the success of our book *Back from Wherever I've Been* (Diehl and Baxter 2000), by researching and publishing a second testimonial book in Tennessee and the first international testimonial book. We will also publish the BRIDGES international newsletter and host the first BRIDGES International Conference.

We will continue to maintain cultural diversity throughout the program, maintaining the program in rural as well as urban areas, and continuing to reach out to ethnic minorities as staff and participants. The program in Tennessee as of 1998 was 81 percent Caucasian, 10 percent African American, 5 percent Native American, and 4 percent other. BRIDGES materials have been translated into Spanish through a SAMHSA grant.

Conclusion

BRIDGES reaches deep into the hearts of its members. Stories abound about how the program has touched people's lives. Several are published in *Back from Wherever I've Been*. Many stories are shared over a cup of coffee at the TMHCA conferences, or increasingly with people from other states at national conferences. There is an instant sense of connection when you meet other people who have been through the program—even when they are new friends from new places.

Maybe BRIDGES reaches its members because it comes from deep in the heart of the people who make it work and from the people who originally conceived of it. Maybe even more it is because it is a response to a heart-felt need by people who come together mutually understanding the value of being heard and valued for who we are and what we have lived through. We can each have the satisfaction of striving for our dreams and goals when we obtain practical information about how to improve our recovery and make some friends to encourage us along our way. We end our BRIDGES classes, and this chapter, with the following affirmation:

> I can be
> All I can be,
> But if it's going to be—
> It's up to me!

References

Diehl, S. M., and E. A. Baxter, eds. 2000. *Back from Wherever I've Been*. Nashville: Tennessee Department of Mental Health and Developmental Disabilities.
Nelson, Barbara. 2001. *BRIDGES Facilitator Trainer's Manual*. Nashville: BRIDGES.

PART V
Conclusion

11
Common Ingredients as a Fidelity Measure for Peer-Run Programs

Matthew Johnsen, Gregory Teague, and Elizabeth McDonel Herr

The Consumer-Operated Services Program (COSP) Multi-Site Research Initiative (MRI) was a large study funded by the U.S. Substance Abuse and Mental Health Services Administration (SAMHSA) from 1998 to 2002. The COSP MRI studied consumer-operated services programs in eight distinct settings across the country over the course of four years. The major study question involved the comparison of two sets of interventions for persons with severe mental illness. In one condition, consumer-operated services were studied as an adjunct to traditional mental health services; in another condition they were compared to traditional mental health services alone. Chapters 3–10 describe the program at each COSP site in narrative, qualitative format. This chapter outlines additional methods used to describe the COSPs participating in the study more formally and scientifically. This approach helped us analyze study data objectively and to spell out the elements of the COSPs for those who might be interested in adopting peer-run programs in their communities. Using both of the approaches in this book to describe the COSPs provides a fuller picture of what actually takes place in these programs than would either approach alone.

This chapter was written solely from the perspective of the authors and does not necessarily represent the official policy or position of the U.S. Department of Substance Abuse and Mental Health Services Administration, the U.S. Department of Health and Human Services, or the federal government.

Defining Common Ingredients of Peer-Run Programs

From the outset, it was clear that the consumer-operated services participating in the MRI clustered into three different program models or variations of consumer-operated services. The program models were drop-in
centers, peer-support services, and educational programs. As outlined in
earlier chapters, the programs describe themselves very differently and
would appear to have different ways of organizing themselves that might,
theoretically, lead to different outcomes. It was clear, however, that while
many of the details of these programs appeared to be different, there were
also a great many similarities among all of them in their organization,
their guiding philosophies, and the ways that they described what was
going on in their programs.

One question raised during the initial deliberations of the steering
committee of the multi-site study was whether, despite these apparent
differences, there is a set of "common ingredients" that is present in most
consumer-operated programs, and that distinguishes these programs
from more traditional mental health programs. Identifying such common
ingredients might contribute to streamlining the analysis of data in our
study and facilitate communication to the public about general program
features associated with outcomes in our MRI. There was a strong push
from the federal project officers at the outset of this study to identify and
measure common ingredients among the eight COSPs.

Although there was recognition that the solicitation and review process for this project introduced variability among the COSPs that were
funded, it was essential to explore to what extent these programs had
cross-cutting elements common to all within a multi-site study context.
If study sites were more different than similar overall, we would face the
quandary of not being able to combine data across the eight study sites
to make generalizable statements about COSPs. Furthermore, the importance of providing a systematic and comprehensive description of study
interventions in the context of performing single-site outcome studies
had been learned from earlier mental health services research efforts, including those funded by SAMHSA and the National Institute of Mental
Health (e.g., McDonel et al. 1997; Linkins et al. forthcoming).

The concept of treatment "fidelity" has been given a great deal of attention in health services research in the past decade. Fidelity measures
provide an objective rating system to assess the extent that components
of a program are faithfully implemented according to the intended program model, theory, or philosophy. In other words, fidelity measures,

once developed, can be used to demonstrate the extent to which actual practice matches program intent. In our MRI, the fidelity measurement approach was used not to verify the match between program intent and practice at each site but to identify program ingredients that might be common across the eight study sites.

Another study challenge involved the recognition that mental health services are dynamic and evolving. As such, traditional mental health services (TMHS) programs were likely to absorb and adopt some principles of peer support and consumer empowerment common in COSPs into their existing programs. Thus, a measure of the common ingredients for COSPs that could also measure the extent to which TMHS programs had implemented these principles or program elements would be invaluable. If participants in a specific COSP site in our multi-site study did not have significant differences in outcomes from participants in the TMHS site, we wanted to be able to explore the possibility that the TMHS site had similar outcomes because of high adoption of COSP-like elements. In the research literature, this problem is known as the contamination of treatment effect into the control group. Alternatively, failure of the COSP site to implement a program different enough from the TMHS site might create a similar pattern of outcomes. In the research literature, this problem is known as implementation failure.

To understand both the similarities and differences among the consumer-operated services in the study, as well as similarities and differences between consumer-operated and traditional mental health services, the project entered into an effort that resulted in the development of a fidelity instrument known as the COSP Fidelity Assessment Common Ingredients Tool (FACIT). Fidelity measures typically examine program implementation at the program level rather than at the consumer level of measurement. These program-level fidelity measures generally rate a program against an agreed-upon list of components within a program model. This chapter discusses the rationale behind studying program fidelity and the development of the FACIT instrument. No published fidelity measures for consumer-operated mental health services existed at the time we began the COSP MRI; other investigators in the field have been working on this issue in parallel with our MRI and are discussed later in the chapter. The chapter also seeks to address three questions: To what extent do consumer-operated services exhibit a set of commonly agreed-upon ingredients? Do these common ingredients differentiate consumer-operated from traditional mental health services? And to what extent are distinct consumer-operated programs different from one another?

The Importance of Fidelity
in Mental Health Services Research

The use of fidelity measures has become a widely accepted methodological tool in mental health services research. Researchers now understand that focusing exclusively on the outcomes of programs has limited value. Finding out whether or to what degree a particular program is successful in achieving particular effects is only part of the story. Applied science also does its work by discovering how effects are achieved, so that we can transfer them to other programs, achieve them repeatedly, and learn what we might try to change in order to improve them. Consider a simple example. Suppose we find out that Program A is very effective in helping people with mental illnesses find and keep jobs that they like. So far, we have produced important information that can support efforts of administrators and advocates to maintain or expand this program. However, our goals are broader; it is important to assist other programs in achieving similar outcomes. By itself, the outcome information can do little to transfer the effect to other programs; organizers and managers of other programs need additional information about Program A: what services it provides, how often services are provided, at what times and in what settings, how it operates and is managed, and characteristics of the people it serves.

If staff of Program B possess a manual with this kind of detailed program information, they can attempt to replicate the program, hoping for the same effects. However, if they are not successful, how can we know what happened? Have they been unsuccessful in doing what Program A does? Or have they been successful in repeating the actions of the first program but there are other reasons for their not achieving the same effects, for example, that aspects of their community or the people served differ from those of Program A? Alternatively, suppose that Program B is also successful in helping people find and keep good jobs. What is the reason for their success? Is it indeed that they have successfully copied Program A's services? Or might it be that they have failed to copy the first program but instead have done something else that was also effective? In either case, without having some way to compare what Program B actually did with Program A's services, there is no way to find out the answers to these questions. By identifying the critical, effective ingredients of a program model, and carefully documenting these ingredients, we can help others to more efficiently deliver services. In the long run, the hope is that this approach will ensure that we can most efficiently use the time and resources of providers and consumers.

There are many program characteristics that one might consider when thinking about program fidelity. Even one program characteristic could carry a great deal of weight in predicting whether positive outcomes are achieved. For example, in thinking about the challenges associated with measuring a consumer-operated program, we may be interested not only in what services it provides, how it operates, and characteristics of the people it services but also in characteristics of the people providing the services. In the case of consumer-operated services, Program B could be almost a carbon copy of Program A but fail because of differences in the characteristics of the people providing the services (professional standing, empathy, class, cultural identity, similarity of experience, and economic level).

A fidelity measure is a tool to answer these kinds of question. It contains precise and concrete operational definitions of the critical aspects or ingredients of a program model. Operational definitions describe phenomena in ways such that they can be measured to produce quantitative information, and the results of the measurement are deemed to reflect the degree or strength of these phenomena. By making these measures quantitative, we can then look for trends, averages, significant differences, and the like. For example, we may find that, on average, programs with at least 50 percent of services conducted outside an office setting are more effective than those conducted within an office-based context. Because mental health service programs are highly complex, fidelity measures must address several features of a program to produce scores that adequately and comprehensively reflect the scope of any particular model.

Developers of fidelity measures have two main tasks—one theoretical, one technical. The theoretical task is to use available knowledge to specify the important features of a model. Ideally, available knowledge is derived from previous research; when there is little empirical evidence, expert opinion may be a crucial source. For example, when McGrew and colleagues (1994) wanted to measure assertive community treatment programs, a well-researched community-based intervention for persons with severe and persistent mental illness, there was insufficient research available to authoritatively define all critical program ingredients. They therefore surveyed recognized experts to obtain additional information (McGrew and Bond 1995). Program features identified as most important through either the literature or expert consensus were then incorporated in a fidelity measure, the Index of Fidelity to Assertive Community Treatment (IF-ACT), that required combining information from a number of sources to obtain a set of fidelity scores (McGrew et al. 1994).

The technical task includes the definition of a series of steps for assessing each program feature. The first step is to specify how it is to be measured, carefully considering the types of information that can be gathered with reasonable cost and effort, and that that can still be used reliably. The next step is to specify what values or scores to assign to various levels of the information obtained. Again using the example of an assertive community treatment fidelity measure, Teague and colleagues (1998) used a 5-point scale for each program feature, defining "anchors" or statements describing the characteristics of a program that would warrant scoring a program at each level. When possible, they used known characteristics of the preeminent example of the program model, the PACT program in Madison, Wisconsin, to reflect the highest rating of 5, and the typical case management program to reflect the lowest rating of 1. The result was a 28-item instrument with each item describing a separate program characteristic. As with the IF-ACT, the resulting Dartmouth Assertive Community Treatment Scale (DACTS) drew information from several sources and methods (Teague et al. 1998).

Fidelity measures serve a number of important purposes (Bond et al. 2000; Teague et al. 1998). First, as suggested above, they may be crucial to helping new programs replicate those that have been proven effective. This is not only necessary as programs are starting out but also may be important later on. Programs may drift away from the model they had originally espoused, and an implementation check may reveal the nature of the problem. For example, McDonel and colleagues (McDonel et al. 1997; Fekete et al. 1998) used data from a qualitative fidelity assessment of ACT programs during a research study to effect a mid-course correction with partially or improperly implemented programs to achieve better outcomes as a result.

Second, a fidelity measure may be especially helpful in choosing appropriate analyses within a multi-site study, where it may be necessary to know what kinds of variations there are among the included programs (Johnsen et al. 1999). In this situation, there may be questions about whether and how to combine outcome data across sites. If some programs within the experimental arm of a study differ significantly from others in terms of component dimensions, it may be these differences (rather than the experimental variable of interest) that are producing different outcomes. Some programs may strongly emphasize a particular program dimension while others may give that dimension little emphasis such that combining their results indiscriminately may make their effects harder to detect. A fidelity measure can help identify which programs are similar enough to be combined in aggregate analyses and which, if any, should be excluded from particular analyses. This function of fidelity measures is important because it prevents precious statistical power from being wasted on analyses that would ultimately be of little use to investigators.

Third, a fidelity measure may complement detailed narrative program descriptions (often found in program manuals) in communicating the nature of the program model (Bond et al. 2000). Typically, program manuals are helpful for obtaining a deeper understanding of complex procedures, or for training purposes, but may be less helpful in understanding which program elements are most critical, or in quantitatively differentiating the model from other types of services. Depending on their structure, fidelity measures can make these kinds of issues explicit. The DACTS, for example, lays out a limited number of discrete features and graphically depicts the range of model-specific performance from least to most preferred. In this way, fidelity measures may serve as either communication tools or training tools, provided their limitations are understood. The DACTS, for example, does not attempt to measure program processes exhaustively, and some of those not included in the scale may be fundamental to a program's operation.

Finally, fidelity measures can provide empirical evidence for a model's most important features: the critical ingredients that are responsible for achieving positive outcomes. If the same fidelity measure is used across a number of sites (or studies), it may be possible to observe relationships between particular program features as measured by the fidelity scale and observed outcomes. This meta-analytic purpose gets to the heart of this kind of scientific enterprise, revealing more about the cause and effect relationships between the independent variable (the intervention and its components) and the dependent variables (outcomes). From a pragmatic standpoint, the better specification of the relationship between intervention components and outcomes, the more likely it is that features of these programs can be more explicitly and efficiently transferred to other programs, allowing careful investment of program resources to yield better outcomes. Building on the methodological history reviewed earlier, the COSP FACIT was developed with an eye to serving all of these purposes.

Measuring Fidelity in the COSP MRI

At first glance, it appeared to the study investigators that there were at least three types of program included within the COSP MRI: consumer-run drop in centers, peer-support programs, and educational programs. This observation immediately raised the issue of combining data from separate programs. In thinking about analysis strategies, we were confronted with a fundamental question: Are there enough similarities among the COSPs to justify the pooling of data across all sites in the MRI? Pooling, or combining, data is one strategy for integrating information from several collaborative research sites. Data pooling can be a powerful tool to identify outcomes and the variables that contribute most significantly to those outcomes. Pooling across multiple sites, each implementing an identical treatment protocol, is the gold standard for studies known as multi-site clinical trials in the medical field, particularly in the area of medication studies. For studies of more complicated interventions, such as psychosocial and case management services, on one hand, the option of pooling data may yield valid results, but it makes sense only if the programs and their effects are similar. On the other hand, if the programs are sufficiently different, their true effects may be masked. So the question of whether to pool can be crucial in multi-site research studies.

To develop a way of measuring program implementation within the COSP MRI, a subcommittee made up of consumers and staff from COSP sites, researchers, and federal project officers for the program met to (1) develop a way to identify the elements that composed the COSP at each site; (2) discuss and determine which of these elements were common ingredients of COSP programs; and (3) provide advice on the development of strategies and procedures to measure both elements that COSPs have in common and those that are not common to all program types but that may be important ingredients of some program models. As byproducts of this activity, participants in the process developed a deeper understanding both of the ingredients that are likely common to all COSPs and those elements that distinguish among particular types. This work was guided by three basic research questions.

1.   Are there common ingredients of all COSPs? That is, are there program characteristics that are fundamental to such programs and that we could expect to find in any COSP?
2.   What distinguishes COSPs from more traditional mental health pro-

grams? Are some or all of these common ingredients not found to any appreciable degree in traditional services?

3. Were there detectable differences among the three program models in our MRI (consumer-run drop in centers, educational programs, and peer support programs)? That is, do different types of programs show strengths—and possibly therefore also lead to stronger effects—in different areas?

The Common Ingredients Subcommittee worked closely with the separate Consumer Advisory Panel (CAP) of the COSP MRI. Although the Common Ingredients Subcommittee included a majority of consumers, it was important that a large and representative group of consumers with experience developing and operating the service programs be available to review and work through issues at length and separately from the researchers to ensure that a resulting measure would be maximally faithful to the intent of COSPs. In fact, in this aspect the COSP fidelity measure development paralleled the methodology used by McGrew and Bond (1995) in seeking expert consensus on the ingredients of assertive community treatment. The MRI represented COSP sites across the country chosen by competitive review process to be part of this federally funded research study. Each site was able to bring to the table multiple consumers with varying perspectives and roles within their COSPs. For example, there were consumers who were executive directors or staff on COSPs, consumers currently receiving services within COSP, consumer researchers, and consumers who were nationally recognized consumer advocates serving as reviewers and contributors to this process.

Identification of Common Ingredients in Peer-Run Programs

The Common Ingredients Subcommittee identified a wide range of possible common ingredients. Some ingredients reflected ways of structuring the organization and others its physical environment. Some ingredients reflected the philosophy and belief systems of the organizations, while others reflected the nature and formality of peer support within the group. Still others reflected activities and other ways that the organization carried out its work of advocacy and education. To the extent that many of these program characteristics might be critical in achieving the effects of COSPs, it would be important to measure their presence in the programs serving all participants in the study.

Early on, subcommittee members recognized important conceptual work by Campbell and Dumont (1998) and by Mowbray and Holter (2000), the latter including preliminary work aimed at developing a fidelity instrument appropriate for consumer-run drop-in centers. These studies provided a useful starting point, and an example of how we might structure our own work. Mowbray and Holter (2000) grouped their criteria into two overarching domains for conceptual clarity. "Structure" reflected the "relatively stable characteristics of providers of care, of the tools and resources they have at their disposal, and of the physical and organizational settings in which they work" (Donabedian 1980, 81). "Process" referred to specific and observable activities in services or in the method of delivering those services (Mowbray and Holter 2000). We organized our own discussion of common ingredients in what came to be six domains: Program Structure; Environment; Belief Systems; Peer Support; Education; and Advocacy. Like the criteria of Mowbray and Holter 2000, these could be grouped into two overarching domains: Structure (which encompassed Program Structure and Environment); and Process (which came to include Belief Systems, Peer Support, Education, and Advocacy).

Ultimately we developed a list of common ingredients and definitions that were shared with the CAP. The CAP considered this list of common ingredients and reached agreement about both the inclusion of particular common ingredients within the list and definitions of these common ingredients. The work of the CAP at this stage was particularly crucial in three respects. First, CAP members included individuals intimately involved with the day-to-day operations of consumer-operated services, and input from these individuals provided an important initial test of the relevance of the ingredients. Second, CAP members represented each of the eight study sites, insuring wider generalizability than one program model. Third, the CAP was able to wrestle with questions about whether common ingredients are, in fact, common across all sites. These modifications were then fed back to the Common Ingredients Subcommittee as it entered the measurement phase of its work. The common ingredients are also described in Chapters 1, 2, and 12 of this book.

Operationalizing Common Ingredients

To operationalize these common ingredients, work groups were charged with identifying recommended data collection strategies for each common ingredient, developing anchored ratings for each common ingredient within the particular domains included in the Common Ingredients

List, and returning to the Common Ingredients Subcommittee prepared to present these ratings for consideration. We tried to ensure that each work group included both researchers and consumers, since both sets of insights would be crucial to effectively carrying out these tasks. In addition, a small number of work group staff participated on more than one work group to insure a consistent approach across domains.

The work groups were allowed to develop more than one anchored rating for some ingredients when necessary to have a more reliable measurement. Thus, the "consumer-operated" component of the Program Structure domain may appropriately have several different indicators (e.g., involvement of consumers on the board of directors, employment of staff who are consumers, participation of COSP members in hiring and budget decisions). Each of these indicators might require the collection of different types of information. Early on, there was discussion about whether the information associated with the fidelity-implementation assessment should not only be gathered at the program level but should also include ratings at the participant level. For example, should questions about the program be addressed to program directors or program staff, who would answer for the program as a whole, or should questions instead be addressed to program participants, who would provide their individual view of these activities?

There are no easy answers to the questions, and while some fidelity-implementation data collection efforts focus exclusively on collecting information from program staff, others employ information from a wide array of sources, including administrators, staff, and program participants. While we reached no decision that would fit across all items, we agreed generally: (1) to address most questions at the program level; (2) to incorporate questions of participants into focus groups rather than adding questions to the follow-up common protocol for the MRI; and (3) to utilize multiple methods where appropriate so that there could be some triangulation in order to validate observations.

The COSP FACIT represents the combined work of the Common Ingredients Subcommittee and its three workgroups. The structure of the FACIT is presented in Table 11.1. Each of the six domains is defined as having from two to seven subdomains, each of which has from one to five items. Each item has an anchored rating scale (typically ranging from 1 to 4 or 5) in which higher numbers represent greater expression of the common ingredient described, and lower numbers represent lower expression of the common ingredient. Overall, the FACIT has 46 items. The overall score is computed by taking the average of all items. In addition, the scores can be computed by domain; in Table 11.1 we present total points within each domain.

Psychometric Properties of the FACIT

In the pilot-refinement phase of development, we used the instrument to assess consumer-operated service programs as a part of the first round of scheduled site visits for the MRI. Such visits by staff of the study's Coordinating Center and outside consultants are a routine component in overall multi-site study administration, performance monitoring, and research. They provide a check on procedural consistency and an opportunity for direct observation and compiling of program information in a consistent manner across sites.

Prior to participating in a site visit, site visitors received training in the administration of the FACIT. This training included an overview of the instrument, instructions about information used in making each rating, examples, and instructions for both independent ratings and conciliations. Instructions were provided about steps to take in verifying information that was inconsistent across interviews, as well as standard operating procedures for how to deal with situations in which the program fell between two anchored ratings.

Two to three site visitors participated in each two- to four-day site visit. Site visitors received documentary information about the COSP and the traditional services associated with the study site prior to the visit. Site visits consisted of tours of programs; interviews with program directors, supervisory staff, and program staff; and focus groups with program participants. In addition, site visitors met with members of local consumer advisory panels and members of the research team. In the course of these activities, site visitors gathered information to assess the program with respect to each FACIT item.

After the first round of site visits, several changes were made in the instrument to improve the interrater reliability. Interrater reliability is an important characteristic of a measure and represents the degree to which different raters consistently achieve similar ratings for the same program component. First, we fine-tuned the language in some anchored ratings. Second, we identified additional questions that site visitors would ask to ensure that they had adequate information to rate all items on the FACIT. Third, we established a consistent process for conciliation to enhance validity that included review of all information from the site visit prior to rating; independent ratings of the program; and conciliation of any disparate ratings, a process that included discussion with other members of the site visit team. The process of independently rating all items prior to joint conciliation means that we had evidence of interrater reliability of the instrument, as well as a final rating for each item that reflected the considered opinion of the team as a whole. Importantly, the people doing the ratings were not the ones who had developed the instrument.

Table 11.2 provides interrater reliability data from the second round of site visits for all items included in the FACIT. Interrater reliability ranges from -.20 to .97. In the second version of the FACIT, while most display good to excellent interrater reliability, two items are poorly correlated (3.3.1 personal empowerment and 4.4.2 informal crisis prevention). Personal empowerment and informal crisis prevention are, not surprisingly, difficult constructs to measure, and more psychometric refinement will be required to adequately capture these two domains in future versions of the FACIT. Across all items, the average interrater reliability is .70, which represents an adequate level of interrater reliability.

Another way of approaching this problem is to look at the extent to which the overall scores from each rater correspond to one another. Computed across all programs, the overall FACIT scores have an interrater reliability score of .954. Because the FACIT is being used in both COSPs and TMHS programs, we have computed separated estimates for each type of program. The average interrater reliability across COSPs is .90, while the average interrater reliability for TMHS programs is .85.

The message taken from these initial examinations is that, at the item level, the reliability of the FACIT appears to be acceptable, and at the total score level, the FACIT would appear to be highly reliable. This is an excellent result for such a comprehensive and newly developed measure, validating the appropriateness of the approach we took to developing the tool.

Are the Common Ingredients Present within the COSPs?

The next important question to be addressed is whether the common ingredients identified in the extended process during the COSP MRI actually are present in the COSPs in the study. We know that the FACIT is a reasonably reliable measure, but we do not yet know if the FACIT is a valid measure. It is one thing to propose theoretically that certain char-

Table 11.1. Organization of the COSP FACIT*
(indicating range of possible points assigned in item or section)

1. Program Structure (10–48)
1.1   Consumer operated
      1.1.1   Board participation (1–5)
      1.1.2   Consumer staff (1–5)
      1.1.3   Hiring decisions (1–4)
      1.1.4   Budget control (1–4)
      1.1.5   Volunteer opportunities (1–5)
1.2   Participant responsive
      1.2.1   Planning input (1–5)
      1.2.2   Satisfaction/grievance response (1–5)
1.3   Linkage to other supports
      1.3.1   Linkage with traditional mental health services (1–5)
      1.3.2   Linkage with other COSPs (1–5)
      1.3.3   Linkage with other service agencies (1–5)

2. Environment (11–50)
2.1   Accessibility
      2.1.1   Local proximity (1–4)
      2.1.2   Access (1–5)
      2.1.3   Hours (1–5)
      2.1.4   Cost (1–5)
      2.1.5   Reasonable accommodation (1–4)
2.2   Safety
      2.2.1   Lack of coerciveness (1–5)
      2.2.2   Program rules (1–5)
2.3   Informal setting
      2.3.1   Physical environment (1–4)
      2.3.2   Social environment (1–5)
      2.3.3   Sense of community (1–4)
2.4   Reasonable accommodation
      2.4.1   Time frames (1–4)

3. Belief Systems (9–40)
3.1   Peer principle (1–4)
3.2   Helper's principle (1–4)

3.3   Empowerment
    3.3.1   Personal empowerment (1–5)
    3.3.2   Personal accountability (1–5)
    3.3.3   Group empowerment (1–4)
3.4   Choice (1–5)
3.5   Recovery (1–4)
3.6   Acceptance and respect for diversity (1–5)
3.7   Spiritual growth (1–4)

4. Peer Support (8–35)

4.1   Peer support
    4.1.1   Formal (1–5)
    4.1.2   Informal (1–4)
4.2   Telling our stories (1–5)
    4.2.1   Artistic expression (1–5)
4.3   Consciousness raising (1–4)
4.4   Crisis prevention
    4.4.1   Formal (1–4)
    4.4.2   Informal (1–4)
4.5   Peer mentoring and teaching (1–4)

5. Education (5–25)

5.1   Self-management/problem solving strategies
    5.1.1   Formally structured activities (1–5)
    5.1.2   Receiving informal support (1–5)
    5.1.3   Providing informal support (1–5)
5.2   Education
    5.2.1   Formal skills practice (1–5)
    5.2.2   Job readiness activities (1–5)

6. Advocacy (3–15)

6.1   Self-advocacy
    6.1.1   Formal (1–5)
6.2   Peer advocacy (1–5)
    6.2.1   Outreach to participants (1–5)

---

*COSP = consumer-operated services program; FACIT = Fidelity Assessment Common Ingredients Tool.

Table 11.2. Interrater reliability and item means for COSP FACIT

	Interrater reliability	Average across all programs (N = 32)	Average across all COSPs (N = 16)	Average rating all TMHS* (N = 16)
1. Program Structure				
1.1.1 Board participation	.91	3.28	4.75	1.81
1.1.2 Consumer staff	.95	3.34	4.88	1.81
1.1.3 Hiring decisions	.96	2.53	3.94	1.13
1.1.4 Budget control	.97	2.42	3.78	1.06
1.1.5 Volunteer opportunities	.99	3.28	4.93	1.63
1.2.1 Planning input	.66	3.33	4.00	2.66
1.2.2 Satisfaction-grievance response	.71	3.31	3.72	2.91
1.3.1 Linkage with TMHS	.54	3.82	3.50	4.25
1.3.2 Linkage to other COSPs	.69	2.77	2.69	2.84
1.3.3 Linkage with other service agencies	.65	3.44	2.91	3.97
2. Environment				
2.1.1 Local proximity	.57	3.06	3.09	3.03
2.1.2 Access	.78	4.19	4.13	4.25
2.1.3 Hours	.81	3.55	3.38	3.72
2.1.4 Cost	.72	3.25	4.56	1.94
2.1.5 Reasonable accommodation	.76	2.94	2.94	2.94
2.2.1 Lack of coerciveness	.58	2.70	3.59	1.81
2.2.2 Program rules	.87	3.72	4.44	3.00
2.3.1 Physical environment	.67	3.13	3.00	3.25
2.3.2 Social environment	.63	4.17	4.56	3.78
2.3.3 Sense of community	.87	3.08	3.69	2.49
2.4.1 Time frames	.71	3.58	3.75	3.25
3. Belief Systems				

3.1 Peer principle	1.81	3.72	2.77	.88
3.2 Helper's principle	2.56	3.56	3.06	.50
3.3.1 Personal empowerment	4.53	4.78	4.66	-.20
3.3.2 Personal accountability	3.88	4.59	4.23	.55
3.3.3 Group empowerment	2.31	3.59	2.95	.79
3.4 Choice	3.09	3.38	3.23	.84
3.5 Recovery	3.25	3.94	3.59	.60
3.6 Acceptance and respect for diversity	4.50	4.44	3.94	.69
3.7.1 Spiritual Growth	2.09	2.38	2.23	.82
4. Peer Support				
4.1.1 Formal peer support	3.03	3.84	3.44	.78
4.1.2 Informal peer support	2.28	4.00	3.14	.93
4.2 Telling our stories	3.03	4.13	3.58	.54
4.2.1 Artistic expression	2.31	3.44	2.88	.89
4.3 Consciousness raising	2.38	3.38	2.88	.63
4.4.1 Formal crisis prevention	3.75	2.68	3.22	.79
4.4.2 Informal crisis prevention	3.00	3.15	3.08	.23
4.5 Peer mentoring and teaching	1.97	3.46	2.67	.90
5. Education				
5.1.1 Formally structured activities	2.56	3.14	2.83	.64
5.1.2 Receiving informal support	2.78	4.31	3.55	.71
5.1.3 Providing informal support	2.13	3.63	2.88	.87
5.2.1 Formal skills practice	2.72	3.06	2.64	.87
5.2.2 Job readiness activities	1.97	2.72	2.34	.93
6. Advocacy				
6.1.1 Formal self-advocacy activities	1.69	3.34	2.52	.84
6.2 Peer advocacy	2.19	4.03	3.11	.81
6.2.1 Outreach to participants	1.59	3.16	2.38	.93

*Traditional mental health services

acteristics typify a group of programs, and quite another to test these as-
sertions empirically, in the real world. Consequently, the first question we
ask is whether we actually find the common ingredients as defined in the
FACIT in the participating COSP MRI programs.

In the absence of previous work operationally defining COSPs, the
question cuts two ways by asking about both the instrument and the
programs. On one hand, is the instrument capable of detecting the ingredients we believe to be there? On the other hand, are the programs
exhibiting the characteristics we believe them to have? The data reported
in this study became the first independent test of the degree to which the
peer-run programs met the very high standards they had proposed for
themselves.

Table 11.3 addresses the validity question and shows both the overall FACIT scores and the scores in each domain for participating COSPs.
The average item score among COSPs on the FACIT is 3.7. The range of
possible scores is 1.0 to 4.6. An alternative way to examine these scales
is to translate them to a 0 to 100 scale (see Figure 11.1). Out of all pos-

**Table 11.3. Performance of COSPs and TMHS Programs
on FACIT by Domain (Second Round Site Visits)**

	Range		COSPs			TMHS programs		
	Min	Max	Mean (SD)	Min	Max	Mean (SD)	Min	Max
1. Structure	10	48	38.81 (3.87)	33	43	24.13 (4.16)	18	30
2. Environment	11	50	38.31 (4.92)	32	45	29.63 (4.31)	24	33
3. Belief Systems	9	39	34.75 (2.05)	33	38	27.38 (5.40)	17	33
4. Peer support	8	35	28.50 (3.07)	25	34	21.88 (5.28)	15	27
5. Education	5	25	17.00 (5.24)	12	25	11.38 (4.17)	5	17
6. Advocacy	3	15	10.38 (2.97)	8	15	5.75 (2.43)	2	9
Overall total	46	212	167.75	157	182	120.13	87	143
Overall average			3.70 (0.22)			2.68 (0.43)		

Figure 11.1. Performance on FACIT by COSPs and TMHSs		
	COSP	**TMHS**
1. Program Structure	75.82	37.17
2. Environment	70.03	47.76
3. Belief Systems	85.83	61.25
4. Peer Support	75.93	51.39
5. Education	60.00	31.88
6. Advocacy	61.46	22.92
Total	73.34	44.65

sible points that could be received on the FACIT, COSPs received 73.3 percent. In other words, the majority of elements that were proposed to be common ingredients of COSPs as outlined in the FACIT were actually observed in our eight COSP MRI programs.

There was some variability in COSP performance by domain. Whereas within the Belief Systems domain, COSPs received 85.83 percent of the possible points and within the Structure domain, they received 75.82 percent of the possible points, within the Education (60.00 percent) and Advocacy (61.46 percent) domains, COSPs did not perform quite as well on average. Interestingly, as we discuss shortly, some COSPs performed exceptionally well on these domains, while others exhibited these ingredients less strongly. Taken as a whole, it would appear that ingredients in four of the domains (Program Structure, Environment, Belief Systems, and Peer Support) are common to all of the participating peer programs in the COSP MRI, while the items in the other two (Education and Advocacy) apply most strongly to a subset of programs.

Are There Differences between COSPs and TMHS Programs?

Table 11.3 also provides evidence to begin to address the question regarding measurable differences between COSPs and TMHS programs. First, it is important to note that at each of the sites, the overall FACIT score was higher for the COSP than for the TMHS program. Were there no difference between these program types, the likelihood of this happening as a result of chance is extremely low (p = .0039). This finding confirms that the implementation of the COSP intervention did indeed take place, relative to the TMHS or control intervention in this study. Consumers were truly receiving two different kinds of services in the two major treatment arms of the COSP MRI.

The average TMHS FACIT item score is 2.68. The difference between the COSP and TMHS overall average item scores is highly significant ($t = 5.377$; $df = 15$ $p<.005$). Moreover, there was no overlap between the range of overall scores for the COSP (3.41–3.96) and traditional mental health programs (2.02–3.11). Thus, the lowest-scoring COSP had a higher overall score than the highest-scoring TMHS program. There was some overlap across domains, but the average performance in each case was invariably higher in the COSP than the TMHS programs. The differences can be visualized in Figure 11.1, which presents these findings in terms of the percentages of possible points that COSPs and TMHS programs received in these ratings.

Within each of the six domains, there was some overlap between COSPs and TMHS programs. On some items, especially within Belief Systems, TMHS programs as a whole appeared to be particularly oriented to consumer values, and a small subset of TMHS programs appeared to have embraced some of the ingredients identified as important for COSPs. We return to this point in the conclusion.

Are There Differences among Various COSP models?

The final research question we addressed was whether there were measurable differences among the COSPs based on the program model they used.

To summarize these differences, we highlight some of the features of the three respective models, or clusters, that were the focus of the COSP MRI. The four *consumer-run drop-in programs* provide an open venue for consumers to receive a variety of services as needed in a specific location. Individuals participate in drop-in activities on a voluntary and noncoercive basis. Service components vary but parallel the range of traditional mental health and social services, including support and activity groups; access to telephones, laundry facilities, and computers; and assistance with entitlements, medication education, clothing, and bus or transportation passes. Both of the *peer-support programs* have a systematic approach consistent with the principles of empowerment and recovery, one offering individual-based support for people with problems associated with substance abuse and mental illness, and the other offering group-based assistance. Like drop-in centers, the peer-support programs frequently help consumers to manage a range of personal concerns, including those associated with work, recreation, housing, health, and personal relationships. The two *educational programs* are organized around the belief that consumers are best able to manage their own disabilities and to address what is wrong with the mental health system when they have accurate and comprehensive knowledge about mental illness and psychiatric services. These educational, or training, programs use well-defined curricula to impart this kind of information, usually in short-term classroom settings. These programs rely on peer support to a somewhat lesser degree than the other models to accomplish their goals, as peer support is defined in the FACIT.

Table 11.4 and Figure 11.2 present information that begins to address the issue of differences among programs. There is notable variability among the three clusters of COSPs, each employing a particular program model. The overall scores for the three types of program are relatively close to one another, with .27 separating the lowest from the highest cluster. Also, that much of the difference between the lowest and highest clusters may be accounted for by differences in the Education and Advocacy domains, in which educational programs received substantially higher total scores than did the other program models. Conversely, the Peer Support ratings for these programs were lower than those of the other programs, which explicitly rely on peer interactions to achieve their impact. Similarly, drop-in centers explicitly provide an environment for services and interactions, and they obtained the highest ratings in this domain. It is important to note that while subjects in the COSP MRI study were randomized, program participants interviewed by site visitors were not. It may be that participation in educational programs requires a threshold of communication, ability, and interest that is not required for other programs.

Programs from all three models had their highest scores in the Belief Systems domain. Interestingly, this is also the domain in which traditional services were able to obtain the highest ratings. Figure 11.2 suggests overall that, while there may be differences in performance across the first four domains, the ingredients are generally present among all COSP models, although they are less so within the two domains of Education and Advocacy.

Table 11.4. Performance of COSP Clusters on FACIT (Wave II)

	Consumer-run drop-in centers			Peer-support programs			Education and advocacy programs		
	Mean	Min	Max	Mean	Min	Max	Mean	Min	Max
1. Structure	39.13	34	43	35.00	33	37	42.00	41	43
2. Environment	42.38	38.5	45	34.00	32	36	36.75	36	37.5
3. Belief Systems	34.75	34	38	35.50	33	38	34.50	34	35
4. Peer Support	29.25	26	34	29.50	29	30	23.25	19.5	27
5. Education	13.25	12	15	16.50	16	17	23.75	22.5	25
6. Advocacy	8.00	8	9	12.00	10	14	13.50	12	15
Total	166.76	157	182	162.50	159	166	175.00	173	177
Overall Average	3.63			3.65			3.90		

Figure 11.2. Performance on FACIT by COSP Models and TMHS

	COSP	TMHS	Consumer-run drop-in programs	Peer-support programs	Education and advocacy programs
1. Program Structure	75.82	37.17	76.64	65.79	84.21
2. Environment	70.03	47.76	80.45	58.98	60.26
3. Belief Systems	85.83	61.25	85.83	88.33	83.33
4. Peer Support	75.93	51.39	78.7	79.63	66.67
5. Education	60	31.88	41.25	57.5	100
6. Advocacy	61.46	22.92	41.67	75	87.5
Total	73.34	44.65	72.74	70.18	77.71

Conclusions

In addressing the three research questions that directed our efforts, we believe that it is possible to identify and validate a set of common ingredients implemented by the consumer-operated services participating in this MRI. Furthermore, COSPs and TMHS programs display measurably different patterns in their expression of these ingredients, with COSPs displaying them to a much greater degree. Finally, using the data available, at an overall level, we were unable to substantially distinguish among programs using the three program models: these differences were small. However, with analyses of larger numbers of programs, it is possible that patterns of strength may emerge from particular program models.

The FACIT as an instrument appears to have some important positive attributes that may support its use in other evaluations. Persons with day-to-day involvement with the eight COSPs were actively involved in the development of both the list of common ingredients and the instrument itself, and this involvement appears to have enhanced the reliability and validity of the instrument. Not only can the instrument be used with a range of different models of consumer-operated services but also it appears feasible to use the instrument with other more traditional mental health services. The fact that traditional services may have adopted the linguistic practices of the consumer movement in espousing empowerment, recovery, and individual autonomy (Anthony 2000) does not guarantee that these principles are embodied in practice. The FACIT may be a useful tool in teasing out this disjunction between rhetoric and practice. Interrater reliability appears to be adequate at the item level and quite high at the overall score level. The FACIT could be effectively employed by TMHS as a tool for measuring the consumer orientation, or consumer friendliness, of their programs and services.

It is important to emphasize that the FACIT was originally developed to help describe (and quantify) consumer-operated services rather than to suggest what a program should be. As the statistics regarding the Education and Advocacy domains make clear, not all COSPs provide services that address these areas, and the results presented here should not be taken as an indication that they should. The FACIT is not intended as a prescription for COSPs, but it could be a valuable tool in helping to identify the current characteristics of a program objectively. While the FACIT provides a reasonably comprehensive menu of possible elements of a COSP, it is unlikely that any one COSP would embody all of the elements contained in the FACIT at their maximum levels.

One question that still needs to be addressed is whether the common ingredients of consumer-operated services are actually active ingredients. That is, do the kinds of things that differentiate consumer-operated and traditional services actually lead to differences at an individual level in empowerment, quality of life, and a range of other potential indicators? It should be understood that the relationship between performance by the program on the FACIT and by individual outcomes of any type has not yet been established. It remains an important question for future study and will be explored in outcome analyses for the COSP MRI.

The development and use of the FACIT is but one prong of a multi-pronged approach to understanding the impact of participation in consumer-operated services on positive outcomes at an individual level. Other components employed in the current study include the development of program descriptions of the sort found in this book, collection of information about the mental health service system delivery network and how the COSP fits within that network, and information about utilization rates of COSP and TMHS. All of these are essential parts of the story of consumer-operated services. We believe, however, that use of a fidelity instrument such as the FACIT can add precision to the storytelling. By carefully identifying program elements, ultimately we may be able to "look under the hood" of the program and better identify those elements the program can use to help its participants to achieve even better outcomes.

References

Anthony, W. A. 2000. A recovery-oriented service system: Setting some system-level standards. Psychiatric Rehabilitation Journal 24(2):159–68.

Bond, G. L., R., Evans, M. P. Salyers, J. Williams, and H. W. Kim. 2000. Measurement of fidelity in psychiatric rehabilitation. *Mental Health Services Research* 2(2):75–87.

Campbell, J., and J. Dumont. 1998. Core competencies of consumer providers: Mapping peer program activities. A report by the Missouri Institute of Mental Health Program in Consumer Studies and Training, St. Louis, MO. Supported through a subcontract with the Center for Mental Health Policy and Services Research, University of Pennsylvania.

Donabedian, A. 1980. *Definition of quality and approaches to its assessment.* Vol. 1 of *Explorations in quality assessment and monitoring.* Chicago: Health Administration Press.

Fekete, D., G. A. Bond, E. C. McDonel, M. Salyers, A. Chen, and L. Miller. 1998.

Rural assertive community treatment: A field experiment. *Psychiatric Rehabilitation Journal* 28(4):371–79.

Johnsen, M., L. Samberg, R. Calsyn, M. Blasinsky, W. Landow, and H. Goldman. 1999. Case management models for persons who are homeless and mentally ill: The ACCESS demonstration project. *Community Mental Health Journal* 35(4):325–46.

Linkins, K., A. Lucca, E. C. McDonel Herr, J. Jacobs, and R. Fox. Forthcoming. A meta-evaluation of the Community Support Program Research Demonstration Grant Program. Monograph to be published by SAMHSA.

McDonel, E. C., G. R. Bond, M. Salyers, D. Fekete, A. Chen, J. H. McGrew, and L. Miller. 1997. Implementing assertive community treatment programs in rural settings. *Administration and Policy in Mental Health* 25(2):153–73.

McGrew, J. H., and G. G. Bond. 1995. Critical ingredients of assertive community treatment: Judgments of the experts. *Journal of Mental Health Administration* 22(2):113–25.

McGrew, J. H., G. R. Bond, L. L. Dietzen, and M. Salyers. 1994. Measuring the fidelity of implementation of a mental health program model. *Journal of Consulting and Clinical Psychology* 62 (4):670–78.

Mowbray, C. T., and M. Holter. 2000. Emerging Program Models: Developing and Testing Fidelity Criteria. Paper presented at the American Evaluation Association Annual Meeting, November.

Teague, G. B., G. R. Bond, and R. E. Drake. 1998. Program fidelity in assertive community treatment: Development and use of a measure. *American Journal of Orthopsychiatry* 68(2):216–32.

12
With Us: Where Are We Going?

*Sally Clay, with contributions
from Bonnie Schell, Patrick
Corrigan, and Jean Campbell*

It was the summer of 1980. As at most state mental hospitals, the grounds at the Augusta Mental Health Institute (AMHI) in Maine were well manicured and green, and they showcased curved driveways and attractive trees that had once been planted with care. Behind the locked doors of AMHI, however, a brown haze enveloped the dimly lit rooms of the psychiatric ward, and an unnatural silence prevailed among the patients who paced endlessly or sat staring blankly in front of the TV, smoking. I was one of those patients, serving out my time in an involuntary commitment. I had been there about three weeks and it was almost time for me to be sent home; I was still in the down phase of my last manic episode, brought further down by the heavy dose of Thorazine I was given. I felt numb and dejected but was unreasonably hopeful at the thought of going back to my apartment, where I would try once again to jump-start my life.

I had spoken to the psychiatrist only once since I arrived at AMHI. The day after my admission he talked to me for less than ten minutes and prescribed the anti-psychotic medication without ever returning to see how it affected my thinking and mood. Now, three weeks later, I sat for my discharge evaluation with him. He complimented me on how well I was doing. He asked me what my plans were. Did I live with anyone? Did I have a job? Did I have friends? Did I have a support system? The answer to all of those questions was no.

I had been hospitalized over a dozen times at this point, but this time I had learned from some of my fellow patients at AMHI that there was a new organization in Portland for families, and that former mental patients were joining. It was after this hospitalization that I joined the fledgling peer support group and then organized a consumer-operated program, creating a support system for myself and others.

We called the program the Portland Coalition for the Psychiatrically Labeled. In the years ahead I went on to organize PEOPLe, Inc. (Projects to Empower and Organize the Psychiatrically Labeled), in Poughkeepsie, New York, and to take part in starting the PEER Center, Inc., in Fort Lauderdale, Florida. None of these programs had the budget or elaborate facilities of the state institutions that kept people out of the community locked away. Neither did they have a professional staff or operations manuals or much oversight. What these ex-patient programs did have was a steady flow of volunteers and budding leaders, buoyed by the promise of re-integration into the community and re-gaining a meaningful role in society.

My experiences parallel those of other consumer/survivors who created peer-run programs like the ones highlighted in this book. Our stories, most of them positive, reflect our fundamental optimism and resiliency. Nevertheless, there are mixed blessings to our experiences, including the four-year experience of the research project. Because we participated as full members of the Steering Committee for the COSP Multi-Site Research Initiative, which guided all aspects of the study, we put ourselves, along with the researchers and the coordinating center, under great stress and in doing so we may have lost connection at times with the need to maintain our own well being.

Obstacles and Pitfalls

As the stories in previous chapters reveal, peer-run programs are widely used by mental health consumer/survivors who seek independence and a place to belong. The COSP fidelity study has shown that peer-run programs do have common structures, values, and activities that lead to their success and make them distinct from traditional clinical programs. Like not-for-profits that serve other special needs groups (alcoholics, trauma survivors, AIDS patients, gays and lesbians, gray whales), a peer-run program for mental health inevitably faces obstacles to its success, pitfalls that threaten its very existence. The difficulties listed below are only a few of the problems common to peer-run programs that cropped up in full force during the COSP study.

Our Struggle: Pulling Up Those Bootstraps

Mental health clients are smugly told, over and over again, that if only we would "pull ourselves up by our bootstraps," we could easily become well and happy and normal like everyone else. By definition, those who start peer-run programs are themselves "psychiatrically labeled," and we have experienced the same emotional and cognitive struggles as have the other members of our group. The result of anyone's first mental crisis, if it leads to involvement with the mental health system, is to fall down several rungs on the status ladder. It is an enormous shock to find yourself, within the space of a few weeks or hours, transformed from promising young student to black sheep, or outcast. Wherever we came from, we have lost any social standing that we once had, and we are now defeated and often alone.

We may or may not accept the idea that we have a brain disease, but we continue to struggle with the fears and confusions that characterize what we have. We hope that our medications will "make it all better," but we know that they provide only a partial "fix." We are still coping with this kind of pain and uncertainty, even as we present ourselves as leaders and mentors for other people.

Our Leaders: Too Vulnerable and Yet Too Mighty

Despite the success and longevity of many grassroots organizations, some fall prey to the dangers inherent in programs started by inexperienced or untrained people who lack their own support system and, worse, are even disparaged by the professionals and agencies that profess to work for the same people and goals. Most consumer/survivors "get into the business" of running a peer program because they have been inspired by their own experience with peers and with self-help. Few of these new leaders have degrees in social work or experience in accounting or business planning or project management.

Few of us have sufficient independent income to work for the cause of self-help without a salary, or even to travel without being sponsored to meetings and conferences that would benefit our programs and our own recovery. A large proportion of consumer/survivors, including leaders and program directors, subsist on Supplemental Security Income (SSI), which means that they have to pay their rent and all of their bills with less than six hundred dollars a month. When I organized the Portland Coalition in 1981, I lived with no income at all for four years and was able to get by only through a trust fund from my family. Bonnie Schell volunteered her time from 1991 to 1995 to start the Mental Health Client Action Network (MHCAN), and later she accepted a half-time wage for a full time job, but she had income from her family as well.

Most other consumer leaders are too proud to admit that they are penniless, and they become angry if they are described in any way as poor or fragile. We do believe in responsible and efficient leadership; it is just that often we come to jobs we love without salaries to compensate for the long hours and without a working vehicle or funds to travel to national workshops and conferences.

New officers of peer-run programs sincerely believe in equality among peers and are hesitant to risk hurting someone's feelings by exercising authority over other people. Often they allow communications to become dominated by whoever can talk the longest and loudest. This results in the silencing of more moderate voices and well-thought-out decisions that might lead to constructive growth. We hesitate to follow the lead of traditional therapists who label their clients as "difficult" or "obstreperous" or "borderline" or "anti-social"; we find ourselves sometimes worn down by the very tolerance we extend to others because we have no strategy to deal with such situations.

Our Anger: When Empowerment Forgets Compassion

Participants in educational, peer support, or drop-in programs gradually overcome the passive dependency that they had to cultivate in order to negotiate the mental health system, and they savor their new feelings of energy and self-worth. This positive energy is what we mean by empowerment. When we learn to redirect our accumulated rage against the poverty and exclusion that we live with, we can heal ourselves and change the lives of our peers. All peer programs are built on a scaffolding of advocacy for social change. Through empowerment, our anger at the "system" is channeled to working with others and learning how to take a legitimate place in our community of choice.

At the same time, there are always some loud complainers and whiners all too willing to let the "old guard," or the original leaders, continue to assume all of the responsibility and the work of an organization. Despite their professed desire for openness and equality, a handful of dedicated leaders find themselves appointed repeatedly to all of the high-level positions, and doing all of the work that goes along with it. These same "consumer stars" (with the unfortunate descriptor of "high-functioning") are the ones noticed by providers and government agencies—the ones picked to write grant proposals and invited to sit on policymaking boards and government committees. Because they want to keep the funder or benefactors of their peer-run agency engaged, the "star" consumers do not say no. It is a recipe for exclusion, resentment, and burnout.

For some consumer/survivors, anger becomes not a means to empowerment but an end in itself, and it turns inward. Jealously simmers, and resentment becomes redirected toward one's own peer leaders. It becomes a desire for power, as disgruntled members covet the authority and status of their leaders and disguise their envy as righteous anger. They want to get their foot in the door of administrative control, although they may be unwilling or unable to carry out the work, skills, and commitment necessary to carry out the positions that they seek. When they do cross the threshold of authority, they do not know what to do with it. This scenario plays out often among nonprofits and new enterprises of all kinds, leaving a trail of ousted administrators, bloody and bitter. It even happened to Steve Jobs at Apple Computer!

Our Burden: Picking Up Briefcases

Another common obstacle to the success of peer-run programs is what Jean Campbell calls "professionalization" (see Chapter 2). This is a scenario that occurs when a peer program joins in partnership or is funded by a professional agency. While the idea of working cooperatively with other community agencies is appealing, and offers the promise of needed funding, technical assistance, and an integrated service system, there is always the danger of "co-option" of a peer program's basic principles and unique benefits. Unknowing people, sometimes even our families and the state agencies that fund us, expect us to function on the same rigid 8:00 to 5:00 schedules and limited, preplanned vacations as so-called normal people.

Keeping financial records and designing programs to fit the mold required by government sources may become a burden to consumer/survivors, whose programs depend on informality and spontaneity for their effectiveness. It is hard to enjoy the freedom and openness of peer support, mentoring, or personalized training when paperwork and reporting requirements take up valuable time and detract from natural warmth and fellowship. External rules and procedures imposed on peer programs by governments and agencies can stifle the unique services that clients say they want and that peer programs deliver.

Traditional community agencies like to dictate who can be served, and how, and this tends to give some people with mental illness more services, while clients who require more flexibility in their system of care get less attention. Peer programs traditionally serve those who "fall through the cracks" of traditional service programs, and those that the agencies refuse to help. For example, a homeless person may not be allowed to join in a men's support group at a traditional agency if he never became eligible for Medicaid. People with personality disorders may be excluded because they do not have an Axis I diagnosis. Persons who are at risk of being homeless or who have addiction or trauma disorders or learning disabilities are often left out of conventional programs, but they are always welcome at drop-in centers. Advocacy programs train patients who are angry about the system that may have shut them out because they are judged "difficult." As consumer/survivors, we treat the untreatable as friends. We make the homeless feel at home. This is what we are good at, but it does not work when too many limits and restrictions are imposed on our way of doing business.

In a bureaucratic environment, consumer/survivor ideas about what is helpful may be dismissed as "non-evidence-based," and less necessary than, say, involuntary treatment programs, drug courts, and compliance with assertive community treatment plans. As a result of this distorted viewpoint, the public is mostly unaware that the unique value of peer-run programs is their embodiment of American values of choice and freedom. Will the measures of research predict positive outcomes for our lives? Can a Managed Care or Health Maintenance Organization require a mental health facility to adopt the common ingredients without perverting them?

Our Choices: People Over Potholes

When mental hospitals closed under deinstitutionalization, former patients were moved to nursing and boarding homes with their needs unaddressed and their problems intact. The funds that had been spent for them in the institutions did not move with them into the community, and thousands of mental health clients were left stranded and vulnerable, with no means of either emotional or material support. Even when the valuable real estate on which state hospitals stood is sold, the profits do not go into resources for community-based mental health but into the state general fund. When I was a peer advocate in New York State, we often joked that the public would rather spend their money on potholes than people, and this was often all too literally true. Organizations that serve the unemployed, medically untreated, and rejected are the organizations that have to put on bake sales and book sales, and who send out begging letters that yield poor results from an equally poor constituency.

Homelessness is commonplace in our nation's urban areas, and poverty is the standard condition for mental health consumers. Most mental health clients served by the public systems of care are unemployed, and the rest are underemployed. In budget crunch times, such as we now experience, peer-run programs are the last to be funded and the first to be cut. Those of us on the bottom rungs of the social-economic ladder can still compute that the amount spent for one Blackhawk helicopter or stealth bomber would fund dozens or even hundreds of mental health programs at home and would pay the yearly expenses of thousands of mental health clients. In the year 2000 the percentage of SSI benefits needed to rent a one-bedroom housing unit in one of the eight COSP sites was: 90.1 percent in Maine, 108.8 percent in Florida, 82.9 percent in Missouri, 95.7 percent in Pennsylvania, 122.1 percent in Illinois, and 113.4 percent in California (Cooper and O'Hara 2003). For example, a mental health client living in Illinois with an income of $600 a month would have to pay $732.60 a month to rent a small apartment.

Another disadvantage inherent in government funding is that any substantial amount awarded to peer programs, and other nonprofits for that matter, is for the most part received for a limited amount of time. When the grant ends, the directors of the programs find themselves spending huge amounts of time writing closeout reports while at the same time making a pitch for more grants. They must justify more and more budgets, with less and less time to devote to the actual people and work of the program. And some good programs that have met a critical simple need—such as training peers to accompany others to their primary care physician—suddenly cease.

Peer programs such as Friends Connection and the St. Louis Empowerment Center are able to avoid some of the funding hassles, because they operate within another organization—Friends Connection within a Mental Health Association, and the Empowerment Center in partnership with their local Mental Health Association and the Depression and BiPolar Support Alliance (formerly, Depressive and Manic Depressive Association). The larger organization can absorb accounting duties for these programs without jeopardizing the independence of the peer program. Until a percentage of sales taxes or income taxes or vehicle taxes is dedicated to the mental health community, consumer leaders will never be able to do their work without looking over their shoulder for the next catastrophe. Like all nonprofits, their programs do not attract venture capitalists as the dot-coms did after the millennium.

Research and Reality

During the first year or so of the COSP study, all seemed to be going smoothly. The initial fear that consumers and researchers would have difficulty relating to each other and working together proved to be largely unfounded. The COSP multi-site project could be viewed as a four-year enterprise that encompassed the daily problems of small nonprofits, the sometimes convoluted requirements of research departments at universities, and the bureaucratic demands and paperwork attached to government funding.

For the nonprofit agencies, it is always a challenge to keep in the good graces of their board of directors or trustees. In a project that lasts for four years, some board members may have their pet projects and have difficulty accepting that grant funds can be spent only on what was approved from the grant proposal. Boards have the power to hire and fire the executive director, and some of them did just that during the research study.

About midway through the multi-site study, in February 2001, the PEER Center was taken over by a group of disgruntled members who commandeered the monthly board meeting and removed the executive director from office. PEER Center, Inc., was the largest and most complex of all of the consumer-operated programs in the study. It boasted over two thousand members and forty employees and owned its own facility with multi-faceted departments. Yet the coup was accomplished with virtually no protest from either its government funders or its own members.

How could such a thing happen? The reasons may be debated for a long time to come, but they certainly included many of the obstacles and pitfalls described earlier in this chapter. Quarrels and jealousy among peers have long posed dangers to peer-run endeavors and plagued their leaders. Events such as this are, in fact, quite common among nonprofit programs of all kinds.

Members of the COSP Steering Committee, which included all key players in the project—researchers, consumers, and federal officers— were aghast at the PEER Center coup. The study continued unabated, but unease and doubt threatened to disrupt the research process. Questions that had been raised earlier in the study—about the efficacy of the COSP research design and the harm it might do to the sites under study—now reappeared.

The Uncertainty Principle

A famous law of modern physics is called the Heisenberg Uncertainty Principle. This principle holds that it is impossible to determine both the location and the speed of a particle at the same time. In other words, the very act of observing alters the subject being observed. Something like this seems to happen in evaluating grassroots programs such as the peer sites in the COSP study. The Consumer Advisory Panel of the COSP from the beginning was concerned about randomizing subjects to programs that, as a matter of principle, seek to attract only consumers who come of their own free will. The mission and character of a consumer organization appears to operate in opposition to classic research procedures. The very heart of peer programs is freedom from the kind of pressure caused by the time and attention demanded by randomization methods in a quantitative study.

Several problems arose as a result of having to expand services beyond the size and scope of the original vision and missions of the organization. The director of Advocacy Unlimited complained that the research study had "mutated" her program by assigning consumers who were not ready for her program's training. In other cases, the infusion of federal funds to "enhance" the peer programs made them victims of their own success, because when the project ended and the funds were removed, the programs could no longer support their increased membership. Further, outreach to people cut off by language differences or living in rural areas without transportation or a fixed address lost importance in the zeal to get the numbers. The increase in numbers did, however, force consumer-run organizations to learn how to relate to consumers they might not have chosen but surely had a mission to serve.

Leadership and Staffing

Disputes over who is the valid spokesperson for the organization or the study evidenced in a few of the peer programs, but were also an issue within the Steering Committee, where the researchers, the consumers, the Coordinating Center, and the federal officers each had a slightly different take on the purposes and promise of the multi-site study.

In most of the peer-run programs, resentments erupted when the consumer leaders had much higher income and responsibilities than the line staff and volunteers. At several of the COSP sites, employees unaccustomed to larger budgets and the enormous amount of work and time required by the research protested that regular operations of the consumer program were neglected. By the end of the study, most of the eight peer-run programs experienced the loss of executive leadership.

At the same time, there was turnover in the Coordinating Center staff and in some of the research staff as well. These latter changes in personnel were seen as normal, whereas any changes in consumer staff were frequently interpreted as an exacerbation of symptoms of mental illness.

Scheduling and Organization

Getting the protocol for research set up and under way was delayed in the beginning by long debates over what questions to include in interviews and what domains were important to consumers. As a result, most of the sites hired interviewers and consumer advisers almost two years before the common ingredients and interviewing instruments were settled upon. Staff at several sites were left "twiddling their thumbs" while they waited for the interviews to begin. When recruitment began in earnest—overnight, it seemed—panic ensued as organizations had to double the number of personnel and provide oversight while meeting the almost weekly teleconference requirements of the study.

Where Did All the Money Go?

The COSP study ended, coincidentally, with an economic downturn in the economy, and the eight peer-run agencies all found themselves strapped for funds to keep their programs going. In each case the greatest loss occurred when the federal funds previously given to the states for community services was redirected to "bombs and potholes" in foreign countries and state highways, leaving human needs unmet and illnesses untreated. New budgets propose how to explore Mars but not how to provide a room with a bed and chair for all Americans on Earth. Unfortunately, programs that serve persons with psychiatric disabilities and differences are subject to the same ranking in importance by funders and policy makers as by their neighbors in the community: at the bottom (Corrigan 2004).

During the COSP multi-site study, the peer-run programs received enhancement funds to meet the needs of the anticipated increase in persons served during the research. Enhancements included boosts in staff and program supplies. All of the programs had to scale down to some degree when the COSP funding ceased. The educational programs had to reduce classes or activities, and the peer support programs had to lay off staff as well as reduce activities. The drop-in programs, which have little control on the number of participants, reported more problems than the others. Both the Portland Coalition and MHCAN drop-ins experienced hardships as a result of increased attendance with decreased funding, including increased demand for basic supplies, such as toilet paper, telephone use, coffee, and computer paper. Most of the programs, however, were able to deal with the cessation of the COSP funds. Missouri, in particular, started cutting hours and people in the third year so that the deficits at the end of year four would seem less overwhelming.

Unlike the cooperative partnership that flourished between the state and peer initiatives in Connecticut, Pennsylvania, and some other states, it seemed that some local funders did not understand the workings of a federal research grant and attempted to trim local funding to equal the federal infusion of funding. Both the Portland Coalition and GROW In Illinois met with resistance from their state agencies. The PEER Center found itself under continual pressure from the state agency in Florida, to do more with less support. Lack of state and county support is probably the single greatest factor in bringing about the downfall and even the demise of otherwise viable peer programs.

Site Updates: We Are Resilient

Information in the following thumbnail sketches was provided to me through personal communications with each of the authors of the site chapters. Some of the material may be sketchy or provisional, but it nevertheless indicates how the peer-run programs weathered both the stress of the COSP multi-site study and the recent cuts in government funding at the end of the study.— S.S.C.

Mental Health Client Action Network (MHCAN)–Santa Cruz, California

Bonnie Schell, director of MHCAN, reported that consumer attendance at her drop-in leapt from 4,100 visits in 1998 to 12,600 visits by the end of the COSP project, and staff increased from 6 to 16. At the end of the study, MHCAN found itself in the position of operating at the same level as before, using the same funds to serve three times the number of people. "We cut our open hours from 38 down to 24 a week," Bonnie said. "We cancelled the newspaper and membership in a video store. We stopped buying refreshments for consumer focus groups and asked some consumers to give up their stipends. We sold a van. We laid off one receptionist, a guitar teacher, an art teacher, and the LCSW who supervised the peer counselors."

MHCAN has successfully applied for new grants, but these do not contribute to operating expenses. At the same time, in California, workman's compensation, gasoline, electricity, and liability insurance have escalated.

"We were more active in the state consumer organization in the early years before the COSP study," Bonnie added. "Now our staff is stretched too thin, as is the budget, to participate in nonlocal client affairs. So for the past two years we have missed out on the Alternatives conferences, the Client Forum, and USPRA (United States Psychiatric Rehabilitation Association) conferences. Our staff people now seem too busy doing intakes and cleaning the kitchen to sit and listen to many consumers. Our program is more businesslike, less informally friendly. We spend a lot of time collecting data on attendees to justify our existence."

Balancing out these undesirable changes, however, were some positive effects from the experience. Bonnie described some of the organizational skills learned: "Five years ago none of us had the confidence to supervise anyone. We all talked and interrupted each other in staff meetings. We didn't know how to plan programs for future years. Now more case managers and psychiatrists refer people to the drop-in center or for support groups. We are invited to more meetings by traditional providers and used to solicit client opinion on program concerns, such as client-centered services."

Portland Coalition for the Psychiatrically Labeled (PCPL)–Portland, Maine

The Maine Department of Behavioral and Developmental Services had long given the PCPL only flat funding for their growing needs; in other words, there was no provision for cost-of-living increases in salaries and expenses. When the enhancement funds were applied to a budget that was lagging because of state cutbacks, they injected new life into the organization. Like MHCAN, under the research study the PCPL found that its membership was growing and its programs thriving; in particular, the vitality of its creative art program allowed the addition of a new art gallery site.

The PCPL was left reeling, however, in the third year of the study, when internal conflicts and the pressures of the research combined to throw the organization and its members out of balance. The executive director took a leave of absence and then resigned. At last report, the state agency was demanding that the Coalition repay some financial irregularities out of their current funding, which had already been cut. Remaining staff members were under pressure to merge their program with Amistad, a professionally run agency nearby.

As noted by a consumer-researcher at the site, "The PCPL is serving more and more people but with less and less resources, and is merging more and more with a quasi-consumer run agency.... I have concerns that PCPL may become defunct or lose its identity altogether and become a branch of the quasi-consumer run agency. If so, it would still be in existence but a shadow of its former self."

St. Louis Empowerment Center–St. Louis, Missouri

Unlike most of the other sites, especially the other drop-ins, the St. Louis Empowerment Center seemed to have weathered the damage caused by cuts in local funding and loss of COSP enhancement funds. The center was open fewer hours and did not have as many perks for members as before. But, as the director, Helen Minth, said, "In all other respects, the Empowerment Center runs the same program as before COSP. We receive excellent support from the traditional mental health services in our community, due in part from the publicity we received during the COSP study." Helen has been busy working out of her home to complete a grant request for more funding.

PEER Center, Inc.–Oakland Park, Florida

The PEER Center faced a major financial crisis as a result of the COSP funding cuts and also financial mismanagement under its new administration. The peer support program and the center's off-campus drop-in center both lost funding. Most of the forty staff members left or were fired, and regular members were frightened away by violent incidents among those who replaced them. Members report that a second mortgage was taken out on the PEER Center, whose first mortgage had been almost paid.

Finally, in the summer of 2002, a group of PEER Center members formed an ad hoc group to represent the membership, calling itself the Members' Advisory Committee. This group demanded the resignation of the persons who had led the forcible takeover of the PEER Center. Although turmoil in leadership at the center continued, and the agency came within a hair's breadth of being closed down, at last report the PEER

Center was rebuilding programs and had found a permanent director. The center is now operating with the help of volunteers and is trying to reestablish its activities and its staff.

One positive outcome of the PEER Center crisis is that members of the PEER Center, by forming the Advisory Committee, reclaimed ownership of their own organization and its programs.

GROW In Illinois

GROW was informed by the state of Illinois in January 2002 that they were among a dozen or so groups that would be cut by 66 percent. Lorraine Keck reports that "the reasons given came on the tails of a struggling economy—that state funding should only go for treatment programs and not self-help or support programs like GROW." She was convinced that without a fight to save their program GROW would not still be around and possibly would not have been able even to finish the COSP project.

As for the long-term effects of the research project, normal operations of GROW programs were altered when traditional services were not allowed to make referrals to GROW, claiming that this would have affected the "recruitment process." As a result, when the study ended, GROW had to start all over again at one of its locations, rebuilding services in the area and renewing relationships with community mental health centers.

Friends Connection–Philadelphia, Pennsylvania

Jeanie Whitecraft, program director, wrote that her program has always enjoyed a good relationship with local agencies. "The Philadelphia County Office of Mental Health & Mental Retardation," she said, "has always supported the Friends Connection Peer Support Program." She added that the administration of the County Office of Mental Health advocates for peer-operated services. "Traditional services have valued our service."

Damages from loss of funding for the Friends Connection have to do more with the overall financial cuts than with COSP cutbacks. The agency lost twenty thousand dollars from county funding, their principal source of income. "We went from three supervisors to one. We also had to cut four line staff positions."

Advocacy Unlimited, Inc.–Connecticut

Advocacy Unlimited is one of the COSP sites whose staff most suffered pressures as a result of the study. During the research there was considerable staff turnover, and the executive director retired in July 2002. The

COSP study called for a large number of people to go through the program in a short time because of delays in starting and the inexperience of the new educators in selecting appropriate students for the program. "Some people that we accepted into the program were not at a place in their recovery where they could take in all the information," the former director Yvette Sangster reported. "As a result we had to add in an additional layer of support in the form of a mentoring group to teach and support them in the field."

Fortunately, Advocacy Unlimited continues to enjoy support from the Connecticut mental health system and from private contributors, and it remains viable after the research.

BRIDGES—Tennessee
BRIDGES is operating quite frugally because of budget restraints. The program has less staff, and support group facilitators are now volunteers no longer paid a stipend. There is currently no money for training new teachers and facilitators, and so the agency is re-exploring opportunities to enlist funding from providers that take part in their trainings.

"None of these changes appears to be directly due to stresses associated with the COSP study," Louetta Hix said. "We have updated our curriculum and it is streamlined and more flexible. A brief inpatient course has been developed and piloted. A Spanish translation has been drafted and a proposal prepared to pilot and evaluate the curriculum. The program manual has been revised to reflect current program procedures and to respond to frequent technical requests from the field."

Preliminary Findings of the COSP Study

At this writing, the analysis of research outcomes is ongoing, so we cannot comment on whether the study has shown "the cost effectiveness of consumer-operated programs for adults with serious and persistent mental illness when offered as an adjunct to traditional mental health services." Nevertheless, baseline studies offer promising indications that further analysis of the data will reveal positive outcomes, particularly in the domains of well-being and cost effectiveness. Hundreds of consumer-operated programs exist today in the United States and around the world. For those of us who met together for the COSP project in Washington, DC, as well as those who have met and made friends over the years at conferences such as Alternatives, NARPA (National Association of Rights Protection and Advocacy), and USPRA, the effectiveness of peer programs has already been demonstrated in our daily lives.

As the authors of Chapter 11 point out, the COSP study demonstrated that peer programs consistently adhere to the common ingredients used to define our organizations. We all value independence, peer support, advocacy, and education, and we all depend on the informality and safety of the environments that we create. Our member/participants are sensitive to the discomfort and even trauma that some have experienced in professional settings, and we are careful to honor the freedom of choice that is so important to developing trust and empowerment. Our peer programs give us a sense of belonging and acceptance.

Significantly, in the fidelity study the same common ingredients we observed in the peer programs were studied by COSP researchers in relation to the traditional programs that served the subjects in our study. Although it seems that professional agencies have, in fact, adopted some core values important to consumers, such as personal empowerment and respect for diversity (see Table 11.2), there remain wide differences between peer and professional services in the Fidelity study, with peer programs following much more closely their identified values and practices than do the providers.

New Directions

In the winter of 2003 Charles Curie, administrator of the U.S. Substance Abuse and Mental Health Services Administration (SAMHSA), reported on interviews that he had had with mental patients about to be discharged from a state hospital:

> I asked them what they needed to make their transition successful. They didn't say they needed a psychiatrist. They didn't say they needed a psychologist. They didn't even say they needed a social worker. They didn't say they needed a comprehensive service delivery system or evidenced-based practices. They said they need a job, a home, and meaningful personal relationships, or to use a direct quote . . . "I need a life—a real life . . . I need a job, a home and a date on weekends." (Curie 2003)

Perhaps we have reason to hope that the wisdom gained by three decades of peer advocacy is finally being acknowledged in professional contexts. In a time of limited fiscal resources, traditional mental health programs are increasingly strained by demands for effective services. A growing number of mental health administrators and policymakers now see peer-run programs as a means to expand the capacity of the mental health delivery system and to promote recovery in cost effective ways. Recent developments in peer research, practices, and organization lead knowledgeable professionals to welcome peer-run programs as key to reform within the mental health system.

In 1999, the Surgeon General's Report (Satcher 1999) recognized self-help as an important adjunct to traditional mental health services and concluded that self-help activities are powerful agents for change in service programs and policy. Two reviews of peer support programs (Davidson et al. 1999; Solomon and Draine 2001) present preliminary evidence that peer support programs are effective across a variety of domains. When the findings of the COSP Multi-Site Research Initiative (1998–2004) are released, the need for larger sample sizes, replications of findings, and generalization of findings to diverse programs, settings, and participant populations will be addressed. Now that the federal and state funders emphasize providing effective services that are evidence-based, establishing peer-run services as an evidence-based practice has become the key to their future as an important adjunct to traditional mental health services and an alternative service for patients to find stability and recovery.

When President George W. Bush announced the creation of the New Freedom Commission on Mental Health in 2001, he stated, "Our country must make a commitment: Americans with mental illness deserve our understanding, and they deserve excellent care" (New Freedom Commission on Mental Health 2003, 19). This statement heralded the first presidential commission on mental health since the Carter Administration created the Community Support System almost three decades ago.

> The initiative is a comprehensive plan that directs the Federal government to remove barriers to equality and community living for people with disabilities. The final report to the President that provides more than 400 specific solutions that agencies can use to support community living is at web site *www.hhs.gov/newfreedom/final/*. (del Vecchio et al. 2004)

After a year of study, research, and testimony, the final report of the commission, "Achieving the Promise: Transforming Mental Health

Care in America" (New Freedom Commission on Mental Health 2003) envisions a future where everyone with a mental illness can recover. The Consumer Issues Commission Subcommittee shared evidence that such programs could offer important lessons in identifying best practices for a recovery-based mental health system, and an array of peer-run services could promote the self-determination of persons with mental illness.

In addition, the commission's final report recommends the involvement of "consumers and families fully in orienting the mental health system toward recovery," noting that recovery-oriented services and supports are often provided not only through consumer-run organizations but also by consumers who work as providers in a variety of settings, such as crisis management and psychosocial rehabilitation programs. It points out that consumers who work in the mental health delivery work force have a key role in expanding the range and availability of services. Such consumer-providers increase the supports that the mental health system offers because they bring different experiences, attitudes, motivations, insights, and behavioral qualities to the personal encounters that facilitate recovery.

The report also identifies as a priority the direct participation of consumers and families in developing community-based, recovery-oriented treatment and support services, and it calls for local, state, and federal authorities specifically to encourage peer-support services. It states, "In particular, consumer-operated services for which an evidence base is emerging should be promoted" (New Freedom Commission on Mental Health 2003, 37).

Hopes for Tomorrow

An essay that appeared in an antipsychiatry magazine more than twenty years ago expresses the experience of many consumer/survivors at that time.

> The solution to emotional problems cannot be found by turning to experts trained in the arts of power and control. The solutions must be found by trusting ourselves and each other in fighting back against the forces which are daily mystifying, robbing and damaging us. (Miller 1983)

At the time, that statement, and *Madness Network News* in general, was considered hopelessly angry and radical. Yet listen to what was recently said by no less than the new administrator of SAMHSA:

> The Commission report found the nation's mental health care system to be well beyond simple repair. It recommends a wholesale transformation that involves consumers and providers, policymakers at all levels of government, and both the public and private sectors.... The new state agendas must be consumer and family driven—not bureaucratically bogged-down. Consumers of mental health services and their family members must stand at the center of the system of care. Consumer and family needs must drive the care and services that are provided. (Curie 2003)

Perhaps the government administrator's words are milder and more inclusive than the anguished statement written by an "ex-inmate" in *Madness Network News*. But the intent of the two views seems to have reached a remarkable convergence: both are saying that the mental health system as it has existed in this country must make a dramatic change, a change to policies that are not only *about* consumers and their families but that are "consumer and family driven"—in other words, they must be policies and services made *with* consumers.

When COSP members—consumers, researchers, and government project officers—met together as a Common Ingredients Subcommittee to identify and define the common ingredients of peer programs, the word *belonging* always came up. All of us agreed that perhaps the greatest benefit of peer programs is the sense of belonging that comes from our participation. Belonging, like recovery and spirituality, is a state that is hard to pin down; nevertheless, the heart of any peer program is the bonding and friendship that we gain from peer support and from relationships with others who have shared our experiences, as well as from the comfortable, accepting environments that we provide. As Janine Elkanich writes in Chapter 4, "It is probably one of the best feelings anyone can have to know that he or she is not alone, and it is one of the most rewarding feelings for the other person to be able to be there for someone in need."

References

Cooper, E., and A. O'Hara. 2003. Priced out in 2002: Housing crisis worsens for people with disabilities. *Opening Doors,* May, no. 21. *www.c-c-d.org/od-May03. htm*

Corrigan, P. W. 2004. *Beat the stigma and discrimination! Four lessons for mental health advocates.* Tinley Park, IL: Recovery Press.

Curie, C. G. 2003. Witness Testimony, Sub. On Substance Abuse Hearing: the New Freedom Comm. Report, Bill Number: Oversight, Hearing Date: November 4, 10:00 A.M. *http://health.senate.gov/testimony/108_tes.html*

Davidson, L., M. Chinman, B. Kloos, R. Weingarten, D. Stayner, and J. K. Tebes. 1999. Peer support among individuals with severe mental illness: A review of the evidence. *Clinical Psychology: Science and Practice* 9(2):165–87.

del Vecchio, P., C. Schauer, C. Marshall, and C. Speight. 2004. 2003 year in review. *CMHS Consumer Affairs E-News,* January 15, vol. 04–04. *www.mentalhealth. samhsa.gov/consumersurvivor/listserv/011504.asp.*

Miller, J. 1983. History of the Psychiatric Inmates Liberation Movement. *Madness Network News* 7(2).

New Freedom Commission on Mental Health. 2003. *Achieving the promise: Transforming mental health care in America: Final report.* DHHS pub. no. SMA-033832, Rockville, MD.

Satcher, D. 1999. *Mental health: A report of the Surgeon General.* U.S. Department of Health and Human Services, Substance Abuse and Mental Health Services Administration, Center for Mental Health Services, National Institutes of Health, National Institute of Mental Health, Rockville, MD.

Solomon P., and J. Draine. 2001. The state of knowledge of the effectiveness of consumer provided services. *Psychiatric Rehabilitation Journal* 25(1):20–27.

Epilogue:
Ourselves and Others

Before I became involved in the Portland Coalition, the PEER Center, and other peer programs, I had spent over twenty years going in and out of hospitals and clinics with severe manic episodes. I had consulted with numerous psychiatrists and therapists, and my life was an endless round of lost family and lost friends, lost jobs and lost homes. When, finally, at the age of forty, I took on the role of peer advocate and started working to help myself and others, I was astonished to find that I finally had a meaningful role in life. I had something to give. I belonged in this world.

It has been heartbreaking for me to write about the Portland Coalition and the PEER Center, programs that I helped to start and the two programs that experienced the most turmoil and personal suffering during the COSP study. Nevertheless, although both programs faltered, they are, for now, both still standing. Consumers and our programs are resilient. Perhaps what happened to all of us personally in the COSP multi-site study—consumers, researchers, and federal officers—will be of use beyond the quantitative information that emerges from the study. Perhaps it will lead us to better understand ourselves and others as human beings and fellow travelers.

Sally Clay
Lake Placid, Florida
September 13, 2004

Appendix A.
Guides to the Text

Table A.1. Glossary

accessibility   Easily approached, entered, or used, especially by someone with a disability.

advocate   A person who "speaks for" an individual, a cause, or a group of people; for example, a lawyer who works for patients' rights.

brain disease   Description of mental illness as a pathological condition of the brain resulting from causes such as infection, genetic defect, or environmental stress.

CAP (Consumer Advisory Panel)   A group of consumers that advise and comment on a professionally run project or organization. Sometimes called CAB (Consumer Advisory Board).

CIT (Crisis intervention team)   A group of people available to help a person in a mental health crisis or emergency.

clubhouse   A social and training program administered by professional staff that includes participation by consumer members but is not consumer operated.

cluster   A way to organize people or programs into a small number of separate groups that are similar within each group. In the COSP project, peer-run sites were organized into drop-in, peer support, and education clusters.

CMHS (Center for Mental Health Services)   A federal agency that focuses on mental health services, evaluation, and exchanging knowledge and information. CMHS is part of SAMHSA within the U.S. Department of Health and Human Services.

common ingredients   A list of components that apply to the peer-run programs examined in the COSP Multi-Site Research Initiative. These characteristics and qualities were drawn up by participants in the study, particularly the CAP.

community education   The use of public presentations or public relations to bring about positive changes in public attitude, for example, running a speakers bureau.

concept mapping A focus group methodology using multivariate statistics to achieve pictorial representations of people's thinking.

confidentiality A policy that no information revealed by an individual will be given to anyone except designated persons, such as medical or advocacy staff. For example, members of a peer support group could promise another member that her comments within the group will never reach anyone not in the group.

consciousness raising   A common result of peer support. Participants discover commonality with each other, and this discovery often produces a dramatic change in perspective from despair to hope and empowerment.

consumer coordinator   Person who plans and coordinates services by or for consumers, and who represents consumers in the larger organization.

consumer movement   The active body of individual mental health consumers and consumer groups who have met and planned for civil rights and improved mental health treatment since the early 1970's.

consumer operated   Consumers constitute the majority on the board of a peer-run program that decides policies and procedures for a program or organization. Staff consists largely of consumers, and consumers have control of the operating budget.

consumer/survivor   A person who uses services in mental health or substance abuse; the term preferred by mental health consumers. Other terms include "CSX," "mental health client," "mental health consumer," and "recipient." (See CSR.)

co-occurring disorder   Two different "diagnoses" given to the same person. Also referred to as "dual diagnosis."

COSP (Consumer-Operated Services Program)   Designation for peer-run programs studied by the COSP MRI.

CSR (consumer/survivor/recovering person)   Designation used in the substance abuse community. (See Consumer/survivor.)

CSX (consumer/survivor/ex-patient)   Designation used in the mental health community. (See Consumer/survivor.)

cultural diversity   Differences (for example, in race, language, or religion) in one community or organization. A neighborhood would be called culturally diverse if African American, Hispanic, white, Italian, and Asian groups all lived there.

DBSA (Depression and Bipolar Support Alliance)   Formerly NDMDA (National Depressive Manic Depressive Association), a patient-directed, national membership organization focusing on mood disorders.

diagnosis   A name of an illness and a description of the illness; usually taken from the *Diagnostic and Statistical Manual* of the American Psychiatric Association, which tries to group clients by their symptoms and the course of their illness.

drop-in center   A peer-run program that offers a comfortable and safe setting for consumer/survivors to meet with their peers, either formally or informally. Many drop-in centers provide other services, such as meals, assistance with housing, and job programs.

DSM (Diagnostic and Statistical Manual)   The book that lists the American Psychiatric Association definitions of mental disorders (illnesses).

dual diagnosis Two different diagnoses given to the same person, such as substance abuse and mental illness. Also referred to as "co-occurring disorder."

ECT (electroconvulsive therapy) Sometimes called "shock treatment."

empirical method A kind of research that is based on believing that facts must come through the senses or a practical experiment, not just through reasoning. A conclusion must be proven by results that can be measured.

empowerment The act of gaining power (such as the power to make decisions, to question, to act, or to vote) that often belongs only to a "higher" group, or a way of helping people who are not in the "higher" group to get this power.

entitlement A government program that guarantees and provides benefits to a particular group. Examples are Medicaid and SSI.

evaluation research A study to see whether a program or a project is doing what it set out to do.

evidence based   A paradigm for health care funding and clinical decisionmaking that relies on evidence from clinical research rather than intuition and hands-on experience.

facilitator   Someone who conducts an activity such as peer support or general meetings. A facilitator may follow an agenda and allow people to take turns speaking but does not control the group.

FACIT (COSP Fidelity Assessment Common Ingredients Tool)   The fidelity study instrument used to examine the consumer-operated sites. (See Chapter 11.)

fidelity A measure that examines program implementation. Fidelity measures generally rate a program against an agreed-upon list of components within a program model. In the case of the COSP project, common ingredients were used as the list of components that were measured. (See Chapter 11.)

focus group   A group of people who have shared an experience (for example, who have all taken the same medication or who have all been sexually harassed) and who are asked about that experience.

follow-up Contact with a person who has received services such as peer advocacy or case management to see whether further services are needed.

Helper's principle   The notion that helping others facilitates one's own recovery. Peer support is a two-way process.

HHS (Health and Human Services)   A major branch of the executive government that includes agencies and organizations related to mental health services, such as SAMHSA and CMHS.

HMO (health maintenance organization) A type of managed care arrangement. HMOs use a "capitated" financing system by which the HMO is paid a fixed amount per person rather than for each visit or by type of service.

informed consent   Agreement by a person receiving treatment, based on information given about the goals, methods, benefits, and risks of the treatment. Informed consent is given with the understanding that the person can change his or her mind about the treatment at any time.

insight   The capacity to see clearly and intuitively; to understand the true nature of a subject. Contrary to medical jargon, insight is the ability to see wellness, not illness.

intervention   A planned therapy, treatment, or action undertaken to change what is happening or might happen in another person's affairs, especially behavior viewed as undesirable.

medical model   A way of identifying or categorizing a condition or behavior as a disorder or illness that requires medical treatment or intervention.

mental health client   A person who uses mental health services. (See Consumer/survivor.)

mental health consumer   A person who uses services in mental health or substance abuse. (See Consumer/survivor.)

mentalism   An ideological framework of oppression that reinforces the idea that mental patients are personally deficient.

mentor   A consumer in recovery who serves as a trusted counselor, teacher, or role model to another consumer.

MHA, NMHA   A local or national Mental Health Association that advocates for mental health issues and often provides local services, such as housing and education.

MRI (multisite research initiative)   A research study that examines several different sites and coordinates the results.

multicultural   Involving two or more different groups of people, each with its own traditions, history, norms, and often language.

mutual support   Support given to and between individuals. In mutual support, consumer/survivors take turns being the "receiver" and "provider" of support. (See Peer support.)

NAMI (National Alliance for the Mentally Ill)   A nonprofit, grassroots, support, and advocacy organization of families, consumers, and friends of people with severe mental illnesses.

NASMHPD (National Association of State Mental Health Program

Directors)   A national organization that represents the policy interests of state departments of mental health.

outcome   The way a treatment or program, or a study or activity, turns out, showing the effect it has on people, or the record or measure of its effects.

peer   A person who has equal standing with another or others, or has had similar experiences as another.

peer advocate   A person who speaks on behalf of her or his peers. The advocate assists other consumers in resolving problems encountered in hospitals and the community, including treatment providers, community service agencies, family members, neighbors, and landlords. **[Appears as "peer advocacy" in COSP definitions.]**

peer counselor   A consumer who is employed by a peer-run program to provide support and encouragement to other members. Peer counseling is often a one-way assistance, in contrast to peer support, which is mutual assistance.

peer principle   The policy in peer-run programs that relationships are based on shared experiences and values. A peer relationship implies equality, along with mutual acceptance and mutual respect.

peer run   See Consumer operated.

peer specialist   A consumer who works with other consumers as a case manager, assisting other consumers to obtain services, jobs, or housing.

peer support   Mutual support and encouragement provided between individual consumers or in a group run by and for consumers.

PI (principal investigator)   The main person running a research study.

pioneer dialogues   Meetings that bring together people from different parts of the mental health system (consumers as well as professionals) to solve problems, make plans, give feedback, and learn about each other's points of view.

prosumer   A consumer/survivor who is also working a professional in the mental health field.

provider agency   An agency that provides treatment or residential services for mental health consumers.

psychosocial rehabilitation   A kind of therapy to improve a person's mental health by looking at how the person can be happier and more skillful in social settings; a realistic plan to achieve self-identified goals.

quality of life   A person's well-being (physical, mental, emotional, social) looked at as a whole, usually by that person.

qualitative studies   Research reporting what people say or write in words, rather than by tabulating numbered answers. Such studies may be based on short answers, personal histories, or focus groups.

quantitative studies   Studies of information that people give in numbers or in a way that can be numbered.

reasonable accommodation   Willingness of an employer to adjust or modify job requirements in order to meet the needs of a person with a disability.

recipient   Someone who receives mental health treatment or services. (See Consumer/survivor.)

recovery   A return to a normal condition; the return of something to a normal or improved state after a setback or loss. Some consumer/survivors aspire to recovery; others believe that they can embrace the changes they have gone through and aspire to a state of "well-being."

RFP (request for proposal)   An announcement that a grant or other funding is available; it also asks for responses (applications) from people who want to get that funding.

risks and benefits   What might go wrong because of a treatment and what good might come of the treatment.

SAMHSA (Substance Abuse and Mental Health Services Administration)   An organization of the federal government, within U.S. Health and Human Services.

substance abuse   Addiction to alcohol or drugs. Sometimes this term is separated from "chemical dependence," which is less severe.

self-advocacy   Consumer/survivors learn to identify their own needs and to speak for themselves, becoming active partners in developing their own service plans with traditional services.

service utilization   The use (or rate of use) of health services or social services.

socioeconomic status   A measure that combines a person's education, work history, and income into a single rating that tries to show where that person is placed in society, and what larger group (for example, the "middle class") that person is part of.

SSDI (Social Security Disability Insurance)   Monthly payments from the U.S. government to disabled citizens who have worked and have paid into the Social Security system.

SSI (Supplemental Security Income)   Monthly payments from the U.S. government to disabled citizens who have not worked in the past and have not paid into the Social Security system.

stakeholders   People who have a share or an interest in something; for example, individuals who receive mental health treatment, their families, and the persons who serve them. Stakeholders can be clients, relatives, professionals, community leaders, agency administrators, or volunteers.

stigma   The shame or disgrace attached to someone regarded as socially unacceptable; specifically, discrimination against a person who has experienced mental illness.

stipend   A small fee paid for someone's work or contribution to an activity.

Often used to provide income and experience to participants in a peer-run program.

systems advocacy Activity to bring about changes at the systems and policy level, such as testifying before the legislature and participating on boards, committees, and task forces.

TA center (technical assistance center) An organization that works to assist mental health consumers and peer-run organizations. There are currently three such centers for mental health consumers. (See Appendix C, Table C.1.)

technical assistance Manuals, instructions, or consultations that give information or support for learning any technical task (such as how to use email or the internet). (See TA center.)

traditional services Mental health services provided by professional staff, usually within the context of a clinic or psychiatric center. As a rule, traditional services do not include peer-run programs.

well-being A good, healthy, or comfortable state.

USPRA (US Psychosocial Rehabilitation Association, formerly IAPSRS) A professional organization of providers, consumers, and researchers.

Table A.2. COSP Contact List

Peer-Run Programs

Advocacy Unlimited, Inc.
   Leslie Woods, Executive Director
   300 Russell Road
   Wethersfield, CT 06109
   Tel: 860-667-0460   Fax: 860-667-2240
   Web site: *www.mindlink.org*

BRIDGES in Tennessee
   Anthony Fox, Executive Director
   Tennessee Mental Health Consumers' Association
   BRIDGES Education and Support Program
   480 Craighead Street, Suite 200
   Nashville, TN 37204
   Toll free: 888-539-0393
   E-mail: *bridges@tmhca-tn.org*   Web site: *www.tmha-tn.org*

The Friends Connection in Pennsylvania
   Jeanie Whitecraft, Division Director
   520 North Delaware Ave., 2nd Floor, Suite 200
   Philadelphia, PA 19123
   Tel: 215-751-1800, ext. 213   Fax: 215-923-2133
   E-mail: *jwhitecraft@mhasp.org*   Web site: *www.mhasp.org/friends*

GROW Branch Center, Illinois
   Carol Mussey, National Program Coordinator
   GROW in America
   P.O. Box 3667
   Champaign, IL 61826
   Tel: 217-352-6989 or 1-888-741-GROW
   Fax: 217-352-8530
   E-mail: *growil@sbcglobal.net*

Mental Health Client Action Network (MHCAN)
   Suzanne Koebler, Executive Director
   1051 Cayuga
   Santa Cruz, CA 95062
   Tel: 831-469-0462   Fax: 831-469-9160
   E-mail: *mail@mhcan.org*   Web site: *www.mhcan.org*

PEER Center, Inc.
    Roger O'Mara, Executive Director
    4545 NW 9th Avenue
    Oakland Park, FL 33309
    Tel: 954-202-7867   Fax: 954-202-7866
    E-mail: *peerctr@peercenter.org*   Web site: *www.peercenter.org*

Portland Coalition for the Psychiatrically Labeled
    Nathan (Nate) Bailey, Executive Director
    P.O. Box 4138, Station A
    Portland, ME 04101
    Tel: 207-772-2208   Fax: 207-772-0887

St. Louis Empowerment Center
    Helen Minth, Executive Director
    1905 South Grand Blvd.
    St. Louis, MO 63104
    Tel: 314-865-2112   Fax: 314-776-7071
    E-mail: *Hminth@aol.com*

Substance Abuse and Mental Health Services Administration (SAMHSA)

    Elizabeth McDonel Herr, Ph.D., Evaluation Specialist
    Crystal Blyler, Ph.D., Community Support Programs Branch
    1 Choke Cherry Road, Room 6-1011
    Rockville, MD 20857
    Tel: 240-276-1911   Fax: 240-276-1970
    E-mail: *betsy.mcdonelherr@samhsa.gov*   Web site: *www.samhsa.gov*

    Crystal Blyler, Ph.D., Social Science Analyst
    Division of Service and Systems Improvement
    Community Support Programs Branch
    1 Choke Cherry Road, Room 6-1009
    Rockville, MD 20857
    Tel: 240-276-1911   Fax: 240-276-1970
    E-mail: *crystal.blyler@samhsa.hhs.gov*

COSP Coordinating Center

Jean Campbell, Ph.D., Principal Investigator
Missouri Institute of Mental Health
University of Missouri School of Medicine
5400 Arsenal Street
Saint Louis, MO 63139
Tel: 314-644-7829   Fax: 314-644-7934

Matthew Johnsen, Co-Chair
Center for Mental Health Services Research
Department of Psychiatry
University of Massachusetts
55 Lake Avenue North
Worcester, MA 01655
Tel: 508-856-8692   Fax: 508-856-8700
E-mail: *matthew.johnsen@umassmed.edu*

Common Ingredients Subcommittee

Matthew Johnsen, Co-Chair
E-mail: *matthew.johnsen@umassmed.edu*

Sally Clay, Co-Chair
E-mail: *zangmo@sallyclay.net*

Consumer Advisory Panel

Zahira Ames-Duvall, Co-Chair
E-mail: *zaduvall@alphaonenow.com*

Sally Clay, Co-Chair
E-mail: *zangmo@sallyclay.net*   Web site: *www.sallyclay.net*

Bonnie Schell, Co-Chair
E-mail: *bonniebelle@mindspring.com*

Kathryn Kidder, Co-Chair
E-mail: *grapenutgallery@juno.com*

Table A.3. Researchers in the COSP study

The following are the research teams who participated in the COSP Multi-Site Study.

COSP Coordinating Center
Jean Campbell
     The Program in Consumer Studies and Training
     Missouri Institute of Mental Health
Matthew Johnsen
     University of Massachusetts Medical School
     Center for Mental Health Services Research

Connecticut
Susan Essock
Yvette Sangster
Nancy Covell
Linda Dunakin
Jo-Anne O'Connor
     Mount Sinai School of Medicine

Florida/California
Nancy Erwin
     PEER Center, Inc.
Gregory B. Teague
     Louis de la Parte
     Florida Mental Health Institute

Illinois
Patrick W. Corrigan
Sarah Diwan
     University of Chicago
     Center for Psychiatric Rehabilitation

Maine
Ruth O. Ralph
David Lambert
Kathryn Kidder
     Edmund S. Muskie School of Public Service

Missouri

E. Sally Rogers
Brian McCorkle
> Center for Psychiatric Rehabilitation
> Boston University

Pennsylvania

Joseph Rogers
> Mental Health Association of Southern Pennsylvania

Mark Salzer
> University of Pennsylvania Center for Mental Health

Tennessee

Wm. Thomas Summerfelt
> Grand Rapids Medical Education & Research Center

Sita Diehl
> Vanderbilt University

Appendix B. Common Ingredients of COSPs, CAP Definitions

Structure	Definition	Extracted issues
Consumer operated	Consumers constitute the majority (at least 51%) on the board or group that decides all policies and procedures. With limited exceptions, staff consists of consumers who are hired by and operate the COSP. Consumers have control of the operating budget. Role opportunities for participants may include board and leadership positions, volunteer jobs, and paid staff positions.	Board of directors or decision-making group Staff composition Budget control Leadership roles for participants
Participant responsive	A COSP responds flexibly to the needs of participants. Consumers have ways to indicate dissatisfaction with their program and to have grievances addressed.	Flexible program Process for complaints or grievances
Linkage to other supports	A COSP offers linkage to other supports, with referrals to other community services, and networking with other consumer groups.	Linkage and referral to other services Networking with other consumer groups

Environment	Definition	Extracted issues
Accessibility	Consumers can walk to the COSP or get there by public transportation; or the program comes to the consumer.	Transportation to the COSP
	Hours of operation are geared to the needs of participants.	Hours of operation
	COSP programs are either free or charge a nominal fee. Program use is not dependent on ability to pay.	Cost of program or activity
	Efforts are made to ensure that consumers with physical and sensory as well as psychiatric disabilities can participate in programming.	Accessible to persons with physical and sensory disabilities
Safety	The COSP provides a noncoercive milieu in which fears due to past traumatization are appreciated and assuaged, including trauma induced by the mental health system.	De-emphasis on clinical treatment or diagnosis
	There is no threat of commitment, clinical diagnosis, or unwanted treatment except in cases of suicide or physical danger to other participants.	Policy for calling police or other agents for involuntary treatment or arrest; policy for expulsion or suspension from the COSP
	Cluster for drop-in: Norms/rules to protect the physical safety of participants are developed by consumers for consumers— either by the participants themselves or by consumer staff— and they are agreed to by all participants.	Rules of daily behavior
Informal setting	Working toward common goals in a comfortable setting creates a sense of belonging and support.	Physical environment
	Rigid distinctions between "provider" and "client" do not exist. While some program components may be structured, there remains a sense of freedom and self-expression. The COSP provides a sense of fellowship, in which people care about each other and create community together.	Relationship between staff and participant
		Spontaneity of participant behavior
		Observed goodwill among participants

	Definition	Extracted issues
Reasonable accommodation	*Cluster for drop-in:* No timeline is attached to participation in the COSP. No pressure to join and no time limit to participation. Schedules and tasks can be flexible and adapted to individual needs. Core consensus: Reasonable accommodation to disabilities of all kinds is advocated and practiced in program and work settings.	Length of time allowed for participation Requirements for membership or participation Reasonable accommodation or flexibility in staff schedules and tasks Reasonable accommodation for all disabilities

Belief Systems	Definition	Extracted issues
Peer principle	Relationships are based on shared experiences and values. They are characterized by reciprocity and mutuality. A peer relationship implies equality, along with mutual acceptance and mutual respect.	Shared values, shared consumer experience Relationships peer to peer, participant to staff
Helper's principle	Helping oneself and others is a corollary of the peer principle. Working for the recovery of others facilitates personal recovery. Help or advice is friendly rather than professional and does not demand compliance. All services at COSPs are based on peer-to-peer relationships, as part of the peer principle.	Peers help peers Help does not require compliance Skilled services provided peer to peer

Empowerment	Personal empowerment: Empowerment is honored as a basis of recovery. It is defined as a sense of personal strength and efficacy, with self-direction and control over one's life. Consumers are expected, but not forced, to be accountable for their actions and to act responsibly. Self-reliance is encouraged. Group empowerment: Belonging to an organized group that is recognized by the larger community contributes to the personal empowerment of the individuals within it. Both personal empowerment and group empowerment can be going on at the same time. As a group, the COSP has the capacity to impact the systems that affect participants' lives. Consumers participate in systems level activities at their own pace.	Personal confidence, efficacy, self-direction, decision-making Individual accountability and independence Pride of membership/ownership of COSP COSP effect on systems Participant participation in system activities
Creativity and humor	Artistic expression: Many consumers find artistic expression helpful in their recovery process. As a result, some COSPs offer group and individual opportunities for artistic expression. Sense of humor: An ability to laugh at oneself and at difficult situations is commonly found among COSP participants.	Use of art and other creative expression

Choice	Participation is completely voluntary, and all programs are elective and non-coercive. Choice of services includes the right to choose none. Consumers are regarded as experts in defining their own experiences and choosing COSP or professional services that best suit them. Problems to be addressed are those identified by the consumer, not by professionals.	Choice in services used Right to choose no services Participant view of personal experience Participant assessment of personal issues
Recovery	We believe in recovery. The recovery process is different for each individual. It is never defined rigidly, or forced on others by a COSP. Recovery describes a positive process that acknowledges strengths and enhances well-being. COSPs regard recovery as a normal human process which is unique for each individual. And like all human processes, recovery takes time and involves a whole range of human experiences. It may include ups and downs and also periods of no apparent change.	COSP definition of recovery Recovery as a positive process, a strengths model Recovery is unique for each individual Recovery involves both time and a range of experiences Acceptance of nonlinear nature of recovery, times when no improvement is seen

	Definition	Extracted issues
Acceptance and respect for diversity	Empowerment and hope are nourished through acceptance of persons as they are "warts and all." All behaviors are understood in ordinary human terms, never according to clinical interpretations. Consumers respect each other for the person they are rather than for the person they should be. Every person is afforded acceptance, respect and understanding based on his/her uniqueness and value as a human individual.	Behavior is regarded in common human terms rather than clinical labels. Stigmatizing attitudes and clinical labels are avoided. Participants are not required to change their fundamental views of self
Spiritual growth	Spiritual beliefs and subjective experiences are respected, not labeled as symptoms of illness.	Spiritual beliefs and affiliations. Subjective experiences are respected

Peer Support	Definition	Extracted issues
Peer support	Individual COSP participants are available to each other to lend a listening ear, with empathy and compassion based on common experience. Similar support may be provided in formal support groups.	Individual and informal peer support. Peer support groups
Telling our stories	Personal accounts of life experiences are embedded in all forms of peer support and education. Open discussion occurs in peer support groups or among individuals. Sharing these life experiences may also be a tool for public education, thus becoming an effective means of eliminating stigma and making consumers more accepted within their community.	Personal testimony in peer support and education. Spontaneity and free expression in conversation or meetings. Personal testimony in public forums

Consciousness raising	Small support or conversation groups allow participants to "tell our stories" or share common experiences. These groups may be formal peer support groups or casual, ad hoc, conversations. Participants receive information about the consumer movement. New participants discover commonality with others, and this often produces the first dramatic change in perspective from despair to hope and empowerment.	Sharing experiences in groups Learning about the consumer movement Positive change of perspective as a result of participation
Crisis prevention	Involuntary commitment is minimized through individual or group peer support, or by peer counselors, or by education and advocacy, by addressing problems before they escalate.	Rate of hospitalization before and after joining the COSP Effect of peer support or counseling
Peer mentoring and teaching	Consumer staff or leaders serve as positive role models to other consumers and to each other. Individual participants act as mentors to others. Consumers teach skills and strategies to other consumers, either formally or informally.	Peer leaders as role models Peers act as mentors Peer as teachers in formal classes or trainings
Self-management/ problem solving strategies	COSP programs or individuals teach and model practical skills and promote strategies related to personal issues, treatment, and support needs. The focus is on practical solutions to human concerns.	Formal educational programs for problem solving Informal exchange of personal experience to enhance individual problem-solving abilities

Education	Definition	Extracted issues
Education	Consumers teach and are taught skills that will equip them for full participation in the community, such as daily living skills, vocational skills, job readiness, communication skills, relationship skills, goal setting and assertiveness skills. Consumers develop and improve social skills in a natural social environment. This is often a first step toward creating or re-establishing valued roles in the community and reintegrating into community life.	Formal or informal teaching and practice of daily living skills, vocational skills, job readiness, communication skills, goal setting and assertiveness skills

Participants reintegrated into the larger community |
| Self-advocacy | COSP participants learn to identify their own needs and to advocate for themselves when there are gaps in services. COSP participants learn to become active partners in developing their own service plans with traditional services to meet their needs.

Consumers learn to deal effectively with entitlement agencies and other services. | COSP participants are better equipped to propose alternative services to meet their needs
COSP participants are more assertive in insuring that they receive the services they need from traditional agencies. COSP participants are more effective in obtaining services needed from other community agencies |
| Peer advocacy | COSP participants assist other consumers in resolving problems they may encounter on a daily basis in hospitals and the community such as problems with treatment providers, community service agencies, family members, neighbors, landlords, other peers, etc. | Individual participants advocate for each other
Formal advocacy program
Outreach to participants |

Systems advocacy	The COSP uses a number of tools to bring about changes at the systems and legislative level. These tools may include testifying before the legislature, participating on boards, committees, and task forces, communicating directly with policy and lawmakers.	Systems advocacy by the COSP or by COSP members or graduates
Community education	The COSP uses public education or public relations to bring about positive changes in public attitude.	Public education efforts

COSP = consumer-operated services program.

Appendix C. National Directories

Table C.1. National Peer Organizations

Founded	Organization	Function	Status
1985	National Association of Psychiatric Survivors (NAPS)	National membership organization	disbanded
1985	National Mental Health Consumers' Association (NMHCA)	National membership organization	disbanded
1985	National Teleconferences	Information sharing and dispersal through Boston University	ended
1985	Depression and Bipolar Support Alliance (DBSA)*	National membership organization for mood disorders	Chicago, IL
1986	National Mental Health Consumers' Self-Help Clearinghouse	TA [technical assistance] center	Philadelphia, PA
1990	Altered States of the Arts	National organization for the arts	Fort Lauderdale, FL
1992	National Artists for Mental Health	National organization for the arts	Catskill, NY
1990	Support Coalition International	National membership organization	Eugene, OR
1992	National Empowerment Center	TA center	Lawrence, MA
1998	CONTAC, Inc.	TA center	Charleston, WV

*Formerly NDMDA (National Depressive Manic Depressive Association).

Table C.2. Web Links for Peer Programs

Web site	Organization	Purpose
www.contac.org	CONTAC, Inc.	Consumer-run technical assistance center
www.cstprogram.org	Missouri Institute of Mental Health (MIMH)	COSP research
www.dbsalliance.org/	Depression and Bipolar Support Alliance (DBSA)	Patient-directed organization focusing on mood disorders
www.madman-bbs.net/accountability/beguine.htm	N.O. List	National Organizing
www.mentalhealth.org/consumersurvivor	Knowledge Exchange Network (KEN)	Information and resources from SAMHSA
www.mhasp.org/friends	The Friends Connection	COSP site
www.mhcan.org	Mental Health Consumer Action Network	COSP site
www.mhselfhelp.org	National Mental Health Consumers' Self-Help Clearinghouse	Peer-run technical assistance center
www.MindFreedom.org	Support Coalition International	Advocacy and social activism
www.mindlink.org	Advocacy Unlimited, Inc.	COSP site
www.peercenter.org	PEER Center	COSP site
www.peoplewho.net	PEOPLE WHO NET	Web page of the Madness groups
www.power2u.org	National Empowerment Center	Peer-run technical assistance center
www.tmhca-tn.org/About_Bridges.html	BRIDGES	COSP site

Note: CMHS = Center for Mental Health Services; COSP = Consumer-operated services program

Contributors

Crystal Blyler, Ph.D., is a social science analyst at the Substance Abuse and Mental Health Services Administration, Center for Mental Health Services. She was government project officer (GPO) for the COSP Multisite Research Initiative (MRI).

Bill Burns-Lynch, M.A., is the former clinical manager and the current director of training and program support at Mental Health Association of Southeastern Pennsylvania (MHASP).

Jean Campbell, Ph.D., was principal investigator for the Coordinating Center for the Consumer-Operated Services Program (COSP) Multisite Research Initiative. A mental health consumer researcher, she is director of the Program in Consumer Studies and Training at the Missouri Institute of Mental Health, University of Missouri-Columbia School of Medicine.

Sally Clay, editor of this book, experienced severe episodes of bipolar disorder for 20 years. She founded and worked for several peer-run programs and in the process learned to maintain personal well-being. She was a member of both the COSP Common Ingredients Subcommittee and the Consumer Advisory Panel. As a member of the research team at the PEER Center, she helped to set up a partnership between the Florida and California sites, called "FLiCA." She maintains a Web site at *www.sallyclay.net.*

Patrick William Corrigan, Psy.D., is a manuscript editor for this book. He was principal investigator for the Illinois COSP site. He has published more than one hundred journal articles and book chapters on areas related to serious mental illness. He was editor-in-chief of a tri-annual journal, *Psychiatric Rehabilitation Skills,* and has authored three books and edited four books. He is also director and principal investigator of the Chicago Consortium for Stigma Research funded by the National Institute of Mental Health.

Dianne Côté, M.Ed., acted as consultant for this book. She was executive director of the Portland Coalition in Maine from 1985 to 1989, director of PEOPLe, Inc., in New York from 1990 to 1993, and director of the PEER Center in Florida from 1996 to 2001.

Janine M. Elkanich was program director of the Portland Coalition for six years. She has an Associate's degrees in medical assistance and accounting and is a single mother. She battled severe depression, anxiety, and anorexia nervosa for nearly ten years but has been in recovery since 1996.

Nancy Erwin, Ph.D., was principal investigator for the Florida site, 2002–04.

Louetta Hix is a member of BRIDGES who says that her life was changed by the peer-run program. After working for BRIDGES, she went back to school and obtained a Master's degree in community practice social work.

Matthew Johnsen, Ph.D. was co-principal investigator for the COSP MRI Coordinating Center. He works for the Department of Psychiatry, University of Massachusetts Medical School.

Lorraine Keck was consumer investigator for the COSP project in Illinois and is a former national program coordinator for GROW.

Elizabeth McDonel Herr, Ph.D., is a social science analyst at the Substance Abuse and Mental Health Services Administration, Center for Mental Health Services. She was government project officer (GPO) for the COSP Multisite Research Initiative (MRI).

Terrance Means was formerly a senior supervisor at the Friends Connection.

Helen Minth is executive director of the St. Louis Empowerment Center.

Carol Mussey is national program coordinator for GROW in the United States.

Ruth O. Ralph, Ph.D., is a manuscript editor for this book. She is a consumer researcher who has conducted mental health research and evaluation for over twenty-five years and was principal investigator for the Maine COSP site. She has written and presented on recovery in mental health. Now retired, she was senior research associate at Edmund S. Muskie School of Public Service, University of Southern Maine.

Joseph Rogers is the president and CEO of Mental Health Association of Southeastern Pennsylvania, a consumer-operated program, and was principal investigator for the Pennsylvania COSP site. He is a longtime leader of the national consumer/survivor movement.

Mark S. Salzer, Ph.D., was co-principal investigator for the Pennsylvania COSP site. He is an assistant professor of psychology at the University of Pennsylvania School of Medicine.

Yvette Sangster founded Advocacy Unlimited, Inc., and was executive director from 1994 to 2002. She is a child-abuse survivor and a consumer of mental health services.

Bonnie Schell, M.A., CPRP, is a manuscript editor for this book and was executive director of MHCAN for nine years. She was editor of the *California Network Newsletter* and is poetry editor of *Mind Freedom Journal.* She served on the California Mental Health Planning Council and received the California Network's Howie the Harp award in 2001. She currently works as director of consumer affairs for Piedmont Behavioral Healthcare in Concord, NC.

James Scott was a peer support staff person at the Friends Connection and currently works at another MHASP program.

Gregory B. Teague, Ph.D. was co-principal investigator for the Florida site and was chair of the COSP MRI Research Committee. He is an associate professor at the Louis de la Parte Florida Mental Health Institute, University of South Florida.

Sam Viar has been involved with BRIDGES since its inception in 1994. He works as a trainer and support group facilitator in Memphis and rural West

Tennessee and in other states. He has been recovering from schizoaffective disorder since 1981. The story included here was used in three workshops to teach basic concepts of BRIDGES.

Jeanie Whitecraft, M.Ed., is the director of the Mobile Services Division at the Mental Health Association of Southeastern Pennsylvania. She developed the Friends Connection Model and currently oversees the implementation of this model in Philadelphia and Montgomery Counties.

With the exception of researchers Blyler, McDonel Herr, Johnsen, Salzer, and Teague, all of the above authors are self-identified mental health consumer/survivors.

Index

501 (c)(3), 9, 123, 125, 202. *See also* nonprofit
abuse, 19, 67, 68, 81, 89, 98, 180, 287. *See also* trauma
acceptance and respect for diversity, as Common Ingredient, 7, 12, 142, 154, 208, 227, 229, 242, 254, 278
accessibility, as Common Ingredient, 7, 10, 92, 101–2, 104, 108, 129, 201, 226, 261, 274
accommodation, reasonable, as Common Ingredient, 7, 10, 144, 226, 228, 265, 275
accountability, 8, 11, 120–21, 187, 227, 229, 276
ACT. *See* treatment, assertive community
addiction, 164, 169–70, 172, 176, 182, 244
advisory board:
    mental health, 74, 191
    MHCAN, 80
    Friends Connection, 170
    hospital, 191, 194
advocacy:
    individual, 6, 14, 30, 112, 118, 179, 187,189–91, 257, 261, 279–80
    legislative, 14, 83, 90, 92, 105, 119–20, 122, 151, 179, 186, 191–95
    lobbying and, 24, 70, 182
    peer, as Common Ingredient, 7, 14, 29, 94, 179, 184–85, 193, 227, 229, 244, 254, 257, 259, 263–65, 280
    protection and, 97, 118–19, 185, 191, 194–95
    self-, as Common Ingredient, 7–8, 14, 195–96, 200, 227, 229, 266, 280
    systems, as Common Ingredient, 6–9, 14, 119, 190, 195, 266, 281
    training, 14, 179
Advocacy Unlimited (AU), 6, 14, 30, 123, 179–96, 247, 252–53
AIDS, 86, 195, 240
Alcoholics Anonymous (AA), 13, 104, 113–14, 141, 156, 161–62, 169–70
alcoholism, 21, 83, 101, 114, 150, 160, 162–23, 166, 169–70, 176, 240. *See also* substance abuse
Alliance for the Mentally Ill, 76, 92, 117, 195, 198, 264. *See also* NAMI
Alternatives Conference, 24, 67, 73–74, 89, 105, 124, 250, 253
Americans with Disabilities Act (ADA), 44, 83, 186
Anthony, William, 27, 56, 236–37
anti-psychiatry, 19, 35, 67–68, 72, 239
anxiety, diagnosis of, 205
arts:
    drawing, 80, 87
    guitar, 69, 80, 250
    music, 80, 93
    painting, 12, 78, 80, 96–97, 101

arts *(continued)*
poetry, 71, 77, 84, 87, 94–96, 133, 166, 206
writing, 12, 33, 76, 79, 154, 157, 179, 185. *See also* creativity and humor as Common Ingredients
assistance:
mutual, 111–12, 114–17, 119, 121
technical, 24–26, 28, 54, 137, 181, 243, 267, 282–83

Baker Act, 126, 135
Baynes, Joan, 142
behavior, rules of, 4, 6, 10, 53, 67, 74, 76, 80, 84–85, 98–99, 106, 121, 131, 188, 226, 228, 243, 274
belonging, 10–11, 13, 74, 127, 154, 162, 168, 240, 254, 257–58, 274, 276
best practices, 200, 256
Bluebird, Gayle, 74
board of directors:
of Advocacy Unlimited, 183
of BRIDGES, 201
consumer control of, 9, 90, 223, 273
of Friends Connection, 172
of MHCAN, 90
of nonprofits, 246
of PEER Center, 126, 128, 137
of Portland Coalition, 98–99
of St. Louis Empowerment Center, 120–21
Boston Mental Patients Liberation Front, 70
brain disease, 241, 261
BRIDGES, 5–6, 14, 30, 197–209, 253
Brown, Neal, ix
Budd, Su, 34, 40
budget, peer-run 249, 253, 273
Burns-Lynch, Bill, 30, 159, 285
Bush, George W., 255
by-laws:
of Advocacy Unlimited, 183
of MHCAN, 80
of PEER Center, 128
of Portland Coalition, 100

California, as COSP site, ix, 5, 21–22, 29, 31, 36, 54, 67–91, 123, 245, 249–50
California Network of Mental Health Clients, 72, 75, 80
Campbell, Jean, ix, 4, 17, 21–28, 31–33, 37, 39–41, 44, 48, 54, 222, 239, 243, 285
Carpinello, Sharon, 32, 50, 52
care, managed, 25, 46–47, 89, 119, 202, 208, 244, 263
caring, as a function, 34–35, 37, 46
Carter, Jimmy, administration, 255
case management, 27, 29, 69, 71–72, 75, 77, 80, 84, 86, 104, 135–36, 161, 169, 218
Center for Mental Health Services (CMHS), 24, 26, 33, 78, 97, 198, 202, 261, 283
Center for Self-Help Research, 86
Chamberlin, Judi, xi, 24–25, 27–29, 31, 34, 36, 38, 70, 76, 124
choice:
as Common Ingredient, 4, 7, 12, 19, 23, 25, 28, 30, 35–37, 40–44, 72, 87, 129, 156, 163, 167, 180–81, 183, 189–90, 193, 227, 229, 242, 244, 254, 277. *See also* consent, informed
Clay, Sally, x, xii, 3, 93–94, 100, 179, 239, 259, 285
club, social, 101, 179, 188, 190, 194
clubhouse, 8, 22, 179, 188, 190, 193–94, 261
Amistad, 251
Fountain House, 57
cluster, 4–8, 14–15, 214, 232–34, 261, 274–75
collaboration, 18, 27, 47, 67, 73, 98, 117, 122, 125, 130, 143, 175, 197–98, 201, 208, 220
Collins, Paul, 133
commitment, involuntary, 10, 25, 120, 126, 189, 194–95, 239, 274, 279
Common Ingredients, 33–34
defining of, ix-x, 9–15, 41, 214–5, 220–21, 261

list of, 6–10, 16, 225–29, 236, 273–81. *See also* by individual ingredient

found in traditional mental health services, 230–32, 244, 254

Common Ingredients Subcommittee, x, 221–23, 257

community:
consumer, 28, 47, 68, 80, 83–85, 90, 92, 99–103, 123, 141, 144–58, 200
re-integration into, 14, 19, 30, 110, 116, 162, 240, 243, 255–56, 280

Community Support Program (CSP), 24, 48, 255

competence:
cultural, 111, 116
peer, 40–42, 44, 112, 121

concept mapping, 41, 262

conferences, consumer/survivor, 15, 24, 27, 36, 67, 71, 73, 82, 89, 105, 124, 174, 187, 192, 206, 208–9, 241–42, 250, 253

confidentiality, 42, 44, 86, 127, 262

Connecticut, as COSP site, 5–6, 30, 123, 179–96, 249, 252–53, 271

consciousness raising, as Common Ingredient, 7, 13, 34–36, 39, 43, 227, 229, 262, 279

consent, informed, 36, 44, 264

consumer affairs, offices of, 26, 104

consumer buddy, 84, 116–17, 168, 204

consumer business, 6, 24, 50, 129, 132–33, 183, 241, 244

consumer expert, 12, 40, 153, 198, 277

consumer leader, 25, 46, 67, 70, 94, 119, 123, 125, 241–42, 245, 248

consumer needs, 34, 37, 117, 132, 162, 194

consumer operation:
as Common Ingredient, 4, 6, 9, 12–13, 36, 48–49, 52–53, 56, 61–62, 64, 273. *See also* peer run

consumer participation, 36, 175, 223

consumer provider, 33, 41, 44–46, 87, 105, 256. *See also* prosumer

consumer satisfaction, 88, 161, 206

consumer voice, 25, 93, 179, 191, 196

Consumer Advisory Panel (CAP), ix, 3–4, 12, 88, 100, 221, 247, 261

Consumer Operated Service Program (COSP), 33, 41, 48, 208, 224:
belief system, 7–8, 10–11, 221–22, 226, 228, 230–35, 275
budget, 9, 16, 70, 73, 76, 78–84, 87–88, 97, 101, 113, 121, 183, 223, 226, 228, 240, 245, 248, 250, 253, 273
category, 7–10, 14
domain, 9, 41–42, 222–25, 230–33, 236, 248, 253
enhancements, 88, 247–51
executive director, 80, 93–94, 97–100, 125–27, 129, 133, 136, 186, 188, 192, 201, 221, 246, 251–52, 286–87
professionalization of, 19, 46, 243
section, 8, 10, 226
steering committee, 87, 214, 240, 246–47
structure, 7–10, 15, 24, 83, 127, 145, 149, 158, 168, 172, 199, 201, 222–23, 226, 228, 230–31, 234–35, 240, 273

Corrigan, Patrick, ix, 143, 239, 248, 286

COSP. *See* Consumer Operated Service Program

Côté, Dianne, ix, 93–94, 100, 126–27, 133, 286

counseling, peer, 8, 30–31, 69–70, 81, 84, 86–87, 111, 135, 165, 167, 250, 265, 269

Covell, Nancy, 179

creativity and humor, as Common Ingredient, 7, 9, 12, 47, 111, 179, 276. *See also* arts

crisis:
intervention, 27, 30, 35, 126, 136, 153, 261
management and support of, 111, 135, 144, 256
prevention of, as Common Ingredient, 7, 13, 225, 227, 229, 279

crisis *(continued)*
    services, 20–21, 24, 42, 49, 56, 61–62,
        79, 93, 109, 130, 153, 204, 241
Curie, Charles, 254, 257

Dana, Woody, 95
deaf, 102
deinstitutionalization, 19, 244
Del Vecchio, Paolo, 24, 48, 255
delusion, 141, 170
demographic, 50, 55, 110
demonstration project, 24, 32, 46, 48
Department of Children and Families
        (DCF), 135–36. *See also* HRS
Department of Health and Human
        Services (DHHS), 213, 255, 263
dependence, 72, 89, 155, 180, 187, 242,
        274
Depression and Bipolar Support (DBSA),
        108–9, 113–14, 119–22, 245,
        282–83
Depressive and Manic Depressive
        Association (DMDA), 54–56, 125,
        245.
diagnosis, 23, 38, 46, 70–71, 80, 106, 155,
        262, 274
    anxiety, 205
    Axis 1, 244
    bipolar disorder, 3, 205, 283
    borderline disorder, 83, 242
    clinical, 10, 189, 274
    co-occurring disorder, 159–61, 167–
        69, 174–75, 262
    depression, 3, 21, 163, 205, 283
    dissociative disorder, 208
    dual. *See* co-occurring disorder
    manic depressive disorder, 70, 72, 75,
        239, 257
    personality disorder, 205, 244
    psychiatric, 36, 38–39, 44–45, 48, 87,
        179, 198. *See also* psychiatric label
    schizophrenia, 3, 70, 157, 163, 169,
        205
Diagnostic and Statistical Manual
        (DSM), 56, 263

dialogue, 15, 18, 26, 93, 265
directive, advance, 208
Disabled People South Africa (DPSA), xi
discrimination, 35–36, 42, 45, 75, 119
    as prejudice, 28–29, 89–90, 180
    as stigma, 4, 12–13, 15, 21, 35, 49, 55,
        70–71, 92, 104, 123, 136, 166, 186,
        194–96, 199–200, 203, 266, 278,
        278
diversity, cultural, 170, 181, 208, 217, 262,
        264
Diwan, Sarah, 143
Double-Trouble, 167, 171
drugs, 85, 94, 99, 162–63, 166, 169–71.
        See also substance abuse
Dumont, Jeanne, 26, 30, 32, 40, 44, 46,
        222
Dunakin, Linda, 179
Duvall, Zahira, 100

education:
    as Common Ingredient, 4–10, 13–15,
        26, 29–30, 33, 35, 45, 48–49, 51–54,
        56, 83, 92, 105, 110–12, 116–17,
        121–23, 137–38, 144, 147–49, 151,
        156, 162, 168, 172, 181–90, 192,
        195, 197–99, 203, 207–08, 214,
        220–22, 227, 229–36, 242, 249, 254,
        278- 80. *See also* training.
    community, as Common Ingredient,
        7, 9, 14, 190, 262, 281
    public, 13, 25, 49,54, 93, 278
element, program, 10, 12, 49, 213–15,
        219–20, 231, 236–37
Elkanich, Janine, 92, 257, 286
emergency room, 21, 93, 103, 191
Emotions Anonymous, 25, 113
employment:
    part time, 87–88, 111, 115–116, 131,
        170, 202
    program, 30, 76, 132, 184
    stipend for, 76, 87, 187, 202, 250, 253,
        266
    volunteer, 32, 36, 53, 83, 87, 110, 113,
        117, 120–21, 132–34, 136, 152, 179,
        184, 189, 199, 201, 204, 206, 226,

228, 240, 242, 248, 252–53, 273. *See also* job

empowerment, as Common Ingredient, xii, 4–5, 7–13, 16, 18–20, 25, 29, 32–35, 37, 40, 44–49, 53, 75, 78, 86, 91, 105–06, 108–24, 138, 152–55, 183, 187, 196–97, 200, 206–08, 215, 225, 227, 229, 232, 236–37, 242–3, 245, 251, 254, 263, 276, 278–79, 282–83

entitlement, 14, 29, 72, 118, 185, 232, 263, 280

environment (domain) 222, 226, 228, 230–31, 234–35, 274

Erwin, Nancy, 123, 132, 286

Essock, Susan, ix

evidence-based practice, 31–33, 46, 244, 255–56

experience:
  common, 13, 35, 40, 146, 278–79
  subjective, 13, 39, 278

family:
  member of, 46, 54–55, 71, 73, 117–18, 148, 153, 166, 193, 198, 201, 208, 280
  negative influence of, 89
  role of, 21, 23, 93, 170, 257
  support from, 32, 42, 51, 75, 83–84, 144, 162, 242

fidelity:
  assessment of, 4, 15, 49, 215, 213–19, 221–23, 237, 263
  and fidelity study, 9, 144, 240, 254

Fidelity Assessment Common Ingredients Tool (FACIT), 9, 15, 215, 219, 223–37, 263

Fisher, Dan, 19

Florida, as COSP site, x, xii, 5, 29, 87, 123–38, 240, 245, 249, 251, 259

focus group, 88, 125, 198, 203, 223–24, 250, 263

Frank, Leonard, 70

Friends Connection, 5–6, 9, 28, 48–49, 159–176, 245, 252, 268

functioning:
  emancipatory, 33–35, 46
  high, 53, 83, 242

normal, 12, 21, 38–39, 241, 243, 248, 252, 277
  social, 32, 49

funding: cuts in, 16, 57, 122, 151, 245, 249–52
  from foundations, 50, 97, 137, 144, 175
  from government, 80, 88–89, 124, 132, 135, 175, 182, 185, 194, 245–46, 249–52
  lack of, xii, 45, 74, 97–98, 106, 112, 122, 135–36, 150–51, 180, 185, 249, 251–53
  management of, 113, 120, 243, 251
  of peer-run programs, 16, 73, 84, 93, 97, 109, 120, 150, 159–60, 182, 202, 243
  resources for, 18, 21, 102
  support and, 120, 151, 202
  with pass-through agency, 120

gays and lesbians, 24, 34–35, 71, 188, 240

grassroots, 179, 192–93, 241, 247

grievance, 119–20, 128, 181–82, 186, 191–92, 226, 228, 273

group, radical, 24, 55, 68, 78, 257

GROW, Inc., 5–6, 28, 52–53, 56–57, 141–158, 249, 252, 268

Gwin, Lucy, xii

Harding, Courtney, 27

healing, 12, 28, 32, 40, 46–47, 67, 86, 103, 146, 148, 152, 181. *See also* recovery

health, behavioral, 46, 73, 143, 160, 173, 175–76, 202

health, mental:
  departments of, 21, 54, 56, 93, 97, 104, 121, 182, 185, 198, 202
  policy for, 20, 44, 92, 119, 190
  system, xi-xii, 4, 10, 17–18, 22–25, 27, 29–30, 34–40, 45–46, 51, 67–68, 70–71, 89, 92–93, 103, 106, 136, 179, 181–82, 185, 187–88, 198, 233, 241–42, 253, 255–57, 274
  services alternative to traditional, 18–19, 32, 36, 38, 42, 54, 57, 70, 112, 130, 135, 255

health, mental *(continued)*
  services, community, 3, 33–34, 45–46,
    56, 67, 112, 114, 116–17, 136, 160,
    244, 252
  services, professional, 6, 19, 23, 27, 55,
    57, 112, 115
  services, providers of, 4, 18, 26–27, 33,
    37–38
  services, public, 26, 48, 68, 70, 110,
    245
  services, traditional (TMHS), 143,
    161, 213–15, 220, 225–26, 228–32,
    235–37, 251, 253–55, 267
  treatment, 6, 19, 23, 37–38, 46, 68,
    197, 200, 203
Health and Rehabilitative Services
    (HRS), 124–25, 136. See *also* DCF
health maintenance organization
    (HMO), 244, 263
helper's principle, as Common
    Ingredient, 7–8, 10–12, 15, 34–35,
    41, 53, 63, 103, 142, 153, 226, 229,
    263, 275
Hispanic, 86, 188
Hix, Louetta, 197, 253, 286
homelessness, 30–31, 52–53, 68–69, 71,
    76, 84, 87–89, 94, 101–2, 108–10,
    117, 122, 129–30, 132, 134–36, 150,
    169, 244–45
hospital:
  commitment to, 189, 239, 27, 279
  psychiatric, 22, 125, 131, 159–60, 163,
    244, 254
hospitalization, 21, 32, 39, 46, 74, 93, 130,
    153, 161, 169, 239, 279
hostel, crisis, 46, 127, 135
hotline, crisis, 115, 126
housing
  assistance, 4, 56, 125, 134
  affordable, 30, 134
  board and care, 68, 72, 244
  fair, 82, 186, 191
  shelter, 20, 69, 101, 117, 150, 162
  supported, 72, 77, 86, 130
  transition, 89, 134
Howie the Harp award, 287

Illinois, as COSP site, 5–6, 52, 56, 141–
    158, 245, 249, 252, 268, 271
illness, mental:
  chronic, 23, 54, 160
  cure for, 86, 146, 186
  diagnosis of major, 130, 205
  people with, 17–18, 21, 24–25, 31,
    33–34, 40, 44, 46–47, 54, 72, 109,
    118, 120, 193, 216, 244
  insight into, 81, 129, 157, 200, 223,
    256, 264
  serious, 3, 22, 33, 45, 48, 50, 52–53, 83,
    112, 115, 127, 143, 217, 253
  severe (and/or persistent), 27, 47, 54,
    127, 136, 141, 143, 160, 213, 217,
    253, 259
inclusion, 18, 25–26, 33, 35, 49, 75
income, 18, 31, 133, 241–42, 245, 248,
    252, 267
incorporation, 34, 100, 123, 125, 181
independent living, 11, 84, 100, 134, 161,
    181
International Association of
    Psychosocial Rehabilitation
    Services (IAPSRS), 105, 250, 254,
    264
investigator, principal (PI), ix, 127, 132,
    143, 265
isolation, 13, 34, 45, 112, 115, 161, 166,
    168, 194, 198

job:
  description, 83, 183
  sharing, 203–4. See *also* employment
Johnsen, Matthew, x, 4, 213, 286

Kaufman, Carrie, 24, 29–32, 50, 52
Keck, Lorraine, 141, 143, 252, 286
Keogh, Con, 29, 141–42, 146, 156–57
Knight, Ed, 18, 32, 46, 48, 52
Knisley, Marti, 160

label, psychiatric, 12–13, 27, 54, 71, 89–
    90, 92–93, 155, 179, 241–42, 278.
    See *also* by specific diagnoses
Loder, Ann, 125

M.I.A.M.I. (Most Important Advocates
      for the Mentally Ill), 124–25
Madness Network News, 24, 70, 257
madness, 12, 17, 73, 86, 157, 283
Mahler, Jay, 30, 75
Maine, as COSP site, ix, 5–6, 29, 87, 92–
      107, 126, 239, 245, 250, 271
McDonel Herr, Elizabeth, 4, 213–14, 218,
      286
Means, Terrance, 159, 286
Medicaid, 45, 69, 75, 88–89, 102, 160, 175,
      186, 244
Medicare, 102, 193
medication, 21, 27, 29, 39, 55, 67, 70, 72,
      80, 83, 89, 95, 118, 122, 133, 136,
      153, 155, 162, 169–70, 190, 194,
      198, 200, 205, 208, 220, 232, 239,
      241.
Mental Health Client Action Network
      (MHCAN), ix, 5–6, 14, 29, 67–91,
      123, 242, 249–50, 269, 283
Mental Health Statistics Improvement
      Program (MHSIP), 26
Mental Patient's Liberation Project, 23
Mental Patients' Alliance, 24
mentalism, 34–36, 47, 264
mentoring. *See* peer mentoring and
      teaching
Millett, Kate, 38
Minth, Helen, 108, 251, 286
mission statement, 34, 75, 79, 200
Missouri, as COSP site, 5, 29, 87, 108–
      122, 245, 249, 251, 271–72
model:
   ACT, 218–19
   clubhouse, 8
   COSP, 232–33, 236
   consumer operated, 8, 36, 48, 214,
      220–21, 236
   medical, xi, 38, 68, 81, 103, 181, 264
   peer run, 8, 36, 48, 214, 220–21, 236
   program, 161, 198, 214–17, 236
   recovery, 18, 195, 277
   rehabilitation, 44, 76
Mood Matters, 72–74, 81
Mouth Magazine, xii

movement:
   consumer, 13, 16, 83, 86, 119, 179, 236,
      279
   disability rights, xi, 9–10, 97, 117,
      180–81
   liberation, xi, 23–24, 34, 36, 70
Mowbray, Carol, 18, 24, 28–9, 31–32, 52,
      56, 222
Mussey, Carol, 141, 143, 287

Narcotics Anonymous (NA), 113
National Alliance of Psychiatric
      Survivors (NAPS), 24, 282
National Association of Rights
      Protection and Advocacy
      (NARPA), 253
National Association of State Mental
      Health Program Directors
      (NASMHPD), 26, 264
National Empowerment Center (NEC),
      xii, 24, 78, 282–83
National Institute of Mental Health
      (NIMH), 48, 56–57, 97, 142, 214
National Mental Health Consumers' Self-
      Help Clearing House, 24, 282–83
Network Against Psychiatric Assault
      (NAPA), 24, 72
New Freedom Commission on Mental
      Health, 18, 255–56
newsletters, 14, 24, 71, 74, 76, 78, 82–83,
      96, 113, 133, 188, 192–93, 208
nonprofits, 9, 68, 76–80, 84, 93, 98, 119–
      20, 134, 150, 172 179, 202, 240, 243,
      245–46
Nothing About Us Without Us, xi, 9, 25
nursing home, 191, 244

Oaks, David, 71
Oastler, Sam, 80–81
O'Mara, Roger, 127
On Our Own, xi, xii, 124
open door policy, 29, 104
ourselves and others, 6, 10–11, 15, 141,
      154, 188–89, 240–42, 256–57, 259,
      275, 279
outpatient, 68, 78–79, 118, 120, 194–95

outreach:
in the community, 24, 29, 75–76, 114,
137, 151–52, 200, 227
to minorities, 114, 118
to participants, 229
to homeless persons, 76
to the public, 14, 172
ownership, 11, 24, 44, 252, 276

Parrish, Jacqueline, x, 78
Participant responsive, as Common
Ingredient, 7, 10, 34–35, 180–81,
187, 199, 226, 273
partnership, 4, 17–19, 23, 25–27, 33,
46–47, 55, 82, 89, 116, 120, 122,
195, 243, 245, 249, 280
peer activities:
coffee, 4, 12, 20, 32, 69, 71, 76–78, 80,
84, 104–05, 109, 130, 153, 165, 209
college attendance, 30, 89, 111, 169–
70, 187
clothing-related, 29, 31, 102, 133, 162,
232
community, 115–16, 148, 150, 166,
168, 175
computer lab, 69, 87–88, 132–34
drop-in, 4, 29, 82, 109, 129, 131, 232,
249
food-related, 20, 31, 84, 101–2, 109,
113, 129–30, 133–34, 162
group, 161, 165–68
recreational, 5, 56, 103, 108–9, 111–
13, 123, 130–31, 148, 162, 164–67,
233
public relations, 89, 183, 281
public speaking, 24, 186–88
social, 21–22, 53, 163, 165
trip-related, 71, 83, 113, 129, 131 166,
168, 172–73
peer mentoring and teaching, as
Common Ingredient, 4–5, 7–8,
13–15, 26, 28–30. See also role
model
peer principle, as Common Ingredient,
7–8, 10–12, 15, 35, 226, 229, 265,
275. See also self-help

PEER Center, Inc., ix, 5, 29, 87, 123–138,
240, 240, 246, 249, 251–52, 259, 283
Pennsylvania, as COSP site, 5, 9, 24, 50,
159–76, 245, 249, 252, 268, 272
People Who, 72, 280
PEOPLe, Inc., 240
Phoenix Rising, 70
Pillows of Unrest, 96–97
Portland Coalition Advocate, 96–97
Portland Coalition for the Psychiatrically
Labeled (PCPL), 5–6, 29, 92–107,
126, 240–41, 249–51, 259,
poverty, 39, 45, 49, 90, 97, 242, 245, 269
prison, 79, 142, 157
Project Acceptance, 24
properties, psychometric, 224–25
prosumer, 110–11, 118, 265.
protest, public, 93–94, 122, 151
psychology, 31, 49, 89, 142, 146, 156, 254

quality:
assurance of, 26, 202, 205–6
of life, 37, 46, 49, 51, 123, 169, 237, 265

Ralph, Ruth, ix, 24–26, 40, 287
Reclamation, Inc., 24
Recovery Inc., 25, 54–55
recovery, as Common Ingredient, 5–7,
11–13, 16, 18–19, 21, 25–30, 33, 35,
40–49, 51, 54–56, 58–59, 61–64, 90,
92, 103–36, 108, 132, 135, 141–42,
144–46, 149, 152–7, 159–71, 173,
175–76, 179, 181–84, 186, 188–90,
194–96, 197–200, 203–5, 209, 227,
229, 232, 236–37, 241, 253, 255–58,
263–64, 266, 275–77
recruitment, 48, 53, 88, 248, 252
referral, 25, 45, 49, 52, 54, 88, 109, 114–15,
117–19, 127, 160–61, 174, 190, 250,
252, 273. See also linkage to other
supports
rehabilitation:
drug and alcohol, 150, 160–61, 168,
173
Medicaid, 45, 75
psychiatric, 18–19, 22–23, 27, 113, 175

psychosocial, 19, 70, 76, 105, 109, 114–15, 175, 220, 250, 256, 265
and recovery, 27–28, 44, 153–54
vocational, 111, 116, 118, 132, 143, 191
relapse, 43, 162, 164

research:
consumer, 26, 88, 143, 251
findings of, 48–49, 51, 232, 253, 255
protocol for, 44, 49, 220, 223, 248
evaluation of, by consumer/ survivors, 17, 25–26, 188, 198, 206
outcomes of, 26, 31–33, 47, 49, 51, 53, 55, 144, 214–20, 237, 244, 253
qualitative, 31, 47, 53–54, 213, 218, 265
quantitative, 3, 54, 217, 219, 247, 259, 265
resilience, 86, 240, 249, 259
respite house, 70, 124, 127, 135
right to choose, 12, 75, 277. *See also* choice.
rights:
civil, 4, 24, 34, 68, 120
disability, xi, 9, 97, 117
legal, 42, 44, 117, 120, 181, 185, 195
of mental patients, 19, 24, 70, 82, 205
Rights of Recipients of Mental Health Services, 93
Rogers, Joseph, 159, 172, 287
Rogers, Sally, x
role model, peer, 13, 28–29, 34–35, 53, 161, 168, 183–84, 194–96, 200, 279
Rowland, William, xi
Ruby Rogers Drop-in Center, 76, 79
safe place, 35, 71, 83, 99, 136, 203
safety, as Common Ingredient, 7, 10, 12, 82–86, 92, 98–99, 120, 226, 254, 274
Salzer, Mark, ix, 28, 30, 159, 171, 287
SAMHSA. *See* Substance Abuse and Mental Health Services Administration.
Sanbourne v. Chiles, 124
Sangster, Yvette, 179, 194, 253, 287

satisfaction, consumer, 11, 14, 33, 37, 53, 88, 161, 206, 209, 226, 228
Schell, Bonnie, ix, 67, 77, 123, 239, 242, 249, 287
Scott, James, 159, 287
Segal, Steve, 18, 31, 52, 86–87
self-determination, 28, 34, 36, 40, 179–81, 188, 256
self-disclosure, 174, 207
self-esteem, 28, 32, 49, 83, 87, 103, 106, 118, 189
self-help,
and mutual assistance, 111, 114–17, 119, 121
clearinghouse for, 24, 282–83
groups for , 18–21, 24, 28, 31, 36, 40, 47, 49–54, 72, 104, 113–14, 121–22, 138
organization for, 36, 57
programs for, 4, 50–51, 73, 85, 122
self-management/problem solving strategies, as Common Ingredient, 7, 14, 90, 145–47, 156, 162, 185, 199, 204–05, 227, 279, 291. *See also* skills
self-worth, 28, 40, 103, 106, 242
services:
community, 76, 124, 159, 248, 256, 273
crisis, 20–21, 24, 42, 49, 56, 61–62, 79, 93, 109, 130, 153, 204, 241
gaps in, 14, 57, 136, 20
mental health (*see* mental health services)
senior (elderly), 71, 73, 89, 131, 195;
setting, informal, as Common Ingredient, 7, 10, 226, 275. *See also* environment
Silverman, Carol, 18, 29–31, 52, 86–87, 240, 253, 267, 277
site visit 9, 224–25, 230, 233
skills:
coping, 20, 26, 29, 41, 44–45, 49, 53, 56, 197, 241
daily living, 6, 14, 22, 47, 75, 113, 134, 149, 153, 162, 169, 183, 203, 280

skills *(continued)*
   interpersonal, 41–42, 112
   leadership, 16, 26, 47, 112, 121, 144,
      148–51, 192, 242, 247, 273
   recovery, 6, 161–62, 203
   training for, 19, 169
Social Security Disability Insurance
   (SSDI), 70, 94, 111, 118, 127, 155,
   266
socialization, 19, 22, 32, 72, 76, 112,
   130–31, 149
socioeconomic status, 217, 245, 266
South Africa, xi-xii, 25
Spanish, 171, 209, 253
specialist, peer, 45, 129, 134–36, 265
spiritual growth, as Common Ingredient,
   7, 12–13, 71, 113, 152, 154, 156,
   188, 205, 227, 229, 257, 278
sponsor, 76, 162, 168, 207, 241
St. Louis Empowerment Center, 4–5, 9,
   29, 108–122, 245, 251, 269
stability, 30, 79, 87, 90, 129, 135–36,
   161–62, 169, 255
staff:
   consumer, 131, 176, 226, 228, 248, 274,
      279
   peer, 163–67, 170–71, 184
   personnel on, 79, 84, 87, 101, 129,
      183–84, 248
   training for, 126, 173
Stigma presentation, 93
substance abuse, 6, 31, 47, 52, 114,
   159–61, 163, 168, 171, 174, 233,
   262–64, 266
Substance Abuse and Mental Health
   Services Administration
   (SAMHSA). 3, 24, 57, 97, 100, 126,
   143, 169, 202, 213, 254, 266
suicide, 10, 47, 72, 86, 135, 205–6, 274
Supplemental Security Insurance (SSI),
   70–71, 82, 94, 118, 127, 185, 241,
   245, 266
support:
   community, 22, 109, 111, 114, 137,
      161–62, 166–75, 179

community, system of, 184, 239–41
   linkage to, as Common Ingredient, 7,
      10, 226, 228, 273. *See also* referral
   mutual, 19, 22, 28–29, 34, 37, 48–49,
      56, 68, 75, 171, 173, 264–65
   network for, 15, 17, 20–21, 32, 45, 51,
      75, 92, 141, 145, 165–66, 168, 171,
      186, 190–92, 201
   peer, as Common Ingredient, x, 4–8,
      12–16, 18–19, 23–24, 27–28, 31,
      33–34, 36–47, 49, 55, 59–60, 62,
      87–88, 103–04, 109, 111, 115–17,
      121, 123, 125, 127, 131, 134–37,
      159–61, 163–173, 175–76, 200,
      214–15, 220–22, 227, 229–35, 240,
      243, 249, 251–52, 254–58, 263–65,
      278–79, 287
   system, 184, 239–41
Surgeon General's Report, 255
symptoms, psychiatric, 12–13, 29, 32, 38,
   42, 49, 51, 53, 55, 75, 79, 81–83, 90,
   94, 115, 164, 169, 200, 248, 278

Take Horses for Instance, 94
task force, 14, 73, 179, 191, 193–94, 281
Teague, Gregory, 4, 213, 218, 287
techniques, research:
   anchored rating scale, 218, 222–24
   baseline studies, 47, 49, 51, 253
   evaluation, 142–43, 171, 236, 263
   interrater reliability, 224–25, 228, 236
   random selection, 32–33, 47, 49–51,
      53–54, 88, 169, 233, 247
   validity, 220, 223, 230, 225, 230, 236
   variables, 49, 51, 214, 218–20, 231–33
teleconference, 70, 72, 248, 282
telephone, access to, 29, 69, 76, 80, 84, 89,
   102, 110, 115, 120, 126, 165, 167,
   206, 232, 249
telling our stories, as Common
   Ingredient, 7, 13, 15 17, 28, 34–35,
   38–39, 62, 278
Tennessee, as COSP site, 5–6, 14, 30,
   197–209, 253, 268, 272

Tennessee Mental Health Consumers'
    Association (TMHCA), 197, 201–2,
    206, 209
therapy:
    individual, 25, 54–55
    time-limited, 6, 45, 102, 275
TMHS. *See* mental health services:
    traditional
timeline, 6, 125, 182, 275
tolerance, 12, 80, 109, 242. *See also*
    Acceptance and respect for
    diversity
Towne, David, 96–97
training program, 6, 169, 192, 233
transportation, consumer:
    bus, 22, 68, 76, 102, 108, 121, 129, 190,
        201, 232
    drivers for, 69, 80, 87, 201
    passes for, 29, 102, 232
    public, 113, 175, 192, 274
    vehicles for, 113, 129, 242, 246
trauma, 10, 42, 57, 70, 106, 180, 206, 240,
    244, 254, 274. *See also* abuse
treatment:
    assertive community (ACT), 217–18,
        221, 244
    coercive, xi, 10, 12, 19, 29, 35–36, 226,
        228, 232, 274, 277
    compliance with, 11, 21, 55, 129, 172,
        244, 275
    day, 25, 118
    electric shock (ECT), 71, 78, 94, 263
    forced, 23, 25, 35, 73, 84, 195

inpatient, 70, 89, 118, 120, 161
involuntary, 12, 25, 36, 46, 55, 72, 126,
    239, 244, 274, 279
outpatient, 78–79, 118, 120, 194–95
plans of, 22, 120, 191, 244
providers of, 199, 280
with seclusion and restraints, 25, 42.
    See also medication
Twelve Steps, 146, 152, 156

Unzicker, Rae, 18, 26

Van Tosh, Laura, 24, 26, 30, 48
Vermont Study, 59–60
Vertz, Karl, 97, 100
veterans, 49, 71, 84, 111, 121
Viar, Sam, 13, 206, 287
violence, 17, 73, 86
Voices & Visions, 77, 80
volunteers. *See* employment

Web site, 133, 183, 185, 188, 192–93, 255,
    283
welfare benefits, xi, 38, 118–19, 160, 180
Well-Being Project, 22–23
well-being, 10–11, 16, 21, 32–33, 44, 49,
    54–55, 68, 92, 98, 162
Whitecraft, Jeanie, 48, 159–60, 169, 252,
    288
Wieselthier, Vicki, 108

Zinman, Sally, 22, 24, 28, 36, 40, 75